CW00515650

IMMIGRATION SERVICE
– 4 OCT 1988
DEPARTED
(1095)
HONG KONG

DEPARTMENT OF IMMIGRATION
PERMITTED TO ENTER
AUSTRALIA,
on 24 APR 1986
For stay of *12 Months*
SYDNEY AIRPORT 54

IMMIGRATION DIVISION BANGKOK THAILAND
A 72 DEPARTED
– 9 FEB 1987
SIGNED

THE INSIDER'S GUIDE TO

CALIFORNIA

IMMIGRATION & ETHNIC AFFAIRS
......Person
30 OCT 1989
DEPARTED
AUSTRALIA
SYDNEY 32

中华人民共和国
广东省公安厅

上陸許可
ADMITTED
15. FEB. 1986
Status: 4-1-   4
Duration: 90 days
NARITA(N)
Immigration Inspector

U.S. IMMIGRATION
160-LOS C-4125

MAY 23 1989

ADMITTED
UNTIL _____ (CLASS)

日本国
ADMITTED
20 OCT. 1988
USED
Status: 4-1-16
Duration   180 days
Port: HANEDA
Narita Air Port
Signature

HONG KONG
(1038)
– 7 JUN 1987
IMMIGRATION
OFFICER

THE INSIDER'S GUIDES

JAPAN • CHINA • KOREA • HONG KONG • BALI • THAILAND • INDIA • NEPAL • AUSTRALIA
HAWAII • CALIFORNIA • NEW ENGLAND • FLORIDA • MEXICO
THE SOVIET UNION • SPAIN • TURKEY • GREECE
INDONESIA • KENYA

The Insider's Guide to California

Hunter Publishing Inc
300 Raritan Center Parkway
CN94, Edison, N.J. 08818

First Published 1989
by arrangement with CFW Publications Ltd

ISBN: 1 55650 163 3

Created, edited and produced by CFW Publications Ltd
5th Floor, 11 Wing Lok Street, Central, Hong Kong.

Editor in Chief: Allan Amsel
Original design concept: Hon Bing-wah
Picture editor and designer: Noel Chan
Text and artwork composed and information updated
using Xerox Ventura software

Printed by Samhwa Printing Co Ltd, Seoul, Korea

THE INSIDER'S GUIDE TO

CALIFORNIA

by Perry Deane Young
Photographed by Nik Wheeler

HUNTER PUBLISHING, INC.
Edison, N.J.

Contents

CALIFORNIA

Crescent City
Del Norte Coast Redwoods
od
nal V
rk

Mt Sha
Mt Shasta
Castle Crag
McClou

Arcata
Eureka

COAST

Shasta Lake

Redding

Humboldt Redwoods State Park

RANGE

Red Bluff

Leggett

Chic

Fort Bragg

Orovi

Mendocino

Ukiah

Upper Lake

Yuba C

Clear Lake

Cloverdale

Calistoga

Geyserville

Napa

Fai

Novato

Vallejo

San Rafael

Richmond

SAN FRANCISCO

Oaklan

Pacifica

Palo Alto

Santa Clara

N

PACIFIC OCEAN

Santa Cruz
Monterey Bay

Salinas

Carmel

Big Sur

Hearst S
Simeon S
Hist. Mor

WASHINGTON
OREGON
IDAHO
MONTANA
NORTH DAKOTA
SOUTH DAKOTA
WYOMING
MINNESOTA
MICHIGAN
WISCONSIN
NEW YORK
NEW
NEBRASKA
IOWA
PENN.
NEW HAMP
NEVADA
UTAH
COLORADO
KANSAS
ILLINOIS
INDIANA
OHIO
NEW JERS
MARYLAND
CALIFORNIA
MISSOURI
KENTUCKY
VIRGINIA
ARIZONA
NEW MEXICO
OKLAHOMA
ARKANSAS
TENNESSEE
SOUTH CAROLINA
TEXAS
LUISIANA
MISSISSIPPI
ALABAMA
GEORGIA
FLORIDA
M

California:
Myths
and
Realities

FANTASIES FULFILLED

Once upon a time, people dreamed of finding a fabulous island called California. It was "on the right hand of the Indies" and "very near to the Terrestrial Paradise." This fabulous island was ruled by black Amazons "and their arms were full of gold."

A fictional account of such a place was published in Spain in 1510 as *The Exploits of Esplandiandon* (Sergas de Esplandian). It was the kind of heroic adventure Cervantes would later satirize with his *Don Quixote*. But the real adventurers Spain sent to explore the New World obviously believed there was such a place. In the 1530s, an expedition sent by Cortez thought they'd found it in the long gnarled peninsula of Baja California. They found no warrior queens and they found no gold, but for more than 200 years, the Spaniards continued to believe they'd found the mythical island. Then in 1746, an exploring padre discovered the mouth of the Colorado River, and proved that California was attached to the mainland.

But the name, California, stuck, not just for the peninsula but for 800 miles (1,290 km) of Spanish territory north of what is now the Mexican border. It is fitting that California began as a fantasy island, because in many ways that is what it has remained. And, maybe, it is also important that the myth cut across racial and sexual barriers of the time. But — most important — was the promise of gold — more than 300 years before any real gold was discovered in California.

Cortez' made his first expedition to Baja in 1533. Several attempts to establish a settlement on the peninsula failed until Jesuits founded a mission at Loreto in 1697. The native population presented a unique challenge to the missionaries. They were the most primitive people ever encountered by European explorers in the Americas. They had only the crudest of weapons, built no kind of shelters, wore no clothes except for a tiny apron on the women, and would eat anything including the boots of their conquerors. Their only sense of time was the annual fruiting season of the *pitahaya* cactus when they would gorge themselves on the refreshing red-fleshed fruit. Having no words for shame, love, vice or virtue, they could make no sense of the missionaries' talk of morality.

The Jesuits responded in kind. One wrote back to Spain that the natives were "stupid, awkward, rude, unclean, insolent, ungrateful, mendacious, thievish... . They are an unreflecting people...who possess no self-control but follow, like animals in every respect, their natural instincts."

The Jesuits would found 20 missions in Baja in 70 years, but their attempts to convert the Indians to Christianity did not succeed. The Indians were brutally put down in uprisings in 1734 and 1736; most of those who survived later died of diseases brought by the Spanish. By the time the Franciscans arrived in 1768, to take up the mission vacated by the Jesuits (who were earlier expelled), the native population had dropped from 40,000 to 7,000. The Franciscans would establish only one more mission in Baja, before moving on to more fertile territories in upper California. (In 1804, the Spanish divided California into Baja and Alta, lower and upper, with the boundary near present-day Rosarito Beach, 20 miles or 32 km south of the current international boundary, which was set at the end of the Mexican War in 1849.)

FATHER SERRA

His name adorns everything from streets, museums, and libraries, to taco shops, car washes, and real estate companies. In the U.S. Capitol, he is one of the two most honored men from California, standing in Statuary Hall.

OPPOSITE: The Mammoth Lakes area in the High Sierras has become one of California's most popular winter and summer resorts.

In September of 1988, Father Serra moved a step closer to sainthood when he was beatified in an elaborate three-hour ceremony in Rome. To mark the event, vandals in San Diego splashed blood-red paint on Serra's statue and scrawled "Genocidal Maniac" on the walls of the Serra Museum. Some 200-odd years after the little padre's death, his "good works" are still a subject of controversy — and he still lacks the necessary two miracles before he is canonized.

converting the heathen Indians in South America.

His was a classic case of enjoying poor health; a few days after he landed in Mexico, he refused to treat an infected insect bite on his foot and was lame for the rest of his life. He would insist on walking when he could ride. Serra's own best friend and biographer, Francisco Palou, described "the severe pains he experienced in his chest, which doubtless were occasioned by striking it with a stone during the acts of contrition he made at the

Pope John Paul II was expected to announce Serra's beatification during his 1987 visit to California, but he chose to avoid the controversy. He merely visited Serra's grave, and said nothing about sainthood. The reasons are perhaps as personal as they are political. For in the life of Junipero Serra, there was much that in the harsh light of modern psychiatry would be regarded as bizarre. Born on the island of Mallorca, Serra could barely see over the lectern when he began studying for the priesthood. Taking the name of St. Francis' best pal and traveling companion, Junipero (pronounced: hoo-NEE-perro), he followed the example of another missionary who became a saint by

end of his sermons, also by putting against his bare chest a lighted torch, in imitation of St. John Capistrano, because in putting it out he used to tear out a piece of skin... ." Palou also tells of Serra inspiring others to similar self-abuse: "During one of his sermons — in imitation of St. Francis Solanus, to whom he was devoted — he took out a chain, and after lowering his habit so as to uncover his back, having exhorted his hearers to penance, he began to scourge himself so violently that the entire congregation broke into tears. Thereupon, a man from the congregation arose and hurriedly went to the pulpit, took the chain from the penitential Father, descended from the pulpit and went and stood in the highest part of the sanctuary. Imitating the venerable preacher, he uncovered himself to the waist and began to perform public penance, saying amid tears and sobs: 'I am the sinner who is ungrateful to God, who ought to do penance for my many sins — and not the father who is a saint.' So violent and merciless were the strokes, that, before the whole congregation, he fell to the floor, they judging him dead. After he received the Last Sacraments where he fell, he died. Concerning this soul we may piously believe that he is enjoying God."

These were among the stories Palou put forward in his 100,000-word biography of Serra published just two years after his death. No mere biography, it was Palou's case for declaring Serra a saint. When the Pope finally responded 204 years later, he, of course, made no mention of Serra's bizarre lifestyle, focusing instead (as Californians always have) on his work among the Indians. While many of the Jesuits regarded the Indians as animals without souls, the Franciscans, at least, saw them as human beings, who could be saved from the devil by accepting Christianity.

A more recent Franciscan biographer of Serra, Omer Englebert, praised Serra's missions in California as a uniquely successful "Christian republic of the communal type". In the peak year of 1828, the California missions had 252,000 head of cattle, 268,000 sheep, 3,500 mules, 34,000 horses, 8,300 goats, and 3,400 pigs — all in an area where horses and livestock had never been seen before the Spanish arrived. The missions also introduced the experimental agriculture that would eventually bring more money into the state than the gold discoveries. One impressed visitor was moved to say he'd finally discovered a country without poor people. Another said, "You would never imagine what orange trees, olive trees, vines and fruit trees of all kinds are growing... . Looking at these mills, these workshops, these machines, these roads, these bridges, these canals, and all these

well-constructed buildings, how can one believe that it is the natives … who have done it."

But the title Englebert chose for his Serra biography is perhaps more telling than the text: *Last of the Conquistadors*. In fact, the lame little padre was the omnipotent ruler of his own little Indian kingdom. There seems to have been no precise plan for what he did. But in California, there were no existing towns or cities as there had been in Mexico. So, Serra

was able to build his little nation at will. There was no private property and the missionary rule was absolute. Until they were converted, the Indians were regarded as savages possessed by the devil, "the enemy". After conversion, they were subjected to near-slave conditions as forced laborers in the mission shops and fields. If they tried to escape, they were chased down and brutally punished. Although Serra claimed to be holding the land in trust for

The Mission at Carmel was the mother church of all California missions and remains an important Catholic shrine as the burial place of Father Serra. OPPOSITE: California's impressive State Capitol in Sacramento.

the Indians, no such legal provisions were ever put in writing. At his death, at the headquarters mission in Carmel in 1784, there were nine missions in operation; 12 more would be built by friars carrying on essentially what Serra started.

THE END OF THE MISSIONS

When an independent Mexican government seized the mission lands and ordered

the padres back to Europe in 1833, the Indians were left with no religion and no title to the land. As Englebert observed: "they vanished, to rejoin other savages and become savage once more with them." Without the Indians, however, the Mexican dons were never able to succeed as the missionaries had in utilizing the vast tracts of land for agriculture and raising livestock. This period of Mexican California was later romanticized, but it was, in

The rugged peaks in King's Canyon are one of several wilderness areas in the Sierras. The restored buildings in Sacramento's Old Town OPPOSITE recall the wild days when the city was at the heart of Gold Rush Country.

fact, a short-lived failure, not helped by the continuing political turmoil back in Mexico itself.

At the time of its independence in 1821, Mexican territory extended into what is now the United States from Louisiana to Oregon. Settlers from the United States and Europe soon began moving into Texas and California. The Donner Party of 87 settlers from Illinois were on their way to Mexican California in 1846, when they took a wrong — and late — turn and got stranded in the deep snows of the High Sierras. Only 47 survived the brutal winter, some of them by resorting to cannibalism and murder.

The Donners were on their way to a settlement founded by a Swiss emigrant named John Sutter. He wanted the area where Sacramento is now located to be called New Helvetia, but everybody called it "Sutter's Fort" and the name stuck. After failing in business in Germany, Sutter had made his way to California, became a Mexican citizen, and was given the largest land grant allowed, 11 leagues or 48,400 acres (19,600 hectares).

Sutter was but one of the "Yankee dons" who helped the Mexicans divvy up the huge acreage left vacant by the padres. Their names have endured even if they were not all that successful. A decidedly non-Catholic — if not outright irreligious — population would thus find its major towns and bays named for the saints and the sacraments. The pragmatic Americans simply adopted these existing names as geographical names — San Francisco was thus named for the bay, Sacramento for the river.

The Yankees were quick to adopt the lifestyle of the Mexican dons even as they were writing home disdaining it. Horse racing and gambling became major preoccupations and endured as the chief pastimes of the Californians. Mexico found, as Spain had previously, that her reach exceeded her grasp; she had more territory than she could possibly defend. In fact, the Americans marched into Monterey and what is now San Francisco and took over without firing a shot. The design of the state flag still in use was taken from that of the "Bear Flag Revolt", a confused month in history when a handful of Americans announced the creation of the Republic of California. An actual declaration of war with Mexico rendered the republic null and void, and most of its "officials" joined the fight. In truth, there weren't that many people in California to wage much of a war, and there were no battles comparable to the Alamo and San Jacinto in Texas.

called the place California. But at the time of occupation, no gold was found — until nine days before the treaty turned over the land to the United States.

On January 24, 1848, James Marshall was working at a new saw mill for John Sutter when he found what he thought was a gold nugget. It proved to be real gold, and the rush was on. Everybody stopped working and began panning for gold. It was a "gold mine" in another sense. Those worried about getting people to make the hazardous

STATEHOOD AND THE GOLD RUSH

In the little Mexican town of Guadalupe Hidalgo, the treaty ending the war was signed on February 2, 1848. The United States agreed to pay $15 million to Mexico, and was granted almost half of that country's territory — comprising the current states of California, Nevada, Utah, New Mexico, Arizona, and parts of Wyoming and Colorado. The date of that treaty reflects a bitter irony in history. The Spanish and then the Mexicans had surely come for gold, or they wouldn't have

trek to California soon found thousands pouring in from throughout the world. California had a non-Indian population of 6,000 in 1840; more than 100,000 in 1850; and 379,994 by 1860. Most of the new territories went through a probationary period, but California was admitted with full privileges as a state in 1850.

The first promoters of California had written back East that the gold was just lying there for the taking — with no mention of the incredible hardships people went through to get there. Those who could afford it went by ship from New York or Charleston down the Atlantic to the Isthmus of Panama, across land to another ship, and up the Pacific coast to San Francisco, the newly-created village that was an overnight boom town.

For every one that made it, there were hundreds who didn't. One who made it described a boat taking settlers from St. Louis upriver to Independence for the trek west; all but one of the 101 passengers died of cholera before they got there. The overland journey was technically possible in three months, but it would often take two and three times that long. "If there is a

California," one man wrote back, "I don't think we will ever see it." There were scorching deserts and impossible mountain walls they hadn't planned for.

And, as if the trip itself weren't bad enough, life in the gold rush country in the rolling hills around Sacramento was often rougher. Conditions were unsanitary, at best, and people died every day from dysentery, cholera, and "the fevers" yet unnamed. "Little did I think that the first digging I did would be digging a grave," one would-be miner wrote.

In fact, a great deal of gold was mined. According to historian James D. Hart, about $245,301 worth of gold was mined in 1848;

$10,151,360 in 1849. The figure would rise to $81,294,700 in the peak year of 1852 then taper off to $17 million in 1865.

Oddly, the major fortunes made at the time were not the miners' but of the various businessmen who sold — at ridiculously inflated prices — to the miners. San Francisco's "Big Four" all started out as merchants in Sacramento. They were soon functioning as banks, and in possession of much of the gold themselves. That led to their interests in dozens of other businesses, most notably, the first transcontinental railroads.

As for James Marshall and John Sutter, they both ended up badly. Not long after he died, Marshall was memorialized by a statue that had cost $10,000, a sum that surely represented more than what he had ever made in a lifetime. For a brief time, he went about making speeches and was on a pension from the state. But, when he showed up drunk at the state Capitol to beg for more, he lost even the pitiful sum he had been getting. He died a pauper; ironically, even the little nugget he found that started the gold rush has come down in history as the "Wimmer nugget", from one of Marshall's co-workers. Sutter started out richer, but fared no better. For decades, he fought to retain his title to the lands the Mexican government had granted him. He had to deal with squatters on the one hand, and the Unites States government legally seizing his property on the other. Late in life, he moved back East to be near Washington to press his cause with Congress for restitution of his land, and payment for his contribution to the great Gold Rush. He never got his gold or his reward and in 1880, at age 77, John Sutter, too, died impoverished.

THE RAILROAD BOOM

With the gathering war clouds in the East, California was just about the best place a state could be in during a war: 3,000 miles (5,000 km) away from it. However, the gold from California played a vital role in the Union cause, and there was a ready market for any and all of its products. The speeded-up war productions also hastened the advances in railroad technology that would allow construction to begin on a transcontinental railroad. Incorporated by the Big Four former hardware store owners in 1869, the Central Pacific Railroad began construction in Sacramento in 1863; the last spike was driven on May 10, 1869 at Promontory, Utah. The same owners (by then called The Octopus) acquired the Southern Pacific Railroad in 1868 and a virtual monopoly on rail traffic to California.

The railroads opened up California to settlers from the East as never before. They also made the great markets of the East accessible to California produce and livestock. Southern California had been a virtual wasteland before this; Los Angeles had a population of only 4,385 in 1860 and only 5,728 in 1870. But with the coming of the Southern Pacific, southern California drew the attention of speculators and developers of all kinds.

The arrival of a competing railroad, the Santa Fe, in 1887, assured Los Angeles' future. In spite of a recent period of boom and bust, when the population went from 10,000 to 50,000 and quickly back to 25,000, the wealthy railroad owners now had a vested interest in promoting the city. Hollywood, Pasadena, and a number of new developments were laid out in the vast open spaces surrounding the original Pueblo de los Angeles. The shift in population would begin slowly, but southern California would set out on a period of growth that has continued to this day.

Once city officials had mastered the water problem — by diverting the Owens River from the Owens Valley in the high Sierras to Los Angeles — the developers would take off full speed and never stop. After the railroads made it easier for people to get to California, and for Californians to ship their products out, other developments speeded life along.

Oil was discovered in Los Angeles and created a big new industry. Then automobiles arrived and not long after, the motion picture.

California: Myths and Realities

Los Angeles has been called the first city of the automobile. It really never was a city in the usual sense, with a central core and everything spreading outward. Parts of the city were separated by distances of 40 and 50 miles (65 and 80 km). But the automobile made such a city possible. It also made much more of California accessible to its citizens. A whole culture centered on the automobile grew out of California and spread. The first use of the word "motel" for what had been a "motor court" took

place in California. "Drive-in everything" became a way of life in California and the rest of America. It included Maurice and Richard McDonald's original hamburger drive-ins in San Bernardino — and reached a climax with the construction of the 12-story-tall Crystal Cathedral, an enormous glass-and-steel church which opens out to a huge parking lot where people can worship in their cars.

You won't find these grand old Santa Fe Railway engines anywhere but in the museums, such as this one in Old Town, Sacramento. OPPOSITE: Another view of Sacramento shows Old Town with the modern cityscape behind it.

THE MOVIES

If the railroads made California easier to get to, and the auto made it easier to get around it, it was the movies that put Hollywood — and California — in general at the center of popular culture in the world. On screen were fantasy flights to every place in the world and beyond, but people knew that the real settings were in California. Not just the sets, but also the people.

Statue of Liberty. The competition that ensued among architects ignored the fact that an impressive gateway to the west already exists. It's called The Golden Gate Bridge and it's in San Francisco. And who in the world can ignore the magnificent symbol for Los Angeles — the Hollywood sign, high up on the mountains overlooking Hollywood and the city. Erected in 1923, the full sign read "Hollywoodland" (for a new development of that name) until 1949. The letters, made of white sheet metal are 50 ft

In movies, and later, television, California's history became everybody's history. The world knew about the Mexican period through *Zorro* and *Ramona*, the 1870s near Stockton through *The Big Valley*, and the 1880s and 1890s in Death Valley through *Death Valley Days*. Would people ever believe that actor Ronald Reagan was anything but the honest, trusting fellow he'd played in the *Death Valley* series? Would he ever have been elected president without that trust? No way.

In 1988, arose a typically irrelevant controversy in Los Angeles over construction of a "Gateway to the West", some kind of monument that would match New York's

(15 m) high and 30 ft (nine meters) wide. For many years, the letters peeled and sagged in ruin; but the sign was restored in 1978, and refurbished again in time for the 1984 Olympics.

While depicting the history and culture of the rest of the world, Hollywood was also creating legends of its own. And not surprisingly, it soon depicted those, too, in film. *Sunset Boulevard* and *A Star Is Born* are just two in that genre. Several famous authors began writing for the movies and some, like F. Scott Fitzgerald in *The Last Tycoon*, wrote about what they saw in movie town. Budd Schulberg's *What Makes Sammy Run?* drew on his first-hand

California: Myths and Realities

knowledge of Hollywood. His father came out with the first wave of moviemakers and Schulberg grew to become one of the best screenwriters in the business. His book, *Moving Pictures: Memories of a Hollywood Prince*, combines his father's memoirs with his own for one of the best insider histories of the movie business.

Aside from providing new material for the movies, World War I also speeded up the development of a new industry in California. The airplane was still being

training programs in the Mojave Desert, and that is where the latest space shuttle flights land today.

During the period between the wars, California suffered, along with the rest of the world, in the Great Depression. But the state also prospered as did few other places in America. It was still where everybody wanted to live; if you couldn't be rich, you could at least be warm. Some extraordinary public works projects, including the Golden Gate and Bay Bridges in San

tested before the war — and where better to experiment than in an area where it's usually warm and never rains. Douglas, Lockheed, and Northrop are just three of the giant aerospace corporations that grew out of small experimental airplane factories in the Los Angeles area.

The government turned out to be another client. It needed space to train its new legions of military recruits, and California had deserts, mountains, seashore, just about any terrain they might ever fight on. Huge areas of the state were transformed into military camps and training grounds. Edwards Air Force Base grew out of one of the most adventurous military

Francisco, highways, bridges, tunnels and dams throughout the state, were completed during this period. And there were expositions in San Francisco and San Diego to celebrate the recovery.

As had happened many times in the past, there was also a nasty selfish turn to this prosperity. When thousands had sought refuge in California, especially the "Okies" from the dustbowl of Oklahoma, the state tried to legally block them at the state line

Behind the scenes on the set of television's *Dynasty*, actors — both equine and human — take a breather. ABOVE: A political rally for candidate Jesse Jackson at the University of California at Berkeley.

as if they were from another country. The "agricultural checkpoints" that still exists on the California borders are a carry-over from that effort to stem emigration in the 1930s. Woody Guthrie, the great balladeer of that period in America, was among those looking for a new life in California. And he sang bitterly of this "Garden of Eden...but believe it or not, you won't find it so hot, if you aint got the do re mi...".

If California was considered important in World War I, it was vital to the Americans

Livermore, once the center of vast vineyards and orchards, you can now buy T-shirts with the slogan, "Better a Shield than a Sword", which is also the title of Teller's last book.

The tumultuous decade of the sixties actually began in the fifties in California. The beatnik poets and writers found it an open and tolerant place for their free expression and easy lifestyles. There was long hair and free love in San Francisco long before they became the norm in the rest of America.

fighting in the Pacific during World War II. The fledgling airplane industry passed from the experimental stage and become one of the state's major industries. From the first basic developments in flight to the most far-reaching plans for "Star Wars", California scientists have been involved, and California corporations have reaped the rewards. It was Edward Teller who first suggested Star Wars to fellow Californian Ronald Reagan, and it was, naturally, the University of California's Lawrence Livermore Laboratory, run by Teller, which got the first major multi-billion-dollar contracts to build this science-fiction shield against nuclear weapons. At stores in the town of

During the 1960s, California became a center for radical changes taking place in American society. Starting with the Free Speech movement at Berkeley, the later movement for "Peace and Love and pass it on" sprang naturally from the sunshine and good times the young people knew best in California. And, typically American, for every progressive change, there was a reactionary step backward. If many of the liberal changes of the 1960s had their start in California, so did the reaction that later took over the country.

There is no understanding or even explaining California politics any more than there is an easy explanation of its people.

California's governor, Earl Warren, was named as a conservative Chief Justice of the U.S. Supreme Court only to become the court's most noted liberal. Liberal Governor Edmund G. ("Pat") Brown was succeeded by the conservative Ronald Reagan who, in turn, was succeeded by Brown's liberal son, Jerry.

When Reagan was governor, he and his wife, Nancy, moved out of the old Victorian house in Sacramento that had traditionally been the governor's mansion, calling it a "firetrap". At their insistence, an elaborate modern mansion was built for the governor, but it was not completed until Reagan's term expired. The Reagans had been fashion-conscious society people, who loved the good life. Succeeding him was Jerry Brown, an ascetic bachelor who had once studied for the Catholic priesthood, and now followed Zen Buddhism. He chose to live in a simple rented room while the new mansion sat vacant until it was eventually sold.

As always, Californians have proved amazingly adaptable to political changes — even managing to be at the center of these changes. Jerry Brown had been at the center of 1960s activism; Ronald Reagan emerged on a national level, as the symbol of the return to conservatism. As president, Richard Nixon tried to establish a "western White House" at San Clemente but scandal soon clouded everything he did. Nixon never seemed that attached to California; he vacationed in various other places during his term as President. The Reagans, on the other hand, always came home to California, spending more than one entire year of his eight-year presidency in the state. As his term came to an end, he would smile and say: "California, here I come." They spent no last Christmas and New Year's in the White House, but instead took two weeks to be with their old friends in California. The Reagans' new home in the Bel Air section of Los Angeles was on the celebrity bus tours weeks before they moved in.

It might seem as if all kinds of changes have taken place in Reagan's California

and Reagan's America. But in so many important ways, the more the change, the more the place and the people have stayed the same.

FROM FRONTIER TO HIGH-TECH STATE

In a relatively short period, California has gone from the frontier state of miners and ranchers to the high-tech capital of the

world, from an inaccessible desert island to the most populous state in America. But, as a recent author warned, it would be wrong to read too much into these outward and visible changes. In fact, there is much to suggest that the pioneer spirit lives on, that when Americans exhaust one frontier, they simply move on to another one. In a book entitled, *The Legacy of Conquest* (W.W. Norton, 1987), Patricia Nelson

Mann's (formerly Grauman's) Chinese Theater OPPOSITE is a rare survivor of the glamorous days of Hollywood Boulevard. The elegant shops along Rodeo Drive in Beverly Hills ABOVE make it one of the most popular and expensive shopping streets in the world.

Limerick observed that "there is, in fact, nothing mythic" about California and the American West. "It has a history grounded in primary economic reality — in hard-headed questions of profit, loss, competition, and consolidation. Behind every trapper lay a trader; before every Indian lay a homeland lost to an encroaching farmer or avid oil man; with every cowboy and every sheriff rode a rancher, eager to add to his herd and the land and water to sustain it. They, and hundreds of thousands like them, meant business. In dozens of ways, their descendants mean business today."

Of course, the real gold ran out a long time ago. But that hasn't stopped the emigration to California. With a population of 26,675,000 in 1986, it is the country's most populous state, and more people are coming every day. In the century following 1860, California's population doubled five times. From 1975 to 1986, more than 5,426,000 new people moved to California. In spite of that, the unemployment rate dropped from 7.2 percent in 1985 to 6.7 percent in 1986. Personal income of California residents in 1986 was $456.1 billion, or 12.9 percent of all personal income in the United States. The 388,243 banks and other corporations in the state reported a corporate income of $21.1 billion. California has the largest manufacturing complex in America; its aerospace industry claims 21 percent of all Defense Department contracts, in addition to its civilian production. The state also leads the nation in agricultural production. Its farmers received more than $14.3 billion in 1985 for their produce.

Big and getting bigger; rich and getting richer. That is the story of California as it moves into the 1990s. Statistics read more like those of a country than those of a state. In fact, Californians like to brag that theirs is the seventh largest economy in the world — and still growing.

Four hundred years after the Spaniards went looking for the sunshine and gold of a mythical California, the lure of the real place endures. Call it high-tech, kiwi fruit or avocadoes, the gold is still there for those who want to work for it.

Whether it's an overnight fad, a serious new trend or a major scientific development, you can bet there's a Californian somewhere back there making a buck off of it. That, after all, was what brought most people here. The others will be content to lie back and enjoy the sunshine, content to live in a place where it's almost always warm.

NATURAL HISTORY

NOT WITHOUT FAULTS

If you want a quick education in geology, bring along your textbooks to California. Here, you will find vivid illustrations of every period and era of the geologic past. Just as California is thought of as a young state in terms of its people, the very land they live on is also "young" in geological terms. Whereas the Blue Ridge Mountains in the East, for example, are so old they've been weathered down, silted over, and covered with vegetation, much of the geologic activity in California is so recent that you can still see where and how the earth cracked and moved. Seismologists explain that the earth is still moving in California almost every day. "California is still an uneasy land," was how an official state report phrased it in 1966.

It has the most varied landscape in America, containing the highest and lowest points among the contiguous 48 states. California's rich earth contains at least 602 different minerals; 74 of them first discovered in California.

While it may not have been a true island surrounded by water, as mythology would have us believe, California was an island in more ways than one. Until the breakthroughs in transportation in this century, the state was accessible only by sea or overland travel of more than three months. While its entire western border of more than 800 miles (1,300 km) lies along the

Pacific Ocean, its eastern border protected by formidable deserts and the sheer impenetrable walls of the High Sierra mountains.

Geologists have identified 12 "geomorphic provinces" in California. What separates and defines each province are the types of rocks, geologic structure, and history of the major landforms in the area. By far, the most impressive of these is the grand Sierra Nevada range of mountains that extends for 400 miles (640 km) from

valleys and basins in Yosemite National Park. The deep snow that still covers the high peaks in wintertime used to be regarded with the fear and dread by the first settlers. But now, it offers months of fun to skiers and has added yet another revenue-earner to California's tourism industry.

Near the Oregon border are two other mountain ranges that form separate geomorphic provinces. These are the Klamath and Cascade mountains. The

northeast of Lake Tahoe south to near Bakersfield. Sierra means "saw" in Spanish; Americans call the mountains "sawtooth" ranges because their jagged edges resemble the edge or teeth of a saw. Nevada is the word for snowfall or snow-covered. The "high Sierras" as Californians call them were formed by a fault block, giving rise to a severe eastern wall that reaches a peak of 14,495 ft (4,418 m) at Mount Whitney. The gentler western slopes are more congenial to man.

About two million years ago, the entire area was covered by ice up to half a mile (800 m) thick. These glaciers shaped Lake Tahoe and some of the more spectacular

Klamath mountains extend 130 miles (210 km) into California, taking up much of the northwest corner of the state. They include the Siskiyou, Salmon, and Trinity mountains. This is one of the last heavily logged areas in the state, but much is protected as federal and state forest preserves with only a few small roadways penetrating the mountain wildernesses. The adjoining Cascade mountains extend 525 miles (845 km) north through Oregon and Washington into Canada. In California, the Cascades consist of more than 120

Above: Deer on the golf course in Yosemite National Park remind the visitor that nature prevails in California's oldest national park.

volcanoes, the most famous being Mount Shasta and Mount Lassen. Both are at the center of national parks. Shasta, rises to a height of 14,163 ft (4,317 m), is visible from Interstate 5. It is a magnificent snow-covered natural monument. Mount Lassen, lying in a more remote area to the southeast, is 10,466-ft (3,190-m) high. Until Mount St Helens erupted in Washington in 1980, Mount Lassen was the only volcano in the contiguous 48 states that had been active (1914–1917) in historic times.

The Great Valley is another of the geomorphic provinces, extending 400 miles (645 km) from Redding in the north to Bakersfield in the south. An alluvial plane between the High Sierras and the coastal mountains, it is one of the richest agricultural areas on earth. The Coast Ranges are parallel mountains extending along much of the coast from just north of Eureka to just south of San Luis Obispo. Here, the north-south ranges run into the Transverse ranges that form the north wall of the Los Angeles basin. Formed by uplifted faults, these east-west ranges include the Santa Monica Mountains on the east, and the San Gabriel and San Bernardino mountains on the west.

The great deserts of eastern California are often separated in two, and sometimes three, different geomorphic provinces. In general, these areas have north-south mountain ranges separated by huge valleys or basins or troughs; they are part of a "basin and ranges" province that includes much of Utah and Nevada. In the great Mojave Desert, all the streams, except the Colorado River, end in dry lakes; more than 50 of these closed basins have one or more dry lakes in them.

California's landscape, however, is best known for being unstable. The fears about devastation in California are often exaggerated. It is not the only place in the United States where earthquakes have occurred. The town of New Madrid in Missouri was leveled by an earthquake in 1811; Charleston, S.C. was heavily

damaged in a quake in 1886; and a massive temblor shook Alaska in 1964. But few earthquakes have captured the world's attention as did the San Francisco quake of 1906. People now laughingly say that if it had been Cleveland, nobody would have noticed — they might even have looked on it as urban renewal. But San Francisco had been a lively pleasure-loving place, long known for the beauty of its setting and the exuberance of its residents. Although 80 percent of the

resulting damage came from the fires that followed the quake, when the dust had settled, more than 3,000 people had been killed, 490 blocks in the heart of the prosperous city destroyed, and 250,000 people homeless. Losses were estimated at $400 million. If it happened once, it could happen again. The legend of "The Big One" grows with every year that passes that no major quake is recorded. The thinking is that California is due for

In Mount Lassen Volcanic National Park, California's majestic pines OPPOSITE rise once again in the area once covered with molten lava and ash. ABOVE: A waterfall sets off the rugged terrain near Lake Tahoe.

another shock even greater than the one that hit San Francisco in 1906, and there are dozens of theories as to when and how bad it will be.

In fact, California is part of a seismic belt around the Pacific, running from Japan across the Aleutian Islands down to Mexico. This belt accounts for 80 percent of the world's earthquakes. Thousands of quakes are recorded in California every year, some 500 of them strong enough for people to feel.

Fault, the longest lateral moving fault in the world. From well south of the Baja Peninsula in Mexico, the San Andreas Fault extends more than 500 miles (800 km) across California, cutting across the city of San Francisco. The most dramatic illustration of the fault's movement is the Baja Peninsula itself. Once part of the Mexican mainland, it broke off during one of the massive shifts along this great crack in the earth. The San Francisco quake was said to have involved a shift of

Since the 1906 earthquake and several smaller but damaging quakes in the intervening years, many buildings in California have been built with earthquakes in mind. But others remain unprotected. The worst danger is from falling beams and plaster — which is why you are warned to quickly get under a table or in a doorway so that the door frame or the table can protect you. You can prepare for the aftershocks, but the truth is, there is very little preparation you can make for the initial shock. It comes unannounced and is over in seconds.

The San Francisco earthquake was the result of movement along the San Andreas

28 ft (8.5 m) in places and affected an area of 100 miles (161 km) on either side of the city. While the San Andreas is the biggest and most feared, there are a number of lesser faults along which minor quakes occur.

"The Big One" has become so much a part of California mythology that it has become a joke. From car salesmen to bar owners, you'll hear commercials warning you to take advantage of their deals "before the Big One comes." In 1988, the Big One fever seemed to have reached their peak. In May of that year, followers of Nostradamus proclaimed that Los Angeles would be destroyed in the worst earthquake ever. A film based on the writings of this sixteenth-century astrologer called *The Man Who Saw Tomorrow*, and the Los Angeles prediction set off a minor panic — well, as near to panic as Californians can get. More than 2,000 copies of the film video were sold the week before the prophesied catastrophe. Observatories were so swamped with anxious callers that some, like the Griffith Observatory in Los Angeles prepared an information kit explaining that earthquakes were not caused

wrong natural disaster (destruction by hail storm instead of earthquake). But that didn't prevent the panicky phone calls — or the run on video stores.

Nor did it prevent the cynical reaction from some quarters. A group calling itself the Skeptics banded together to combat such non-scientific nonsense. Claiming more than 2,000 members in California, its founder said the group was formed by "people who found themselves going crazy living next door to someone trying

by extraterrestrial events and, by the way, "there will be no planetary alignment or conjunction in May."

The video was actually a timely re-release of a 1981 film produced by David Wolper and narrated by the late Orson Welles. Asked about the impending doom of his home city, Wolper said he planned to be out of town that week in May. But he had the typical Californian's response to the prospects: "If the quake does happen, we'll sell a lot more copies, maybe enough to rebuild my house." The *New York Times* pointed out that the filmmakers were confused about the Nostradamus' texts, and had the wrong year and the

to fix their cars with crystals."

The final word on the Nostradamus scare of 1988 and the perpetual earthquake scare was spoken by a devout Californian who told *People* magazine: "In spite of its many faults, California is still the best place in the world to live."

OPPOSITE: Skateboarding at the Youth Festival in front of San Francisco's elaborate City Hall, as fine as many state and national capitols. At Cinco de Mayo Festival in Los Angeles ABOVE a Hispanic couple sell jewelry and colorful dancers RIGHT seem part of an equally colorful Mexican mural.

San Francisco

VISIONS OF SAN FRANCISCO

San Francisco was long known in California as "the city", simply because there was nothing to compare with it in terms of population — and sophistication. San Franciscans, of course, still call it "*the* city". Perhaps no other American city is loved so passionately by its residents as is San Francisco. At the time of the great earthquake and fire in 1906, a crusty old boxing manager said: "I'd rather be a busted lamppost on Battery Street in San Francisco than the Waldorf-Astoria in New York."

The city has two official songs, both of which are all-time national favorites: *San Francisco,* sung by Jeannette MacDonald as the title song of the 1936 movie, and the more recent *I Left My Heart in San Francisco.* So many songs, poems, and books have been written about the place that the name alone has come to signify beautiful people, fabulous restaurants and hotels, magnificent views of mountains and the bay — and, above all, a sense of fun. There is the usual American respect for wealth and success, but in San Francisco it is tempered with a delightful irreverence and the knowledge that for every success story, there's one that goes the other way, from "riches to rags".

In 1970, French president Georges Pompidou said San Francisco "is remarkable not only for its beauty. It is also, of all the cities in the United States, the one whose name, the world over, conjures up the most visions and more than any other incites one to dream." English author and television personality Alistair Cooke called it "the most individual and engaging of American cities." Adlai Stevenson said the United Nations would have worked much better if it had stayed in San Francisco. And Robert Kennedy said, "I love this city. If am elected, I'll move the White House to San Francisco."

A BIRD'S-EYE VIEW

The best place to begin to understand and appreciate the unique qualities of San Francisco is atop the 500-ft (152-m) -high **Coit Tower** on Telegraph Hill, in the heart of the city. In 1876, a group of citizens bought the top of the hill and presented it to the city so that the view could be enjoyed by all. From the open-air viewing platform, you can see almost the entire 46.38 sq miles (120 sq km) of San Francisco. The beauty of the setting is striking, and it is easy to understand why so many people consider themselves lucky to live here. The reason San Francisco ranks third among Californian cities in population (only 750,000) is its limited size; by comparison, Los Angeles covers 463.7 sq miles (1,200 sq km). The same area in and around San Francisco would accommodate more than six million residents, or twice the population of Los Angeles. However, the density of population is several times that of Los Angeles, or any other place in California, and this accounts for the real spirit of neighborhood you find here that other Californian cities lack.

Through the huge open arches of the Coit Tower, you can see the famous **Golden Gate Bridge** to the west. Few man-made structures inspire the kind of awe and affection that San Franciscans continue to feel for this spectacular engineering masterpiece, and nearly every citizen is an authority on the subject. You can see **Sausalito** tucked into a bay at the opposite end of the bridge and **Belvedere** and **Angel Islands** in the bay. Unmistakable is the solid-looking **Alcatraz**. Although the name is Spanish for the amiable pelican, Alcatraz has a feared reputation as the world's worst top security prison; the currents around it are so fierce that only one man has successfully swum away from it.

OPPOSITE: The Transamerica pyramid rises dramatically behind one of San Francisco's older landmarks, the Sentinel or Flatiron Building which is now headquarters of Francis Ford Coppola's Zoetrope Studios.

Still farther to the east is the sprawling university town of **Berkeley** and the city of **Oakland**. Its beautiful **Bay Bridge** would be a major landmark in any city that didn't have a Golden Gate.

Spread out over the 42 steep hills of San Francisco are row upon row of beautiful old Victorian houses. So treasured are these old houses that city law prohibits any change in existing structures and new residential buildings must incorporate bay windows into the design. But the special appeal of San

Francisco lies in its people, and downstairs at the Coit Tower you begin to understand why. A sign there advises that it is not true that the tower was built in the shape of an upturned fire hose nozzle; it was simply judged the best design for the setting. But the fire hose legend has a basis in fact. Lillie Hitchcock Coit (1843–1929) specified in her will that $125,000 was to go to "adding beauty to the city which I have always

The fountains at San Francisco's Civic Center provide a resting place for two young people in the latest of punk chic. OPPOSITE: The turrets and bay windows of old San Francisco are so revered all new housing construction must follow a similar design.

loved." But Lillie Coit loved to ride on fire trucks — so much so that she was dubbed the mascot of one hook and ladder company. She also dressed as a man, gambled in the North Beach saloons, smoked cigars, and generally entertained San Francisco with her antics while outraging her relatives, one of whom took a shot at her in a San Francisco hotel, causing her to move to Europe where she became the darling of royalty in several countries.

At the foot of the hill, down some old wooden steps, is a beautiful flower garden known as **Grace's Garden**. Grace Marchant, one of Mac Sennett's bathing beauties in the days of silent films, moved into a little house on the hillside in the 1940's and started cleaning up the garbage dump that people had made of the unused hillside. It became a garden spot so loved by her neighbors that they got together and bought the property when Grace died a few years ago to ensure that it would always remain Grace's garden.

At the ocean end of **Golden Gate Park**, one of the world's most beautiful city parks, are two huge windmills, one of which is now working again. Designed as part of the park's irrigation system, the windmills deteriorated through disuse until a private citizen raised the money to restore one of them. In 1988, the police department announced that the mounted patrols in the park would have to be discontinued due to a shortage of funds. But the horse patrols had always been there, and soon another private subscription assured that they would always be there.

THE SPIRIT OF SAN FRANCISCO

A more famous gesture was the public subscription of $10 million which returned the cable cars to use after having been closed down in 1981 due to safety hazards in the old equipment. This gesture assured federal and city grants of more than $60 million, enabling the complicated cable system to be restored to its original working condition.

The public spirit of San Franciscans was never more in evidence than in the days following the devastating earthquake and fire in 1906. It remains the worst natural disaster ever to befall an American city. More than 3,000 people were killed, 28,000 buildings were destroyed, and 250,000 people were left homeless. With amazing determination, the city cleared the ruins (at a cost of more than $20 million) and rebuilt on the spot. Within three years, more than 20,000 structures had been replaced and the city was making plans for a World's Fair.

But the earthquake had exposed more than a fault in the earth's crust to San Franciscans. The magnificent Beaux Arts City Hall building stood in ruins, exposing a spindly steel superstructure where the dome was supposed to be. Corrupt city officials and builders had swindled the city out of millions of dollars, but City Hall was only the most obvious place where the public had been shortchanged.

"They was all a-grafting," said one old-timer about the tradition of corruption in the city. Despite its Spanish name, San Francisco was an American place from the very beginning. The Spanish and Mexicans had their capital in Monterey, with only a small mission and garrison fort in what is now San Francisco. U.S. Navy Captain John B. Montgomery sailed into the bay and took possession without ever firing a shot, raising the United States flag on July 9, 1846. He also named the new town's square in honor of his ship, the *Portsmouth*, and the waterfront street (at that time) after himself. The tiny settlement had been called Yerba Buena, for the "good herb" or sweet grass that grew on the dunes there; but the American invaders renamed it San Francisco.

With the end of the Mexican War and the discovery of gold, San Francisco was suddenly a boom town. The miners found their gold in the territory to the east, but it was to San Francisco that they came to spend it. Twice during those raucous years the city was taken over and run by vigilante committees. The very rich built elaborate mansions on Nob Hill, where they could be safe from the boisterous city below.

Sailors from around the world called it the "Barbary Coast", because navigating in and out of San Francisco's red-light district could be as treacherous as sailing the Mediterranean, with its pirates. The city became a pleasure capital and, in spite of its political corruption, gained an international reputation for its love of the arts and pure fun. At the time of the earthquake (5:13 am on April 18, 1906), the great actor John Barrymore was staying at the St Francis Hotel and the great opera tenor Enrico Caruso at the Palace Hotel, where he had checked in the day before with 54 steamer trunks and 50 self-portraits. One Los Angeles newspaper headlined its report on the earthquake: "San Francisco Punished", to which San Franciscans responded with a rhyme:

If, as they say, God spanked the town
For being over-frisky,
Why did He burn all the churches down
and spare Hotaling's Whiskey?

(Hotaling's, a popular saloon, survived both the earthquake and the fire.)

The earthquake caused extensive damage for a hundred miles along the San Andreas fault line, from Eureka to Salinas; in San Francisco alone, the damage was estimated at more than $400 million.

By the time the great Panama–Pacific International Exposition was held in 1915, the city had been reconstructed from the ashes and rubble of the earthquake and fire. The Palace of Fine Arts is a permanent reminder of what the exposition meant in restoring the pride of the city.

In the 1930's, San Francisco again faced disaster, along with the rest of the world, in the Great Depression. But, once again, the city pulled itself out of the economic crisis with two extraordinary construction projects: the Golden Gate Bridge and the San Francisco–Oakland Bay Bridge. An international exposition staged on Treasure Island

OPPOSITE: A coffee shop in the Haight–Ashbury section of San Francisco recalls a time when "The Haight" was the center of Flower Power, the capital of world hippiedom.

in 1939 proclaimed the successful completion of these projects, indicating to the world that San Francisco was a survivor with strength and style. World War II brought even greater prosperity to the city, when it served as one of the major ports for the Pacific theater.

In the 1950's, while the rest of America was lulled by the do-nothing spirit of the Eisenhower years, San Francisco was home to the "beat" generation. San Francisco columnist Herb Caen was the first to call the

peace and love, "Flower Power". The hit song and theme of it all was: "If you're going to San Francisco, be sure to wear some flowers in your hair...". The original "be-ins" and "love-ins" were staged in San Francisco's Golden Gate Park, near the Haight–Ashbury district, a neglected slum when the "flower children", or hippies, laid claim to it as their national capital.

With the bitter divisions over the Vietnam War, the movement that had begun with flowers in San Francisco ended with blood

dropout poets and artists "beatniks", which name eventually became a badge of honor. Poet Lawrence Ferlinghetti's City Lights Book Store in North Beach became the cultural center of that movement, with Allen Ginsberg, Gregory Corso, and Jack Kerouac frequently in residence.

The area was fertile ground for the Free Speech Movement, which was born at the University of California in Berkeley in the fall of 1964 — and set the stage for the social and political activism that would spread throughout America in the coming decade. But San Francisco gave its own special stamp to this political action. It was a peculiarly gentle persuasion that emphasized

and tear gas in Washington, DC. But the city had made its mark on the decade, not least of all through its folk and rock 'n' roll music. Joan Baez was the Joan of Arc of free speech, civil rights, and peace and love — and she would always call San Francisco and Carmel home. Bill Graham's Fillmore Auditorium (a converted roller-skating rink in Haight–Ashbury) became the Mecca or La Scala of rock 'n' roll and launched any number of careers, including Graham's own.

During the "me" decade of the 1970's, old-time San Franciscans became concerned that the place was turning into another New York. The once-low and gentle skyline was fast becoming a wall of skyscrapers; the developers were "New Yorking" it to death, some said. At the center of this new conglomeration of buildings was a pyramid rising 48 stories to a point. Designed by William Pereia as the headquarters of Transamerica Corporation, the building was at first greeted with derision. But, with time, this too became another distinctive piece of San Francisco's fabric, a dramatic reminder that the city is not only a cultural center but also the banking and insurance capital of the American West.

Also in the seventies, a number of serious social issues confronted the populace. The city was stunned when it learned that a local religious leader, Jim Jones, had led his followers (most of them from San Francisco) in a mass murder-suicide — more than 900 men, women, and children lost their lives in the remote commune of Jonestown in Guyana. And when a bright, energetic mayor, George Moscone, and the city's first gay supervisor, Harvey Milk, were assassinated by an embittered ex-fireman and supervisor, the people of San Francisco were united in their outrage.

In the eighties, the city was the first to discover the dreaded virus that would become known as Acquired Immune Deficiency Syndrome, or AIDS. San Francisco has been especially hard hit because of its very large homosexual population. But the city's program for helping AIDS victims is superior to that of any other American city. One doctor said, "If I had AIDS, I would crawl to San Francisco to get help."

George Moscone's name lives on in a huge new convention and visitor center. And in 1987, Art Agnos — another man of strength, vision, and compassion — was elected mayor to carry on the programs Moscone didn't live to see enacted.

Though leveled by fire, destroyed by an earthquake, and hit by violence and disease, the spirit of the place endures. It isn't so much that one leaves one's heart in San Francisco, but that it gives its heart to you.

CHRYSOPYLAE: THE GOLDEN GATE

CHRYSOPYLAE: THE GOLDEN GATE

GOLDEN GATE BRIDGE

Just as Winston Churchill claimed to have created the nation of Jordan "with the stroke of a pencil", so the famed Golden Gate was born with the pen-stroke of a brash young United States Army explorer and map-maker, James C. Fremont.

Considering the area was a virtual wasteland which the Spanish had never seen any use for, it was somewhat pretentious of Fremont to label the narrow entrance to the huge San Francisco Bay "The Golden Gate". In 1846, long before gold was discovered in the hills beyond, Fremont explained that ancient Byzantium had its "Golden Horn", so the territory of

The botanical Conservatory in Golden Gate Park OPPOSITE was shipped from England and reconstructed after the conservatory in London's Kew Gardens was demolished. ABOVE: Few man-made structures inspire the awe and affection that San Francisco's Golden Gate Bridge does; even the Pope insisted on visiting it.

California should have its "Chrysopylae", or Golden Gate. Never mind that the area still belonged to Mexico; by the time it became part of the United States three years later, the Gold Rush was on and the name became known around the world.

Although the opening into the bay is relatively narrow, it was still a treacherous sea passage, 318 ft (97 m) deep with fierce ocean currents proving a formidable obstacle to any serious plans for a bridge. In 1917, an international bridge builder by the

name of Joseph B. Strauss arrived in San Francisco with a grand plan for connecting northern California with the San Francisco peninsula by means of the most magnificent bridge the world had ever seen. Construction didn't begin until 1933, and Strauss would later say: "It took two decades and 200 million words to convince the people that the bridge was feasible; then only four years and $35 million to put the concrete and steel together."

It was an awesome project and 11 workers were killed, despite elaborate safety precautions; another 19 workers were saved by safety nets. The bridge was suspended between two enormous towers the height of a 65-story building; only the Empire State Building was taller at that time. The other statistics are equally impressive: enough steel wire in the cables to circle the earth three times, and enough concrete to pave a five-foot (one-and-a-half meter) -wide sidewalk from San Francisco to New York. The central span of the 9022 ft (2,750 m)

bridge is 4,200 ft (1,280 m) across, the longest at that time.

When President Franklin Roosevelt pushed the button that opened the bridge on May 27, 1937, some 200,000 people walked across the amazing structure. Fifty years later, more than 800,000 people showed up when the city celebrated the anniversary of the bridge, still its most famous landmark. When Pope John Paul II visited San Francisco in 1987, his only sightseeing request was to see the Golden Gate Bridge. Tolls are charged for southbound traffic only: $1 Sunday through Thursday and $2 on Friday and Saturday. There is no charge to pedestrians, and the bridge offers the city's most picturesque and popular walking and jogging course. There are few man-made structures one can describe as breathtaking — the Golden Gate Bridge is one.

GOLDEN GATE NATIONAL RECREATION AREA

With the bridge as its crowning jewel, the Golden Gate National Recreation Area was established in 1972, incorporating several existing parks and newly-acquired private land on both sides of the bridge. With more than 34 million acres (14 million hectares), it is the largest urban park in the world and the most popular of all United States national parks. On the San Francisco side, the park includes the entire oceanfront down to San Mateo County. Also included in the park are Angel and Alcatraz islands in the bay.

Angel Island
The largest island in San Francisco Bay, Angel Island is now a nature preserve, inhabited only by park rangers, wild birds, and deer. For many years, the United States Public Health Service maintained a hospital there for examining immigrants, and during World War II, the buildings were used to house Italian and Japanese prisoners of war. Angel Island is a favorite picnic spot for San Franciscans, and there is a regular ferry service from the Embarcadero which also calls at Alcatraz.

Alcatraz

Alcatraz, or The Rock, is a barren 12-acre (five-hectare) island that became known as the most formidable prison in America. Originally a Spanish fortress, it became an American military prison and "disciplinary barracks" in the 1850's. In 1933, it became part of the federal prison system — the prison of last resort, where the most notorious inmates were jailed and from which there was no return. The most unruly and infamous prisoners were brought here from all over America, and were kept in line by rigid discipline and the latest in "electric eye" surveillance. Abandoned as a prison in 1963, the island was occupied from 1969 to 1971 by American Indians wishing to draw attention to their plight. In 1972, it became part of the National Park Service. Today, you can wander about the grim gray cell blocks while listening to cassette tapes of former inmates and guards describing conditions as they were on Alcatraz.

Marin County

From the northern end of the Golden Gate Bridge, the National Recreation Area extends for 23 miles (37 km) to the town of Olema. This area includes much of picturesque Marin County, in particular, Mount Tamalpais and the Muir Woods.

At 2,604 ft (794 m), **Mount Tamalpais** is the highest mountain on the west side of San Francisco Bay. Located 15 miles (24 km) north of San Francisco, by way of U.S. 101, Tamalpais has three camping areas and numerous hiking trails and viewing points. For more information, ✆ (415) 388-2070.

Muir Woods, 17 miles (27 km) north of San Francisco by way of U.S. 101 and State Highway 1, is a true shrine to environmentalists. It preserves the memory of John Muir, the Scottish-born naturalist who was instrumental in getting Yosemite named a national park and also in establishing a commission in 1896 which created 13 national forest preserves. Muir Woods is the closest place to San Francisco where you can walk among the ancient redwood trees. Some of the 250-ft (76-m) -high giants are more than 1,000 years old. The 500-acre (200-hectare) grove of redwoods was dedicated in 1908 under the Act for the Preservation of Antiquities and was incorporated into the national park in 1972. For information on Muir Woods, ✆ (415) 388-2595.

For general information on the Golden Gate National Recreation Area, write care of the park headquarters, Fort Mason, San Francisco, CA 94123, or ✆ (415) 556-0560.

GOLDEN GATE PARK

Golden Gate Park is truly one of the great city parks of the world, and unique in its appreciation of beauty and fun. Even the city's own brochure describes it as a "space for both the silly and the solemn". Roughly three-quarters of a mile by four miles (one

The cells at Alcatraz OPPOSITE, now maintained as a part of a national park, tell of a time when it was one of the world's most feared and secure prisons. The Japanese Tea Garden ABOVE in Golden Gate Park is an authentic reproduction complete with magnificent carved gates constructed by master craftsmen from Japan.

kilometers wide and six-and-a-half kilometers) long, the park cuts a green swath from the oceanfront through the city's residential areas. Originally a wasteland of sand dunes and scrub oak, the park began to take shape in 1870 through the creative use of manure from the city streets. The plantings from all over the world eventually became one of the greatest botanical gardens in America. The beautiful Victorian greenhouse, or Conservatory of

Flowers, was shipped from England around Cape Horn and reassembled in the park in 1879. The **Strybing Arboretum and Botanical Gardens**, in another area of the park, have more than 6,000 plants on display including the California redwood. But Golden Gate Park is not a pristine nature preserve; it is used by thousands of people every day for outdoor sports and nature walks. The soccer fields are at the ocean end of the park, and the Kezar football stadium at the other (east) end; in between is a golf course, tennis courts, baseball fields, polo stadium, a

Young Japanese girls in San Francisco reflect a happier time in a state where Orientals suffered a history of legal oppression.

fly-casting pond, and a delightful miniature yacht racing pool with its own elegant little clubhouse. There is also a buffalo paddock, the five-acre (two-hectare) **Japanese Tea Garden** (its magnificent gates recently restored by skilled temple craftsmen from Japan), the 1912 carousel in the children's playground, and the Dutch windmills that were once part of the park's own irrigation system. The city's major science and art museums are also located in the park. (See ART MUSEUMS, page 51.) The park is a wonderful place to just wander about, or you can take a guided tour. For information, ✆ (415) 221-1311.

THE CABLE CARS

It's not unusual to visit a national landmark, but in San Francisco you will also be riding on one when you climb aboard one of the unique cable cars. It is the only system of its kind in the world, and in 1973, the city celebrated the cars' first 100 years. In 1982, it seemed the cars might have had their day, as the peculiar underground cable system was beyond repair. However, a vigorous local campaign raised $10 million which, with $50 million in state and federal funding, enabled the entire system to be dug up and restored. In mid-1984, the city celebrated the return of its beloved old cable cars. You can study the mechanism that powers the cable cars firsthand at the **Cable Car Museum, Powerhouse, and Car Barn**, on the side of Nob Hill at Washington and Mason Streets. ✆ (415) 474-1887. The Car Barn is a three-story red-brick structure dating from 1907. Here you can see the original prototype cable car, models of other cars, and the cable mechanism itself. The cable cars were the brainchild of Andrew Hallidie, who was appalled by the sight of horses and mules trying to negotiate San Francisco's steep hills. The current system involves a circular, or "endless", steel cable $1\frac{3}{8}$ in (3.5 cm) thick and 11 miles (18 km) long that is let out at a speed of $9\frac{1}{2}$ mph (15 kph). The cable cars move by grasping on to the moving cable and stop by letting go. There are now 37 cable cars in

operation, 26 on the Powell Street line and 11 on the California Street route. It's a unique and historic way to see the city, and 14 million people ride the cars each year.

SANFRANCISCO'S LOCALITIES

NOB HILL

The name "Nob Hill" comes from the British corruption of the Hindu word "nabob" or "nawab", a person of wealth and power. The nabobs who got rich off the mines and the railroads claimed this hilltop as their own in the 1870's. It was 376 ft (115 m) above the rabble of San Francisco, with a steep grade that discouraged the uninvited and prompted the hill's residents to build their own railroad, which is still in service as part of the city's cable car system. Some of these palaces were so grandiose — Mrs Mark Hopkins' in particular — that the whole city laughed at them. But their lofty perch and their wealth couldn't save them from the earthquake and fire of 1906. All but one of the mansions on Nob Hill were destroyed; James G. Flood's sturdy brownstone has endured as the Pacific Union Club, where successive generations of capitalist barons still hold forth. Some of the names of the mansions have survived in the hotels and parks. The Mark Hopkins Hotel is on the site of the Hopkins mansion; Huntington Park is where that family's house once stood; and the Fairmont Hotel is on the former estate of James G. Fair. The Fairmont serves as the "St Gregory Hotel" in the television series, *Hotel*. Here you will find the penultimate in San Francisco hotel accommodation: the Fairmont's penthouse rents for $5,000 a day, but comes complete with a butler, maid, and limousine service. **Grace Cathedral** sits on land donated by the Crocker family after their two mansions were destroyed by the 1906 fire. Erected in 1910, the cathedral is the largest Gothic structure in the American West; its huge gilded brass doors are copies of the fifteenth-century work of the Italian master, Lorenzo Ghiberti, for the Baptistery in Florence.

UNION SQUARE

Union Square is famous as a hotel and shopping center, but it is also a thing of beauty in and of itself. The banks of flowers at every corner are arranged so beautifully you forget they are there to be sold. The 2½-acre (one-hectare) square was set aside as a public park in 1850, the same year the city was incorporated. It got its name from a series of violent pro-Union demonstrations staged there just prior to the Civil War. The 97-ft (29-m) column at the center of the square commemorates a later war, Commodore George Dewey's victory at Manila, in the Philippines, in 1898. The most historic of the hotels around the square is the St Francis, which dates from the time when "hotels" were nothing more than tents, with cots for beds. The St Francis prided itself on being the first hotel in San Francisco to provide sheets. Rousted out of his bed in the St Francis by the 1906 earthquake, the actor John Barrymore was one of thousands who took refuge in Union Square, where he was promptly pressed into service by the United States Army. Said his actor-uncle, John Drew, "It took an act of God to get Jack out of bed and the United States government to get him to work." A grand new St Francis opened in 1904, only to be gutted by fire two years later. An elegant banquet was staged in the embers of the old ballroom to celebrate the hotel's reconstruction within the same walls; it reopened in 1907 and a 32-story tower was added in 1972.

Underneath Union Square is a four-level parking garage built in 1941, with enough space for 1,000 cars. Don't count on finding a space, though; parking is a problem throughout the city, but especially in the more popular tourist areas.

CHINATOWN

The old Chinatown was truly a closed oriental city within the larger city of San Francisco. It had the largest oriental population outside China, and it was a place of mystery and intrigue, not to mention danger. That Chinatown of opium dens, brothels, and gambling parlors was destroyed by the earthquake and fire of 1906. But the new Chinatown that replaced it is still an exotic and foreign place. Police are warned not to chase a suspect underground, because it is believed a labyrinth of escape tunnels still exists there; and the most recent oriental gang war took place not in the 1800's but in the 1970's.

Until the 1950's, the Chinese had their own telephone system that depended on the remarkable ability of operators to remember 30,000 names instead of numbers. Few other immigrant groups have met with the intense hostility the Chinese faced in California in the early days. They were willing to work hard for much lower wages, and were the victims not just of vigilante actions but of legal discrimination as well. Orientals could not testify against whites in the courts, and Chinese immigration was prohibited by state laws passed as late as 1902. In the face of all this, the Chinese developed their own Chinese Benevolent Association, or "Six Companies" (or tongs), that looked after the community and represented the Chinese in all disputes with Californian and United States officials.

Today's 24-block Chinatown is a relatively peaceful place. A huge stone "Gateway to Chinatown" was erected in 1970 as a bridge of understanding with the rest of the city. Even the modern banks and telephone booths are built in pagoda style. For a glimpse of authentic temple life, you can visit the **Kong Chow Temple** at Clay and Stockton Streets, the **Tien Hou Temple** at 125 Waverly Place (dedicated to the Queen of Heaven in 1852), and a more recent symbol of cultural assimilation and endurance, **Buddha's Universal Church** at

720 Washington Street, which was completed in 1961. Three museums in Chinatown offer exhibits on the role of the Chinese and other immigrants from the Orient: the **Chinese Historical Society**, 17 Adler Place; the **Chinese Culture Center**, 750 Kearny Street; and the **Pacific Heritage Museum**, 608 Commercial Street.

The best way to see Chinatown is on foot, and you may want to make an adventure out of discovering a little dim sum place or an elegant restaurant on your own. If you prefer

a guided tour, one of the best is offered by cooking instructor Shirley Fong-Torres. For information on her "Chinatown Walking Tours with Wok Wiz", write to P.O. Box 1583, Pacifica, CA 94044, or ✆ (415) 981-5588.

The following are some of the older, more established, restaurants in Chinatown:
Cathay House, 718 California Street. ✆ (415) 982-3388.
The Celadon, 881 Clay Street. ✆ (415) 982-1168.
Empress of China, 838 Grant Avenue. ✆ (415) 434-1345.
Great Hunan, at two locations: 531 Jackson Street, ✆ (415) 982-1708, and 941 Kearny Street, ✆ (415) 781-3888.

A newsstand in San Francisco's Chinatown, an exotic city within a city. OVERLEAF: The Palace of Fine Arts, the only surviving structure from the 1915 Panama-Pacific International Exhibition. Originally built of plaster, it was strengthened in 1967 and in one wing houses the Exploratorium, considered by many to be the best science museum in the world.

Imperial Palace, 919 Grant Avenue. ✆ (415) 982-4440.
Louie's of Grant Avenue, 1014 Grant Avenue. ✆ (415) 982-5762.
Sun Heung Chinese Restaurant, 744 Washington Street (since 1919). ✆ (415) 982-2319.

NORTH BEACH

North Beach, more than any other part of San Francisco, best expresses both the city's

raucous and sophisticated past. Here, great writers such as Mark Twain, Bret Harte, Robert Louis Stevenson, and Rudyard Kipling once walked, and might still walk if they were to come back. The literary whimsy even extends to the name: "North Beach where there is no beach; with Washington Square where the statue is not of Washington but of Franklin." In fact, it was once much closer to the waterfront and there was a "north beach" before a huge landfill was created.

The area was once famous for its "Barbary Coast" brothels and bars, and was where most of the Italian immigrants settled. A legacy of the past endures at the intersection of Columbus and Broadway, where there are several striptease places, **Enrico's** sidewalk cafe, where you can sit and watch the crowds outside Finnochio's, famous (for 50 years) for its drag shows.

In addition to Enrico's, several nice old coffee houses carry on the Italian tradition

in North Beach. At **Puccini's**, there is a jukebox filled with all the classic favorites of Italian opera. The **Cafe Roma** is housed in an old Italian bakery where you can dine either on a back patio or in the original bakery where the walls are covered in delightful frescoes of naked cherubs carrying trays of cookies and cakes. **Mario's Cigar Store** also has a wonderful old Italian ambience, but its main attraction is its grilled eggplant sandwich, which attracts customers from throughout the city.

Washington Square is at the heart of North Beach and here you'll find any number of comfortable old bars and restaurants. This is the traditional gathering place for San Francisco's highly literate journalists, mainly at the **Washington Square Bar & Grill**. Across the square is **Mama's**, one of the city's most popular breakfast places. Although the restaurant has now expanded to a branch on Union Square, this is the original where "Mama" Fran Sanchez often does the cooking, as she has done for 35 years. There's nothing dainty about Mama's breakfasts — the omelets, waffles, and pancake plates are so huge it's a meal that can last all day.

THE EMBARCADERO

Being a peninsula, San Francisco has a waterfront on three sides. The oceanfront is taken up by the Golden Gate National Recreation Area, but most of the rest is still a busy working port area, or embarcadero. If you ask any devout San Franciscan about Fisherman's Wharf, he will respond with an adamant, "Don't go." Where once it was an authentic haven for colorful Italian fishermen to pull in and sell their catches, it has become almost the exclusive domain of tourists, overrun with restaurants and shops that in one writer's opinion make it a parody of what it once was. Two of the oldest seafood restaurants on Fishermen's Wharf are **A. Sabella's** and **Alioto's No. 8**. A. Sabella's, dating back to the 1920's, is located at 2766

Taylor Street at Fisherman's Wharf. © (415) 771-6775. Alioto's is at No. 8 Fisherman's Wharf and claims to be the oldest restaurant on the pier. © (415) 673-0183.

However, if you despair at what you find on Fisherman's Wharf, look at a map and you'll see that this is only a small part of the vast waterfront; there are many other places to explore, some as "authentic" as the old Fisherman's Wharf.

One of the most popular restaurants in the city is **Pier 23**, where local celebrities including Mayor Art Agnos and football hero Joe Montana often eat. What is special about Pier 23 is not just the ambience created by the clientele, but also the waterfront vistas, with freighters docking and unloading at the next pier. Across from Pier 23 is the **Fog City Diner**, where a wide variety of dishes is served dim sum style.

Further along the Embarcadero (at Broadway) is another seafood restaurant with a less cluttered view of the bay. This is **The Waterfront**, on Pier 7. © (415) 391-2696.

SOUTH OF MARKET

Following the lead of New York's "Soho" area, San Francisco has created what some are calling "SoMa", or South of Market. For many years, this former warehouse and slum housing district was referred to as "south of the slot", but after the $126 million Moscone convention center was built, the whole area was revitalized. It is now home to dozens of very popular restaurants and discotheques, experimental theaters and art galleries, and a design center called **Showplace Square**.

On **Folsom Street**, in the heart of the South of Market district, there is a new "Restaurant Row". The best of these places are: **Taxi**, **South Park Cafe**, **Julie's Supper Club**, **Rings**, **Southside** (a bar and dance place which also has very good food), **Milano Joe's**, and **Hamburger Mary's**.

CULTURAL LIFE

San Francisco is the only city in California, and one of the few in America, that has world-class opera and ballet companies and a major symphony orchestra. Opening nights for all three are major dress-up events for the city's high society. But, in the true spirit of San Francisco, the day after opening night at the San Francisco Opera in September, the public is invited

to a free performance of *Opera in the Park* at the band shell in Golden Gate Park.

The San Francisco Opera and San Francisco Ballet perform in the **Opera House** at the Civic Center, a wonderful *beaux arts* building in the complex surrounding City Hall. You get some idea of the city's place in the cultural life of California when you realize that this is the only functioning opera house in the state. The San Francisco Symphony performs in the new **Davies**

Although locals shun Fisherman's Wharf as too touristy, some of the old fishing boats OPPOSITE still dock there. ABOVE: Children at play in the Mission District, the largely Hispanic quarter surrounding the old mission.

Symphony Hall, a modern addition to the center.

The box office for the Opera House is located at Van Ness Avenue and Grove Street, ℂ (415) 864-3330; and the symphony box office is located at Davies Symphony Hall, ℂ (415) 431-5400. Ticketron and Bass agencies also have ticket offices throughout the city. To charge by phone with Bass, ℂ (415) 762-2277, and for a recorded message on performance schedules, ℂ (415) T-E-L-E-T-I-X. For Ticketron information, or to charge by phone, ℂ (415) 392-S-H-O-W. While cultural events of every description are often sold out long in advance, it is sometimes possible to get reduced-rate tickets on the day of a performance through the STBS office on the Stockton Street side of Union Square. The STBS office is open only from noon to 7 pm and closed Sunday and Monday; all sales are cash and there are no reservations. ℂ (415) 433-S-T-B-S.

ART MUSEUMS

When one looks around at all the beautiful private houses and public parks, it would seem that San Franciscans look on their city itself as a work of art. With this generous attitude toward the place, it's not surprising that many of the city's wealthiest families have helped to establish here some of the greatest art museums in America. The main museum is the **M.H. de Young Museum** in Golden Gate Park. This is the city's most diversified museum, with exhibits ranging from ancient Egypt up to the beginning of this century. Adjoining the older museum is a new wing built to house the Avery Brundage Collection. This **Asian Art Museum** was opened in 1966, and more than 1,000 objects are on display at any one time in changing exhibits from the permanent collections. One of the most unusual art museums in San Francisco is the **California Palace of the Legion of Honor**. Situated on a plateau near Land's End in Lincoln Park, the building itself is worth a visit. Modeled after the Legion of Honor building in Paris, it was built to house an all-French

collection by the Spreckels family. Alma de Bretteville Spreckels was an early patron of Rodin, among other French artists of the time, and the familiar Rodin sculptures (such as *The Thinker*) shown here were among the first cast by the sculptor. The Achenbach Foundation for Graphic Arts is also located in the Legion of Honor museum. All three of these museums are now administered by the Fine Arts Museums of San Francisco. Admission to individual museums is $4 for adults, $2 for seniors and children. One ad-

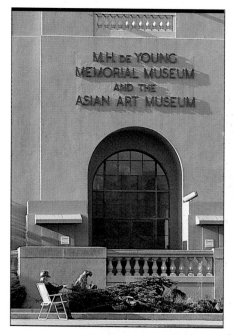

mission, however, admits you to all three museums on the same day. For more information, ℂ (415) 221-4811 for the M.H. de Young Museum; ℂ (415) 668-8921 for the Asian Art Museum; and ℂ (415) 221-4811 for the Legion of Honor museum; for a taped message on museum activities, ℂ (415) 750-3659.

The **San Francisco Museum of Modern Art** was the first museum dedicated solely to modern art in California. Located in the War Memorial Veterans Building at the

In Golden Gate Park you will find the M.H. de Young Museum ABOVE, one of the great art museums of America. OPPOSITE: A revolutionary bookstore south of Mission.

Civic Center (Van Ness Avenue and McAllister Street), the SFMMA features lively exhibits that are frequently changed and with a special emphasis on abstract expressionism and photography. Admission is $3.50 for adults, $1.50 for seniors and children. © (415) 863-8800.

HISTORICAL MUSEUMS

Ironically, the mission that gave San Francisco its name is not known by that name

itself. The Mission San Francisco de Asis was the sixth established by Father Serra and was located beside a stream already named for Our Lady of Sorrows ("Dolores" in Spanish). Still called **Mission Dolores**, the original building, dating from 1782–1791, survived the 1906 earthquake and is the oldest structure in San Francisco. Located at 16th and Dolores Streets, in the heart of the Mission District south of Market Street, the

building is now maintained as a museum, its religious functions being taken over by a much larger church constructed nearby in 1916. The mission is open daily from 9 am to 4:30 pm. © (415) 621-8203.

Perhaps because they'd been able to seize the place without ever firing a shot, the United States government set about building a huge and sturdy fort on the south side of the narrow Golden Gate opening to the suddenly busy and valuable Bay of San Francisco. Constructed between 1853 and 1861, **Fort Point** is a classic four-tiered fort whose thick walls were built to house 600 soldiers and to mount 126 cannon. "None were ever fired in anger", the National Park Service guides — in Civil War-era Union uniforms — will tell you. Even if there weren't a fort there, you would want to visit the site because it is located right under the Golden Gate Bridge, at the base of the south tower. There is no charge for admission and the fort is open daily from 10 am to 5 pm. To get to the fort, take Lincoln Boulevard to Long Avenue, which ends at the fort. © (415) 556-1693.

Located in Aquatic Park, at the foot of Polk Street, the **National Maritime Museum** features two floors of exhibits on San Francisco's long and lively association with the sailing trade. Opened in 1939, the museum offers a good background for viewing the several historic ships docked nearby. Open 10 am to 5 pm daily. © (415) 556-2904. At the Hyde Street Pier, located at the foot of Hyde Street, between Fisherman's Wharf and Aquatic Park, several historic ships are docked, including the *Balcutha*, a steel-hulled square-rigger built in Scotland in 1886. There is a $2 admission charge for the *Balcutha*. For more information, © (415) 556-6435.

The Presidio in San Francisco is one of the most beautiful military reservations in America and the **Presidio Army Museum** is located in one of its oldest buildings, the Old Station Hospital, part of which dates back to 1860. The Army played an important role in the city's early history by keeping order and getting the city back on its feet following the earthquake of 1906. All

The original "Mission Dolores" ABOVE somehow survived the Great Earthquake of 1906 and is now preserved as a museum. OPPOSITE: A surfer is alone with the gulls on San Francisco's Ocean Beach.

of this is explained in exhibits at the museum, with no charge for admission. The Army Museum is located at Lincoln Boulevard and Funston Avenue. ✆ (415) 561-4115.

First opened in 1874, the **Old Mint** is a rare example of Greek Revival architecture in the West. Now maintained as a museum, it houses period rooms displaying Western art and collections of gold coins. Its most spectacular display features a mound of gold bars worth $4 million. The Old Mint is located at Fifth and Mission Streets. ✆ (415) 974-0788.

Founded in New York and San Francisco in 1852 by Henry Wells and William G. Fargo, Wells Fargo became the banking and overland stagecoach line of the American West. The banking and shipping operations were separated in 1906 and Wells Fargo continued to grow as one of the region's major banks. In 1986, Wells Fargo absorbed the Crocker Bank, one of California's major financial institutions. The **Wells Fargo History Museum** takes up two floors of the bank's headquarters at 420 Montgomery Street. The centerpiece of this collection is a real Wells Fargo overland stage coach. The museum is open 9 am to 5 pm Monday through Friday; no charge for admission. ✆ (415) 396-2619.

course is located at 34th Avenue and Clement Street. Green fees are $8 weekdays, $12 weekends. ✆ (415) 221-9911. There is a nine-hole course in beautiful Golden Gate Park, not far from the windmill and the ocean. Fees at the **Golden Gate Park Course** are only $2.50. ✆ (415) 751-8987. One of the most difficult courses in northern California is located at Half Moon Bay, just 25 miles (40 km) south of San Francisco off Highway 1. **The Half Moon Bay Golf Links** are at 2000 Fairway Drive in Half Moon Bay. ✆ (415) 726-4438. In the Napa Valley, about 45 minutes from San Francisco, is a new championship course, the **Chardonnay Club**, 2555 Jamieson Canyon Road, at the intersection of Highways 29 and 12. ✆ (707) 257-8950.

PROFESSIONAL SPORTS

San Franciscans aren't nearly as fanatic about their home teams as fans in Los Angeles, but you may have trouble getting tickets to games of the popular National Football League's San Francisco Forty-Niners. There are nearly always tickets at the gate for the more frequent professional baseball games of the San Francisco Giants and the more successful Oakland Athletics (or "A's") across the bay. The Forty-Niners and the Giants both play in the windy **Candlestick Park** stadium, located eight miles (12.8 km) south of downtown off U.S. 101. Football games in August, September, and October are played at 1 pm, while baseball games in July, August, and September are played at 1:05 pm and 7:35 pm. For information on the Forty-Niners, ✆ (415) 468-2249; and on the Giants, ✆ (415) 467-8000. For information on the express bus service from downtown to Giants games, ✆ (415) 673-M-U-N-I. For information about Oakland baseball games, ✆ (415) 638-0500.

SPORT AND RECREATION

GOLF

No one in San Francisco would ever admit it, but it's surely because of the frequently damp weather that golf is not the major sport here that it is further south in drier, sunnier parts of California. Still, there are several courses in and near the city, two of the most picturesque being public courses operated by the city. Some of the greens on the 18-hole **Lincoln Park Golf Course** even have a view (from near Land's End) of the Golden Gate Bridge. The start of the

Some of the greens at the Lincoln Park Golf Course in San Francisco offer spectacular views of the ocean and the Golden Gate Bridge.

VICTORIANA

In most American cities you'll find that a little jewel box of a house built in the late 1800's has somehow escaped the wrecking ball and is now preserved as a public treasure. In San Francisco, you'll find that almost a whole city has been so preserved, not by government edict but through the concern of its citizens. Even though 514 blocks of the old city were destroyed in the fire following the 1906 earthquake, there are still more than 14,000 examples of this elaborate architecture dating from 1850 to 1900.

There are three basic schools of Victorian architecture found in San Francisco. The Queen Anne school was copied from a style popular in England in the 1860's and features rounded corners, hooded domes, and wooden shingle siding; the Italianate style was popular from 1850 to 1875 and is seen in doorways framed by narrow columns; the Stick, or Eastlake, style took Italianate to delightful extremes and into the twentieth century with horseshoe arches and corners perched on columns.

You can see fine examples of all of these if you wander through any of the older parts of the city. However, if you want to be sure you're seeing the best examples, you should follow a tour laid out by the **San Francisco Convention & Visitors Bureau**. This tour starts at California and Franklin Streets and zigzags up to Lafayette Park, then on up Pacific Street and down Scott to Alta Plaza Park, and down Divisadero and back down to Scott and around Alamo Square.

Two houses are maintained as museums. The Foundation for San Francisco's Architectural Heritage has its headquarters in the **Haas-Lilienthal House** at 2007 Franklin Street and the house is open for tours; for information, ✆ (415) 441-3004. The Society of Colonial Dames maintains the **Octagon House,** which dates from 1861, at Gough and Union in Cow Hollow. The house is open for tours three days a month; for exact times, ✆ (415) 885-9796.

Several groups offer walking tours of the more interesting areas. The best of these are: Heritage Walks, 2007 Franklin Street, ✆ (415) 441-3004; City Guides (Friends of the Library) at Civic Center, ✆ (415) 558-3981; and Downtown Community College Center, 800 Mission, ✆ (415) 239-3660.

THE FUN OF GETTING THERE

In San Francisco, you may find that getting there is half the fun. There is no city anywhere that can offer as many different — and fun — ways of getting around on public transportation.

CABLE CARS

The best known, of course, are the cable car routes, three in all: the **Powell-Hyde Line** originates at Powell and Market Streets and ends at Victorian Park, not far from the Maritime Museum and Aquatic Park; the **Powell-Mason Line** also starts at Powell and Market, but terminates at Bay Street near Fisherman's Wharf; while the **California Street Line** goes from the foot of Market Street up and over Nob Hill to Van Ness Avenue. The fare on the cable cars is $1.50, or 15 cents for seniors. Tickets must be purchased before boarding and can be bought from automatic machines at the major stops.

"MUNI"

"Muni" is the pet name for the **San Francisco Municipal Railway**, which operates all the rail facilities including the cable cars. The Muni is a streamlined electric version of the cable cars, operating underground downtown and aboveground in the outer city. Fares on the Muni are only 75 cents, and exact change is required. For $5 you can purchase an all-day Muni pass from any of the ticket machines (it is also good on the cable cars). For information on routes and schedules, ✆ (415) 673—M-U-N-I. A free pamphlet called *Tours of Discovery* - describes nine tours of the city using Muni trains and is available by writing to the San Francisco Municipal Railway at 949 Presidio Avenue, San Francisco, CA 94115. ✆ (415) 673-6864.

BART

An acronym for the city's newest and most modern transportation system, **Bay Area Rapid Transit**, BART is a $5 billion space-age underground and underwater system that links Daly City and San Francisco with Oakland, Berkeley, and other spots on the East Bay. The 71 miles (115 km) system is described as "the tourist attraction that gets people to other tourist attractions". The fares on BART depend on your destination and all tickets must be bought from machines at any of the 25 stations. A free brochure, *Fun Goes Farther on BART*, is also available at the stations. For other information, write to: BART, 800 Madison Street, Oakland, CA 94607, or ✆ (415) 788-B-A-R-T.

BUSES

Bus services operate throughout the bay area. In addition to the regular electric buses you see on the city streets, there is also a regular service to the outlying areas. **AC Transit** operates buses to Oakland, Berkeley, and other East Bay areas from the Transbay Terminal at First and Mission Streets. ✆ (415) 839-2882. **Golden Gate Transit** operates out of the same terminal, with a service across the Golden Gate Bridge to Marin and Sonoma counties. ✆ (415) 332-6600. Also operating out of the Transbay terminal at First and Mission Streets, **Samtrans** has a service to the San Francisco International Airport and other areas as far south as Palo Alto. ✆ (415) 761-7000.

FERRY SERVICES

Once a vital link between San Francisco and other parts of the bay area, more than 50 ferry boats were in service when the Golden Gate and Bay bridges put them out of service. In recent years, the ferries have come back as a popular way of crossing or seeing the bay. **Golden Gate Ferries** leave from the south end of the Ferry Building at the foot of Market Street and make

regular runs back and forth to Sausalito and Larkspur. The fare to Sausalito is $3.50; and to Lakspur $3 on weekends, $2.20 on weekdays; there is a 50 percent discount at all times for senior citizens and handicapped persons. ✆ (415) 332-6600. The **Red & White Fleet** of ferries has offices at Pier 41, Fisherman's Wharf. ✆ (415) 546-2896 or (800) 445-8880. Fares are $4 for adults and $2 for children. Boats leave from Pier 43½ on a regular daily schedule to Sausalito, Tiburon, and

The recently restored cable cars in San Francisco offer the visitor a chance not just to visit but also to ride on a National Landmark and enjoy a unique transportation experience.

Angel Island. Special excursion cruises are also offered during the summer months.

AIR TRANSPORT

The sixth busiest airport in the world is located just 14 miles (23 km) south of San Francisco. The San Francisco International Airport is serviced by all of the major American and international airlines, and has complete customs and immigration services.

SAN FRANCISCO RESTAURANTS

A part of local lore in San Francisco is that there are so many restaurants (4,200) in the city, every resident could be seated at one time. This is a slight exaggeration, but the number of restaurants for the population is still much higher than in New York or any other American city. San Franciscans love good food, and they love to eat out three meals a day. You will find almost as many locally famous breakfast places as you will dinner places.

The following are some of the best restaurants in the city:

Big Four, 1075 California Street in the Huntington Hotel on Nob Hill. ℰ (415) 771-1140.

Bix, 56 Gold Street, was opened by Doug Biederbeck after the success of his Fog City Diner. Bix is more formal and more expensive, but it has quickly caught on as one of the more favored "in" places of San Francisco's high society. ℰ (415) 433-6300.

Brasserie, 950 Mason Street in the Fairmont Hotel on Nob Hill. Open 24 hours. ℰ (415) 772-5199.

Buena Vista, 2765 Hyde Street on Fisherman's Wharf. ℰ (415) 474-5044.

Campton Place Restaurant, 340 Stockton Street, downtown. ℰ (415) 781-5155.

Dish, 1398 Haight Street beside Golden Gate Park, is a classic San Francisco neighborhood restaurant, featuring tastefully prepared "health" and "natural" foods. ℰ (415) 431-3534.

Faz Restaurant and Bar, 132 Bush Street in the financial district, features their own smoked fish and game and all fresh ingredients. ℰ (415) 362-4484.

Fog City Diner, 1300 Battery, became an overwhelming success among locals and tourists alike. Doug Biederbeck opened this place after his success with Prego's in Los Angeles. ℰ (415) 982-2000.

Hayes Garden Cafe, 482-A Hayes Street at the Civic Center. ℰ (415) 861-6044.

Janot's, 44 Campton Place, downtown, is a superb place for lunch, with French cuisine and modern decor. ℰ (415) 392-5373.

Lori's Diner, 366 Mason Street, offers a delightful trip back to the 1950's, with thick burgers and shakes and decor to match. Open 24 hours. ℰ (415) 392-8646.

Maltese Grill, 20 Annie Street, south of Market, has Northern Mediterranean cuisine served in a cozy cave atmosphere. ℰ (415) 777-1955.

Max's Opera Cafe, 601 Van Ness Avenue, features big New York-style delicatessen sandwiches served up by opera-singing waiters. ℰ (415) 771-7300.

Mission Rock Resort, 817 China Basin Street, south of Market Street, is an authentic waterfront place that is somewhat rustic, but popular for breakfast and lunch because of the spectacular view of the bay from the deck. ℰ (415) 621-5538.

Natoma Cafe, 146 Natoma Street, South of Market, is another favorite spot for breakfast and lunch only; closed Saturdays and Sundays; no alcoholic beverages and no credit cards. ℰ (415) 495-3289.

Pier 23 at Pier 23 is one of the current "in" places in San Francisco. Owned by Peggy Knickerbocker, it is popular with local celebrities from Mayor Art Agnos to football hero Joe Montana. ℰ (415) 362-5125.

The Ramp Restaurant, 855 China Basin Street, South of Market, on the waterfront, has American food with live music Thursday through Sunday nights. ℰ (415) 621-2378.

Teddy Bears Restaurant, 131 Gough Street near the Civic Center, features hearty American food. 2,600 teddy bears look down from the walls of the Teddy Bear Lounge. Live music every night until 2 am. ✆ (415) 621-6766.

Top of the Mark is just what it says, at the top of the Mark Hopkins Hotel on Nob Hill. Even if you don't eat or drink here, it's worth the trip up for the best panoramic view of the city you'll find short of the Coit Tower. Prices are fairly moderate by luxury hotel standards and the Sunday brunch is lavish at any price. ✆ (415) 392-3434.

Upstairs at the Cliff House in the Cliff House at 1090 Point Lobos at Ocean Beach. A light fare of omelets and salads is featured in the daytime. A favorite (and rare) spot from which to watch the sun set over the Pacific. ✆ (415) 387-5847.

White Horse Restaurant, 635 Sutter Street, downtown, is an English-style pub with hearty chops-and-potatoes fare to match the decor. ✆ (415) 673-9900.

ETHNIC RESTAURANTS IN SAN FRANCISCO

So many different nationalities have made the city home that almost no cuisine is truly foreign. The city's own guide to restaurants actually lists "Californian" among the ethnic or foreign places.

CHINESE

Hunan Restaurant, 924 Sansome Street in North Beach, was one of the first in the United States to serve the fiery Hunan cuisine. ✆ (415) 956-7727.

Tommy Toy's Haute Cuisine Chinoise, 655 Montgomery Street in the financial district, has received many awards for Toy's elaborate menu of French and Chinese cooking. ✆ (415) 397-4888.

FRENCH

Ernie's, 847 Montgomery Street in the financial district, has won the Mobil five-star award for 25 straight years; elegant and expensive. ✆ (415) 397-5969.

Jack's, 615 Sacramento Street in the financial district, has been in the same building since 1864 and remains a landmark for its fine cuisine. ✆ (415) 986-9854.

Le Piano Zinc, 708 14th Street in the Upper Market area, features jazz piano music as a backdrop for a chic Parisian setting. ✆ (415) 431-5266.

The Shadows, 1349 Montgomery Street on Telegraph Hill, is a French chalet overlooking the bay. ✆ (415) 982-5536.

IRISH

You don't often find Irish places listed separately from American, but this place is special. At the **United Irish Cultural Center**, 2700 45th Avenue, you'll find down home (to the Irish) cooking and live music that will make you want to get up and do the jig — it's allowed. ✆ (415) 661-2700.

ITALIAN

Milano Joe's, 1175 Folsom Street, South of Market, features classic Italian food and is one of the most popular restaurants on the new restaurant row. ✆ (415) 861-2815.

Ristorante Firenze, 1421 Stockton Street in North Beach. ✆ (415) 421-5813.

Washington Square Bar & Grill, 1707 Powell Street in North Beach. ✆ (415) 982-8123.

JAPANESE

Ichirin, 330 Mason Street, downtown, has the usual sushi bar, but also a tempura bar and tatami room. ✆ (415) 956-6085.

Yamato, 717 California Street in Chinatown. ✆ (415) 397-3456.

MEXICAN

There are Mexican restaurants throughout the city of varying age, size, and quality. Here are some of the best:

Cadillac Bar, One Holland Court (off Howard Street, between Fourth and Fifth Streets, South of Market), can be a bit loud with guitars and mariachis playing at full blast, but it can also be fun if you're in the mood for it. ✆ (415) 543-8226.

Corona Bar & Grill, 88 Cyril Magnin, downtown. ✆ (415) 392-5500.

La Posada, 2298 Fillmore Street in Pacific Heights, is a rare outpost of old Mexico in this upscale neighborhood, but it offers the finest in Mexican cuisine at reasonable prices. ✆ (415) 922-1722.

Leticia's, 2223 Market Street in the Upper Market area. ✆ (415) 621-0441.

By all accounts, the most authentic and oldest Mexican restaurant in San Francisco is the **Roosevelt** (it was named for Teddy) **Tamale Parlor**, corner of 24th Street and York. ✆ (415) 550-9213.

SAN FRANCISCO HOTELS

Almost from the days when the first gold miners came back with money to spend on a lavish night on the town, San Francisco has boasted America's most luxurious hotels. Nob Hill was where the first of the gold and silver millionaires built their fabulous private mansions and that is where the city's better hotels are located, some on the site of the old mansions and preserving the pioneer family names. Union Square is the other center of luxury hotels in San Francisco. There are more than 40 hotels in and around the beautiful old square, convenient to the city's premier shopping district. Of course, there are many newer luxury-class hotels in other parts of the city, but the most interesting development in recent years has been the popularity of smaller hotels, many of them restorations to a turn-of-the-century elegance befitting the Victorian residential areas. Not least among the places to stay are the many bed and breakfast places available in San Francisco. This is a way to stay in one of the old homes, but "bed and breakfast" does not mean cheap lodging, as it does in Europe; this has become one of the most elegant and expensive American means of lodging.

NOB HILL

The "big four" hotels that help to sustain Nob Hill's name and reputation are the Fairmont, Huntington, Mark Hopkins, and Stanford Court.

Fairmont, 950 Mason Street, has 596 rooms, seven restaurants, 10 lounges, and a supper club with world-class entertainment. Rates from $140 to $260. ✆ (415) 772-5000 or (800) 527-4727.

Huntington, 1075 California Street, is on a much smaller scale and is preferred by many celebrities. 143 rooms, two restaurants, and one bar. Rates from $140 to $230. ✆ (415) 474-5400 or (800) 227-4683.

Mark Hopkins Inter-Continental, 999 California Street, has 406 rooms, two restaurants, and one lounge. Rates from $145 to $235. ✆ (415) 392-3434 or (800) 327-0200.

Stanford Court, 905 California Street, has 402 rooms, two restaurants, and two bars. Rates from $155 to $245.✆ (415) 989-3500 or (800) 227-4636.

Stepping down from the luxury class, but still on Nob Hill, there are several small hotels that give you the classy address at a fraction of the cost.

Ellesmere, on Nob Hill at 655 Powell Street, has 48 suites with rates ranging from $99 to $250. ✆ (415) 477-4600 or (800) 426-6161.

Nob Hill Inn, 1000 Pine Street, has 21 rooms, with rates from $85 to $200. ☎ (415) 673-6080 or (800) 874-8770. **Nob Hill Suites**, 955 Pine Street, has 19 suites. Rates from $65 to $95. ☎ (415) 928-3131.

UNION SQUARE

Some of the city's grandest old hotels are located in this beautiful old shopping and hotel district. Most are now

Campton Place, 340 Stockton Street, has 126 rooms. Rates from $180 to $240. ☎ (415) 781-5555 or (800) 647-4007. **Four Seasons Clift**, 495 Geary Street, has 329 rooms. Rates from $155 to $235. ☎ (415) 775-4700 or (800) 268-6282. **Hyatt on Union Square**, 345 Stockton Street, has 693 rooms, three restaurants, and three lounges. Rates from $165 to $220. **Meridien San Francisco**, 50 Third Street, has 675 rooms. Rates from $140 to $205. ☎ (415) 974-6400 or (800) 543-4300.

owned and operated by the major chains, but much of their local charm lives on. The most historic are the St Francis and the Palace.
St Francis, now a Westin Hotel, 335 Powell, right on Union Square, has 1,200 rooms, five restaurants, and five bars. Rates range from $135 to $260. ☎ (415) 397-7000 or (800) 228-3000.
Palace, now a Sheraton Hotel, 2 New Montgomery Street, has 528 rooms, three restaurants, and three lounges. Rates from $95 to $165. ☎ (415) 392-8600 or (800) 325-3535.

The other luxury hotels in the Union Square area include the following:

Nikko San Francisco, Mason and O'Farrell Streets, has 525 rooms. Rates from $140 to $205. ☎ (415) 394-1111 or (800) N-I-K-K-O-U-S.
Portman, 500 Post Street, has 348 rooms. Rates from $185 to $320. ☎ (415) 771-8600 or (800) 533-6465.
Ramada Renaissance Hotel San Francisco, 55 Cyril Magnin (Market and Fifth), has

The old and new city are strikingly revealed in these pictures of two famous hotel lobbies in San Francisco. The modern high-rise atrium of the Embarcadero Hyatt Hotel OPPOSITE features a bold new sculpture and, the lobby of the Fairmont Hotel ABOVE reflects the generations' old elegance of Nob Hill.

1,050 rooms. Rates from $125 to $185. ✆ (415) 392-8000 or (800) 368-0700.
San Francisco Hilton, 333 O'Farrell Street, has 1,907 rooms. Rates from $105 to $215. ✆ (415) 771-1400 or (800) 445-8667.
Sir Francis Drake, 450 Powell Street, has 415 rooms. Rates from $105 to $180. ✆ (415) 392-7755 or (800) 227-5480.

There are also dozens of less-expensive and cozy hotels in the Union Square area. These include:
Bedford, 761 Post Street. Rates from $85

single double. ✆ (415) 673-6040 or (800) 652-1889.
Beresford, 635 Sutter Street. Rates from $55 to $60. ✆ (415) 673-9900 or (800) 533-6533.
Galleria Park, 191 Sutter Street. Rates from $94 to $110. ✆ (415) 781-3060 or (800) 792-9639.
Golden Gate Hotel, 775 Bush Street, is a turn-of-the-century hotel with antique

The North Beach area of San Francisco holds onto some of the charm and decadence that gave the city a reputation among sailors throughout the world. OPPOSITE: At Mario's you'll find the same old world atmosphere that drew the original Beatniks to this Bohemian setting. ABOVE: It's not the raucous "Barbary Coast" it once was, but Columbus Avenue still offers some spicy entertainment.

furnishings. Rates from $45 to $69. ✆ (415) 392-3702.
King George, 334 Mason Street. Rates from $69 to $75. ✆ (415) 781-5050 or (800) 227-4240.
Mark Twain, 345 Taylor Street. Rates from $50 to $64. ✆ (415) 673-2332 or (800) 227-4074.

SMALL HOTELS

Atherton, 685 Ellis Street, is one of the great bargains in downtown accommodation at $49 a night single or double. Rate includes free breakfast and newspaper. ✆ (415) 474-5720 or (800) 227-3733.
Cornell Hotel, 715 Bush Street, Powell, is between Union Square and Nob Hill and has a special weekly rate of $315 single or $395 double that includes seven breakfasts and five dinners in the Jeanne D'Arc Restaurant. ✆ (415) 421-3154.
The Majestic, 1500 Sutter Street, is a 60-room, five-story Edwardian gem opened as a grand hotel in 1902. Rates from $95 to $160. ✆ (415) 441-1100.
Queen Anne, 1590 Sutter Street, has 49 rooms in an 1890 building. Rates from $89 to $139. ✆ (415) 441-2828.

BED AND BREAKFAST

Albion House, 135 Gough Street near the Civic Center. Rates from $67 to $110. ✆ (415) 621-0896.
Annabella Victoria, 1801-A Laguna Street, in Pacific Heights. Rates from $52 to $150. ✆ (415) 567-8972.
Archbishops Mansion Inn, 1000 Fulton Street, at Alamo Square, a fabulous *belle epoque* house, was home to local archbishops for many years. It is now one of the city's most elegant little inns. Rates from $100 to $250. ✆ (415) 563-7872.
Edward II, 3155 Scott Street. Rates from $45 to $200. ✆ (415) 922-3000.
Grove Inn, 890 Grove Street, at Alamo Square. Italianate Victorian dating from

the 1870's. Rates from $33 to $55. ✆ (415) 929-0780.

The Mansion, 2220 Sacramento Street, in Pacific Heights, is an 1887 Queen Anne house with 19 rooms. Rates from $74 to $200. ✆ (415) 929-9444.

Sherman House, 2160 Green Street in Pacific Heights, is an 1876 Italianate mansion and carriage house. Rates from $170 to $600. ✆ (415) 563-3600.

Victorian Inn on the Park, 301 Lyon Street, overlooking the "panhandle" of Golden

If you accept that San Francisco is the gay capital of America, you will understand that there is a congenial mixture of lifestyles here that you don't often find even in the most cosmopolitan cities. In other words, none of the really popular dance clubs are exclusively gay or straight — you'll find cross-over crowds at all the bars. And if two men or two women dancing together — or someone dancing alone, for that matter — offends you, then you'd do best to stick to Fisherman's Wharf and the Top of the Mark.

Gate Park, is an 1897 Queen Anne house. Rates from $75 to $125. ✆ (415) 931-1830.

Washington Square Inn, 1660 Stockton Street in North Beach. Rates from $65 to $160. ✆ (415) 981-4220.

SAN FRANCISCO NIGHTLIFE

Although the nightlife in San Francisco has calmed considerably since the raucous days when sailors regarded it with fear and longing as the Barbary Coast, it is still a pleasure-loving city where having a good time is high on the list of life's priorities.

DISCO DANCING

But if you're out for some wild dancing, you can't beat the clubs of San Francisco. The most popular clubs that are predominantly straight all feature live entertainment and disco dancing. These are: The **I-Beam**, 1748 Haight Street, ✆ (415) 668-6006; **Club DV8**, 55 Natoma Street, South of Market, ✆ (415) 777-1419; and the **DNA**, 375 11th Street, South of Market, ✆ (415) 626-1409. **The Kennel Club**, 628 Divisadero, is another popular club that has a mainly straight clientele every night except Wednesdays and Saturdays, when it becomes a gay club called **The Box**. For information on either club, ℂ (415) 931-1914. **The Stud** is the city's oldest gay leather bar, but the disk jockeys and the music they play here are so popular you'll find a happy mix of all the city's lifestyles, with men and women in evening dress dancing alongside the various leather outfits. The Stud is located at 399 Ninth Street, South of Market. ℂ (415) 863-6623.

UNIQUE PERFORMANCES

There are several performance groups that are unique to San Francisco, expressing the city's special blend of politics and humor that is rare in other American cities. The most famous of these is the **San Francisco Mime Troupe**, a non-profit collective of actors formed in 1961 to perform free in the city parks. The group now has a national reputation, no longer as a silent mime troupe, but as outspoken political theater at its best. For information on the schedule of performances in July, August, and September, ℂ (415) 285-1717.

Showbus offers a wacky combination of sightseeing and zany San Francisco theater. The audience boards a real city bus and sits back for a traveling show of comedy, music, and dance. For information on tickets and departure times, ℂ (415) 661-S-H-O-W.

Backstage at the O'Farrell Theater in San Francisco, performers get ready for another show.

Ladies Against Women was started in 1977 by the Plutonium Players in San Francisco and now carries its "Ladyfesto" on tours throughout the country. A spoof of right-wing politics, the ladies take such stands as these: "Make America a man again. Invade abroad." And this: "Abolish the environment. It takes up too much space and is too difficult to keep clean."

The **Sisters of Perpetual Indulgence**, like the Ladies, are not sisters at all. They are not so much a performance as a disturbance group — making nervous such staid old groups as the Democratic National Convention. A bunch of hairy men dressed in nuns' habits, their reason for being is the wicked pun that cuts through the hypocrisy of politics. Sista Boom Boom took her name from the fifties sound; Sister Freeda Peeples was the group's first black member.

Cross-dressing is an accepted part of the San Francisco tradition. The annual *High Jinks* show was a chance for the all-male Bohemian Club members to strut their stuff in ruffles and bows. Although the club, founded by actual artists and writers in 1878, has now become the exclusive province of super-rich barons of the military industrial complex, the annual drag show endures — with reliable leaks about how lovely the U.S. Secretary of State looked in a dress. The Bohemian, of course, is a private club, but there is one place where you can see the San Francisco drag tradition on outlandish display five nights a week. This is the famous **Finocchio's**, 506 Broadway in the North Beach area. For 50 years, Finnochio's has featured the best in female impersonator shows found anywhere in America. The lavish, Las Vegas-style revues are staged every night except Monday and Wednesday, starting at 9 pm. ℂ (415) 982-9388.

San Francisco also has several traditional theaters where you can see the latest in American drama and musical productions. **The American Conservatory Theater** performs at the **Geary Theater**, 415 Geary Street, with a regular schedule from October through May. The same theater houses the **American Musical Summer Festival** in the summer months. For more information on either schedule, ✆ (415) 673-6440. Two other theaters regularly stage popular plays on the way to Broadway or on tour from New York: the **Curran Theater**, 445 Geary Street, ✆ (415) 243-9001; and the **Theater on the Square**, 450 Post Street, ✆ (415) 433-9500.

Three comedies have proved so popular in San Francisco they have been given open-ended billing: *Beach Blanket Babylon Goes Around the World* is in its 15th year at the **Club Fugazi**, 678 Green Street in North Beach, ✆ (415) 421-4222; *Party of One* is an original musical comedy on the joys and tribulations of being single, at the **Zephyr Theater**, 25 Van Ness Avenue, ✆ (415) 441-7787; and *Greater Tuna* is the city's longest-running comedy and focuses on a day in the life of Tuna, Texas, with two actors playing 20 characters, at the **Mason Street Theater**, 340 Mason Street at Geary, ✆ (415) 668-T-U-N-A.

HIGH LIFE

The many new high-rise hotels and office buildings have extended San Francisco's elegant supper club high life from the Top of the Mark at the Top of the Mark Hopkins Hotel on Nob Hill to several other new high spots throughout the city.

Although it's only on the 19th floor, the **Top of the Mark** still reigns supreme on Nob Hill, where generations of San Franciscans have memories of special evenings spent looking over the city spread out below. The Top of the Mark has a Sunday brunch from 11 am to 3 pm and serves cocktails until 1:30 am every night. ✆ (415) 392-3434.

Here are some other vantage points from the upper stories of modern San Francisco: **Carnellian Room** is on the 52nd floor of the Bank of America Building, 555 California Street, ✆ (415) 433-7500; **Cityscape** is on the 46th floor of the San Francisco Hilton, One Hilton Square, ✆ (415) 776-0215; **One Up** is on the 36th floor of the Hyatt on Union

Square, Stockton and Sutter Streets, ✆ (415) 398-1234; **Victor's** and **Oz** are both located on the 32nd floor of the Westin St Francis Hotel on Union Square, Powell at Geary, ✆ (415) 956-7777 for Victor's and (415) 397-7000 for Oz (there is a strict dress code at Oz); the **Crown Room** is on the 24th floor of the Fairmont Hotel on Nob Hill, 950 Mason Street, ✆ (415) 772-5131; and the **Starlite Roof** is on the 21st floor of the Sir Francis Drake Hotel on Union Square, Sutter and Powell Streets, ✆ (415) 392-7755.

SAN FRANCISCO FESTIVALS

The frantic rush for gold in the 1850's brought people from nearly every country in the world to the then-tiny port city of San Francisco. This cosmopolitan atmosphere has endured through the several ethnic neighborhoods in the city, but also in its major parades and festivals. In most cases, parades and festivals are held on different dates each year, so for specific dates you should check with the **San Francisco Convention & Visitors Bureau**, 201 Third Street, San Francisco, CA 94103. ✆ (415) 974-6900.

Columbus Day celebrations are held during the first week of October in honor of America's Italian roots. In addition to a parade, the week-long festival features a procession of Madonna del Lume and the blessing of the fishing fleet from the church of saints Peter and Paul at Fisherman's Wharf.

The Chinese offer one of the most raucous (with fireworks galore) of the city's ethnic celebrations. The Year of the Horse 4688 will be blasted in with a parade through Chinatown on February 10, 1990. The parade will be preceded by a week of special events in the Chinese and Asian communities.

The Irish take to the streets for **Saint Patrick's Day**, March 17 in 1990.

In recent years, the Japanese have presented one of the city's most beautiful events, with the annual **Cherry Blossom Festival** in early April.

The city's Spanish and Mexican past and present are honored in the annual **Cinco de Mayo** parade and festival, although they are not always held on May 5, but usually the weekend before.

Finally, **San Francisco's Gay Pride Parade** is held in June each year. Although the spirit of carnival prevails in the annual parade, there is an underlying tone of defiance and seriousness since the city's first openly gay supervisor was assassinated and, in more recently, because of the AIDS crisis.

include Gucci, Tiffany, Jaeger, Brooks Brothers, Louis Vuitton, Gump's, and Hermes.

The Neiman-Marcus building is a striking Philip Johnson design that would be a treasured piece of modern architecture in most cities. However, it was the subject of a bitter controversy here because it involved the destruction of a beautiful old *beaux arts* building, the City of Paris, which featured a delightful neon Eiffel Tower on top. The rotunda of the older

SHOPPING IN SAN FRANCISCO

Beverly Hills has Rodeo Drive, New York has Fifth Avenue — San Francisco has all this and more in the fabulous shopping area in and around old **Union Square**. It is not just the premier shopping district in the city, it is also the heaviest concentration of retail outlets and sales anywhere in the country. The most famous fashion houses in the world — Saks Fifth Avenue, Burberry's of London, Bally of Switzerland, Neiman-Marcus of Texas — are right on the square, and hundreds of others are located in the blocks nearby. The latter

building was preserved and incorporated into the new design, providing the very elegant setting for Neiman-Marcus' restaurant.

The **Crocker Galleria** is one of several new enclosed malls that have enlivened and expanded the city's shopping possibilities. Not far from Union Square, the Crocker Galleria features a magnificent glass-fronted atrium and covers the block bounded by Post, Kearny, Sutter, and Montgomery Streets. More than 50 shops and restaurants are located under the glass-domed structure modeled after the Galleria Vittorio Emmanuelle in Milan.

Located in what might once have seemed an impossible area for a successful shopping district, **Ghirardelli Square** has its place in history for several reasons. Completed in 1964, it was the first inner city project in which a seemingly useless old warehouse or factory building was renovated into an elegant mall of shops. The success of San Francisco's Ghirardelli Square has since inspired hundreds of imitators, from Monterey to Charleston, S.C. One of the buildings dates back to 1864, when it was used as a woolen mill; however, it is famous locally as the home of the Ghirardelli family chocolate factory from 1893 until its present conversion. Covering the block bounded by North Point, Polk, Beach, and Larkin Streets, Ghirardelli Square is located on the northern waterfront area and now includes more than 70 shops and restaurants.

The Powell-Hyde cable car line will get you within easy walking distance of Ghirardelli Square and also to a newer factory building conversion called **The Cannery**. This old building dates from 1893 and was used as a cannery by the Del Monte Company for many years. There are 50 shops and restaurants in the complex, some with a lovely view of the bay, and others fronting a colorful courtyard busy with jugglers and mime performances. The Cannery is located at 2801 Leavenworth Street.

The **Embarcadero Center** is yet another huge new shopping area and a plus in San Francisco, where parking is always difficult — there is plenty of parking. It's free on Sundays, and at a discount other days with validation from any of the 175 shops and restaurants in the area. First planned in 1959, construction of the Center began in 1966 on the site of the city's old produce market. Work was completed in 1982 on the four towers and the Hyatt Regency Hotel. The center complex is located on the Embarcadero between Sacramento, Clay, and Battery Streets.

In the heart of Fisherman's Wharf, you'll find another gleaming new shopping complex called **The Anchorage**. Oldtime local residents may find it a bit

garish; visitors might call it fun. The 2½-acre (one-hectare) center is bound by Jefferson, Beach, Leavenworth, and Jones Streets.

Pier 39 is just two blocks east of Fisherman's Wharf, and many local people prefer it. An abandoned shipping pier has been transformed into an ongoing waterfront festival and one of the city's most popular attractions. The 45-acre (18-hectare), $54 million complex includes two levels of restaurants and shops with

spectacular views of the bay, and a 350-berth marina. The family entertainment area includes a fabulous Venetian carousel.

Japan Center is surely the city's most exotic shopping area. Covering three square blocks, it was designed by the famous architect, Minoru Yamasaki and completed in 1968. In addition to the best of Japanese restaurants and sushi bars in the city, the five-acre (two-hectare) complex includes an array of Japanese art galleries, bookstores, and numerous other shops offering oriental specialties.

A youngster takes advantage of the annual Pumpkin Festival at Half Moon Bay south of San Francisco. The Crocker Galleria OPPOSITE is just one of the many new enclosed shopping centers near Union Square.

Northern California

MONTEREY AND THE CENTRAL CALIFORNIA COAST

One of the most beautiful highways in California and the world is the Pacific Coast Highway, California 1. It snakes along the rugged coast south of San Francisco all the way to Santa Barbara, and on into the vast megalopolis of southern California. In remarkable contrast to the southern routes, you will find almost no development along much of Route 1 on the central coast. But Highway 1 is very narrow by modern standards and often crooked; it is no highway for those in a hurry. In other words, it is best to relax, take your time and enjoy the scenery. If you should happen to get behind a slow truck, or any of a million campers and vans on the roads, you will have to slow down anyhow because there just aren't many places where the road is wide enough for passing. It is possible to drive from San Francisco to Los Angeles on the coastal road in one day, but that is rushing it through some of the state's most beautiful scenery. Slow down, stop along the way, and enjoy the views.

SANTA CRUZ

Santa Cruz is called the "new Berkeley" by some in San Francisco because it is the site of a very liberal branch of the University of California, where the activist students do seem a throwback to earlier days at Berkeley. The 2,000-acre (800-hectare) campus sits atop gently sloping hills overlooking the town. Santa Cruz is a lovely old town of tree-lined streets with Victorian houses comparable to San Francisco's but, here, many of them are surrounded by beautiful yards and gardens. The Chamber of Commerce can provide not only a map for a self-guided walking tour of the downtown area, but also a map of the surrounding farms, where you can go and pick your own fruits and vegetables. The approach roads to Santa Cruz appear like a massive study in deep, nearly

black, green — miles and miles of artichokes and brussels sprouts in fields that reach to the very edge of oceanfront cliffs.

The town was named for Mission Santa Cruz, the twelfth and one of the least successful of the 21 California missions. Heavily damaged by earthquakes in the early 1800's, the mission buildings were abandoned in the face of a feared pirate attack in 1818 and left to ruin after 1833. In 1931, a smaller replica of the mission church was built; it is now maintained as a **museum.**

Located at 126 High Street, it is open from 9 am to 5 pm daily.

The town's main attraction is a fabulous old **boardwalk,** California's oldest, and one of the few amusement parks located right on the beach. Situated at the northern tip of Monterey Bay, it stretches along a mile and a half (two and a half kilometers) of beachfront, lined with shops, galleries, rides, and games. The **Giant Dipper** is a

The rugged coastline at Big Sur OPPOSITE has long been a haven for artists and writers and much of that earlier spirit lives on in the lodges and campgrounds. ABOVE: Emerald Bay in Lake Tahoe, one of the purest, deepest, and highest bodies of water in the United States.

wooden roller coaster built in 1924; the carousel dates to 1911.

The cool damp climate in Santa Cruz is ideal for raising begonias, and the colorful National Begonia Festival is held at the **Antonelli Begonia Gardens** every year, the weekend after Labor Day. The Gardens are located at 2545 Capitola Road, nearly three miles (five kilometers) south of Santa Cruz; ✆ (408) 475-5222. Another event that celebrates nature is the annual Welcome Back Monarch Butterfly Festival at the **Natural Bridges State Beach,** at the western edge of Santa Cruz. The beach is famous for the bridges and arches constantly being carved into the soft sandstone. In mid-October, the festival welcomes back the Monarch butterflies which arrive by the thousands every year and stay to the end of February. For more information, ✆ (408) 423-4609. If you're looking for strange sensations, visit the **Mystery Spot** at 1953 Branciforte Drive, just over two miles (three kilometers) north of Santa Cruz. It is a 150-ft (46-m) -wide clearing in a grove of redwoods where normal gravity doesn't seem to apply. Walking uphill, you seem to be on a flat surface; two people standing on a level block appear to be at a great distance from each other; and you can roll a ball uphill as easily as down. The Mystery Spot is open from 9:30 am to 4:30 pm daily; admission is $2.50 for adults and $1.25 for children five to 11-years; children under five are admitted free. ✆ (408) 423-8897.

MONTEREY

Formerly the Spanish and Mexican capital of California, Monterey is known to many as the somewhat decadent setting of John Steinbeck's *Cannery Row.* In recent years, everything here — including the huge cannery buildings for sardines and tuna — has been restored to an elegance the place never knew as a working port town. In fact, the only criticism you'll hear about present-day Monterey is that it's too pretty.

Discovered by the Spanish explorer Vizcaino in 1602, Monterey was named for the viceroy of Mexico, the Conde de Monterey. Vizcaino had described the bay in such elaborate terms that later explorers went right by it without recognizing it. However, the sacred mission of Father Serra found it, planned it as their capital and headquarters. All too soon, Serra saw that he had to put some distance between his Indian "neophytes" and the bawdy Spanish soldiers if he was ever going to train the Indians in the straight and narrow path. So, he moved on to Carmel; Monterey remained the civilian and military capital.

Several United States citizens and even a military contingent were already living peaceably in the Mexican capital in 1846, when United States forces took over the presidio without firing a shot. The state government was formed in meetings in Monterey and it remained the seat of government until Sacramento was made the capital in 1854.

Bypassed by government (for Sacramento) and business (for San Francisco), Monterey became a beautiful old relic of California's Spanish and Mexican years. Robert Louis Stevenson described it well in *The Old Pacific Capital* in 1879. The whaling and fishing industries and the canneries, with some very wealthy citizens at the top of the social scale and a very colorful working class made up largely of Mexicans below, kept the city prosperous. These people were celebrated in one of John Steinbeck's early novels, *Tortilla Flats,* the author's first major success. A native of nearby Salinas, Steinbeck moved to Monterey as a young man, and most of his major works drew on the life he knew in the agricultural valley and in the old port town of Monterey. His later work, *Cannery Row* was based on the adventures of a contingent of genial bums and a marine biologist friend, with whom he had earlier written *The Sea of Cortez,* a non-fiction account of life in what is also called the Gulf of California. The lovable bums in Steinbeck's book would be astounded to see the present-day transformation of

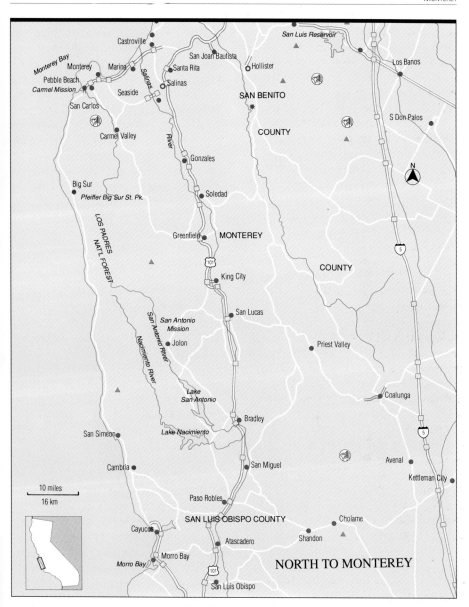

Castroville

Monterey Bay
Monterey Marina
Pebble Beach
Carmel Mission
San Carlos
Seaside
Salinas
San Juan Bautista
Santa Rita
Salinas
Hollister
San Luis Reservoir
Los Banos

SAN BENITO

COUNTY

S Don Palos

N

Carmel Valley

River

Gonzales

Big Sur
Pfeiffer Big Sur St. Pk.
Soledad

LOS PADRES NATL FOREST

Greenfield MONTEREY

5

San Antonio River

King City

COUNTY

San Lucas

San Antonio Mission

Nacimiento River

Jolon

Priest Valley

Lake San Antonio

Coalunga

Lake Nacimiento

San Simeon

Bradley

5

Cambria

San Miguel

Avenal

Kettleman City

10 miles
16 km

Paso Robles

SAN LUIS OBISPO COUNTY

Cholame

Cayucos

Atascadero

Shandon

Morro Bay
Morro Bay
101

NORTH TO MONTEREY

San Luis Obispo

Cannery Row. Gone are the smelly fish factories and canneries; on the same spot are elegant restaurants and hotels, boutiques, and all manner of fancy shops.

Don't despair of such gentrification, it has saved the old buildings from ruin. And Monterey — it has carried on the old flavor of the city in the "new" shops and restaurants. Along the old waterfront, you'll find a small-scale **Fisherman's Wharf,** its creaking old docks still jammed with working fishing boats. There are small shops where you can buy cups of chowder and all kinds of fresh seafood to go. The oldest and best restaurant is at the very end of the wharf — **Rappa's**, a busy comfortable place which has been there since 1951. For more information, ✆ (408) 372-7562 — you can buy fresh fish not only for yourself, but also for the hundreds of sea lions you'll hear honking from their habitat under and around the old wharf. The citizens of Monterey are ferociously protective of these sea creatures that live by the hundreds under the old docks. Jet skis and speed boats are prohibited in the areas where the sea lions live. If some of the restoration work seems too pretty, the sea lions — with their rude honking through the night — are a great leveler.

The beautiful old stucco and tile-roofed houses from the Spanish and Mexican period are found throughout the city. The more important ones come with plaques and signs

distance of Fisherman's Wharf and the historic district. First opened in 1904, the Monterey reopened in 1986 after a total restoration. It is a cozy, friendly place, and a free breakfast comes with the room. For enquiries, write The Monterey, 406 Alvarado Street, Monterey, CA 93940; ✆ (408) 375-3184. For a more lavish and elegant setting, the **Spindrift Inn** in Cannery Row is recommended. Located right on the beach, the Spindrift is close to the aquarium and everything else in Cannery

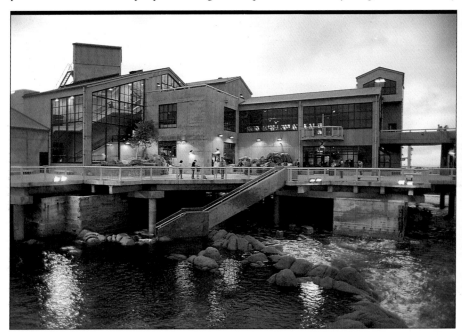

explaining their role in history. For a self-guided tour of the downtown area, the Chamber of Commerce provides an excellent map. Many historic buildings are clustered in a park around the **Presidio Museum** in the heart of town. **Colton Hall**, where the state constitution was drawn up, and the **Allen Knight Maritime Museum** are also worth visiting. For more information, write Monterey Peninsula Chamber of Commerce, 380 Alvarado Street, Monterey, CA 93940; ✆ (408) 649-1770.

Of the many fine old and new hotels in Monterey, one of the most comfortable is the recently restored **Monterey**, at 406 Alvarado Street. It is within walking

Row. Rates are $129 to $229 per night. For $45 an hour, you can rent the hotel's chauffeured Rolls Royce, minimum three hours, maximum four people. For information, write Spindrift Inn, 652 Cannery Row, Monterey, CA 93940; ✆ (408) 646-8900.

One of Monterey's crowd drawers in recent years has been the **Monterey Bay Aquarium.** First opened in 1984, it was built at a cost of $40 million and is the largest in the United States. Its exhibits are considered the most innovative anywhere; along with the huge kelp forest and shark tanks are smaller "touch pools" where youngsters (and oldsters) can reach in and touch a bat ray, or stroke a "starfish" or decorator crab. Located in one of the old sardine factories on Cannery Row, the Monterey Bay Aquarium is open 10 am to 6 pm everyday; it is closed on Christmas Day. Once you turn off Highway 1 into Monterey, there are signs marking the way to the Aquarium; ✆ (408) 649-3133.

PEBBLE BEACH

This beautiful 17 miles (27 km) stretch of beach, nestled among the windswept pines along the rocky coast between Monterey and Carmel, is famous for its golf courses and annual tournaments. The **Pebble Beach Golf Links** is one of the greatest courses ever built, with an extraordinary view of the beach and ocean from many of the links. Golf enthusiast Bing Crosby started an annual tournament at Pebble Beach in 1946 and it has since become one of golf's biggest tournaments. Now known as the Nabisco Golf Championships. It carries an annual pot of $2 million and contributes an additional $2 million to charities of PGA tour events. Accommodation is available at the **Lodge at Pebble Beach**, originally named the Del Monte Hotel. The first hotel was, in fact, a log lodge, which was built in 1908 and burned in 1917. The present structure first opened in February 1919 and has remained one of the world's premier golfing resorts. The Golf Links and the Lodge are a luxury resort, and green fees and room rates are expensive. For more information, write to The Lodge at Pebble Beach, 17-Mile Drive, Pebble Beach, CA 93953; ✆ (408) 624-3811. Two less expensive courses are: **Spyglass Hill** and the **Del Monte Course** both 18-hole, 72-par. For information and reservations, ✆ (408) 624-6611.

Golf is Pebble Beach's main claim to fame, but there is also an **Equestrian Center** where numerous events for serious horse enthusiasts are held. Watch out for the annual California Challenge Polo Match and the Annual Dressage Championship.

Another traditional event at The Lodge is the Pebble Beach Concours d'Elegance,

an automobile show held on the lawn between the Golf Links' 18th hole and the Lodge's Club XIX restaurant. Started in 1950, it has become a major charity event and a premier competition among the world's great automobiles. The Concours d'Elegance is held in August. The publicity office at The Lodge can provide more specific information.

Just north of Pebble Beach is a new resort built by architect Henrik Bull — the **Inn at Spanish Bay.** Before building the 270-room

resort, Bull restored 176 acres (71 hectares) of sand dunes in the area, hauling in 675,000 cu yd (516,000 cu m) of sand. The low stucco and tile-roofed buildings were designed to blend in with the dunes, "to look as if they'd always been there," and were landscaped with local plants.

A new championship golf course designed by Robert Trent Jones, Tom Watson, and Frank Tatum, the **Spanish Bay Golf Links**. It is located at 17-Mile Drive

The Monterey Bay Aquarium ABOVE AND OPPOSITE represents one of the most spectacular conversions of the old cannery buildings that once supported the city; the Aquarium has itself become a major new tourist attraction.

and Congress Road. For information or reservations, ✆ (408) 624-6611.

CARMEL

Father Serra retreated to Carmel when he could no longer put up with the "liaisons" between the Spanish soldiers and his Indian "neophytes" at Monterey. Since then, lovely "Carmel-by-the-Sea" has become home to a wide diversity of artists, writers, and celebrities such as folk singer Joan Baez and Clint Eastwood, "Dirty Harry" of the movies. Eastwood owns a popular bar here and has just finished a term as mayor of Carmel. The writers' colony in Carmel dates to 1904, and has included such American authors as Lincoln Steffens, Upton Sinclair, Sinclair Lewis, Jack London, and the poet Robinson Jeffers who used the area as a setting for many of his later poems.

At the south edge of town is the **Mission San Carlos Borromeo del Rio Carmelo.** Although it has always been called the Carmel Mission, the name Carmel actually antedates the mission. It came from the Carmelite friars who accompanied the explorer Vizcaino and named the river for their order in 1602. The mission, named for a sixteenth-century Italian cardinal, served as Serra's headquarters for all the missions; he died here. Serra's remains are buried at the foot of the altar in the church built in 1794. That structure is still intact, although it stood in ruins from 1840 until a major restoration in 1936. Pope John XXIII elevated the church to the status of a basilica in 1960, and in 1987, Pope John Paul II visited the site. The old mission has been a functioning parish church since 1933 and the mood inside the garden walls here is decidedly, refreshingly, religious. No tourists are allowed in during services, and the only request for contributions is a tiny sign in the museum and gift shop which suggests a $1 donation.

The mood is casual and comfortable in Carmel. The streets are lined with beautiful old twisted sea pines. Nothing is over two or three stories high; even the tract houses seem tucked into their own cluster of pines. The chain motels are built in low village-inn style, and flowers are found everywhere. Most of the more popular bars and restaurants have open fireplaces to counteract the chilly fog. Clint Eastwood's place is called the **Hog's Breath Inn,** at Fifth and San Carlos Streets, ✆ (408) 625-1044. Across the street, at the same intersection is a popular restaurant, the **Casanova,** ✆ (408) 625-0501. Some comfortable inns: **Dolphin**

Inn San Carlos Street and Fourth Avenue, ✆ (408) 624-5356; **Horizon Inn**, Junipero and Third Avenue, ✆ (408) 624-5327; The **Sandpiper Inn**, 2408 Bayview, at Martin Street, ✆ (408) 624-6433; **Wayfarer Inn**, Fourth Avenue and Mission Street, ✆ (408) 624-2711.

BIG SUR

Big Sur is one of those wild places that are dear to the hearts of Californians — a special blend of Nature's eccentric artwork — and man's. Beatnik author, Jack Kerouac, born in the factory town of Lawrence, Mass., wrote *Big Sur*, the story of an early counter-culture hero who settled there; Henry Miller,

The beautifully restored Mission San Carlos Borromeo del Rio Carmelo ABOVE AND OPPOSITE was headquarters for all the missions and it was here that Father Serra died and was buried. A museum is open to the public and a refreshingly religious air is maintained throughout the compound.

born in New York and a resident of Paris most of his life, came home to die in a secluded house in Big Sur.

Located 25 miles (40 km) south of Carmel, the Big Sur area is the southernmost point where the redwoods grow and the giant trees literally heighten the dramatic landscape, where the sheer cliffs rise straight up from the pounding surf, and where the steep rugged mountains of Los Padres National Forest loom behind. The name is an English corruption of the Spanish name for

White, Miller's official best friend, still holds court. The library and White's stories are open to the public.

Carmel's restaurants and motels are built like mountain lodges, nearly all have nice old paneled bars, high ceilings with broad exposed beams, and big stone fireplaces. Everything in Big Sur is right on Highway 1. One of the more expensive lodges is the **Ventana Inn**; ✆ (408) 667-2331. Less expensive are **Fernwood Park**, ✆ (408) 668-2722; and the **River**

the river, El Rio Grande del Sur, Big River of the South. Even today, there is almost no development along the narrow Highway 1 that meanders through the wilderness around Big Sur. There are numerous camp grounds, the best at the **Pfeiffer Big Sur State Park**, which is set in a thick grove of redwoods. It has a lodge with a restaurant.

The few commercial places along the road still look and feel like the 1950's; and here writers and artists are still regarded with special respect. The house where Henry Miller lived is not open to the public, but huge signs announce the **Henry Miller Memorial Library** at a sharp bend in the road. Here is where Emil

Inn, which has a very good restaurant with seating on an outdoor porch overlooking the river; ✆ (408) 667-2700.

SAN SIMEON

The signs now identify it as "Hearst's Castle", although William Randolph Hearst himself liked to call it "The Ranch". This was just another quirk of the controversial newspaper tycoon who built this grandiose monument to himself and led one of the most extravagant lifestyles ever seen in America.

The name San Simeon was borrowed from an adjoining ranch; Hearst's mother liked to called it "La Cuesta Encantada", The Enchanted Hill, a more fitting name any visitor can appreciate. The setting alone is worth the trip. As far as the eye can see, north and south, there is the rocky shore and the gentle hills rising up behind. It was an actual ranch when Hearst's father owned it, almost 244,000 acres (100 hectares) with 50 miles (80 km) of beachfront; a small tract compared to the many millions of acres the mining magnate owned in the United States and Mexico. William Randolph Hearst grew up spoiled, the only child of a refined and doting mother and a barely literate millionaire father. He ran a nationwide chain of newspapers that had the potential to wield extraordinary power in America, but Hearst's own muddled thinking and writing usually canceled that out. He was a man of contradictions. He single-handedly got the United States into war with Spain, only to become a bitter isolationist during World War I and World War II. Starting out as an enlightened Democrat and friend of the common man, he later became a violent anti-union leader; he helped elect Franklin Roosevelt and then turned on his administration with a vengeance. He wrote piously about fidelity and the sanctity of marriage while living openly with a mistress.

But through these 60 turbulent years in American politics, Hearst remained constant to San Simeon, this enchanting landscape on the then nearly inaccessible coast of California and the castle he was building for himself there. The family had built several ranch houses on the property since Hearst was a child, but he began work on the castle in 1919. After 30 years and millions of dollar spent, he had still not finished with it, and today, you can see an enormous wing that was never completed.

Hearsts' newspapers are credited — or, more accurately discredited — with having originated "yellow jounalism", and are now considered part of journalism's sordid past. What endures is "Hearst's Castle". Although Hearst died in

1951, the state did not take over the 127 acres (50 hectares) at San Siméon until 1957 — and then only reluctantly. Much to everyone's amazement, the public was standing in line to get a glimpse inside. Hearst's Castle is a rare state park that has been in the black from the start. More than a million people now visit the site every year. In 1985, a modern visitor's center was constructed just off Highway 1. It cost $7.5 million, almost as much as Hearst spent on his fabulous castle in the sky.

There is an excellent interpretive exhibit in the visitors center which does an accurate job of describing Hearst's strange career and his life at San Simeon. The Hearst Corporation still owns all the surrounding property and, in the early days, it was feared that his family's frequent visits would affect any objective presentation of

Once the exclusive preserve of the eccentric William Randolph Hearst and his invited guests, San Simeon or "Hearst's Castle" is now open to anyone with the price of admission. One of the purest and most beautiful designs on the cluttered mountain top is the Neptune Pool (OPPOSITE) designed after a Greek temple pool. Indoors, there is an equally extravagant heated pool featuring classic statuary and good mosaic tiles.

the man's life. The new exhibits, however, explain in detail how he lived openly with actress Marian Davies for the last half of his life. She was the real mistress of San Simeon. They would often import trains or planeloads of actors and actresses from Hollywood for one of their spur-of-the-moment costume parties. Hearst loved to dress up, just one of the frothy details you'll find in Davies' remarkably shallow memoir, recorded on tape and published after her death in the book, *The Times We Had*. The book revealed that she may have been a B-grade actress, and a lightweight intellectual (with girlish schemes to shake hands with Hitler and Mussolini), but she was a shrewd businesswoman. When Hearst's extravagance plunged the Hearst Corporation $125 million into debt in 1937, Miss Davies rescued him with a $1 million loan.

San Simeon is the enduring monument to Hearst's unbelievable extravagance. From his first visit to Europe as a boy with his mother, Hearst set about buying up its greatest art treasures. Miss Davies tells about his shipping an entire medieval monastery to San Simeon, and leaving it boxed up along the road for years because, he couldn't decide where to put it. Even now, guides tell you, there are four floors of a huge warehouse filled with Hearst's art treasures. When he came close to bankrupting the family corporation, many of his pieces were put on sale at Gimbel's and Saks Fifth Avenue. The sale lasted two years, and more than 700 pieces were sold each day.

Visitors to San Simeon are warned that you must walk a minimum of 150 steps on any of the four tours of the castle. First-time visitors are advised to take Tour #1 which focuses on the interior of the main house. Tours cost $10 for adults and $5 for children aged six to 11; children under six are free. Advance reservations are recommended for the peak summer months; © (800) 444-7275 or (619) 452-1950. The tours last about two hours, but you should allow an extra hour to go through the exhibits in the visitors center because the guides at the castle are not well-versed on their subject. A roomful of objects is dismissed as "old Catholic art"; a Greek sarcophagus as "a really ancient burial urn".

The winding road up to the castle goes through the old ranchlands; a herd of zebras now graze where Hearst once had the world's largest private zoo. (The animals were put in regular zoos during World War II.) Arriving at the base of the steps leading up to the castle, you behold not a castle but a cathedral. The stonework in the façade was taken from a fifteenth-century Spanish convent, and much of the woodwork tapestries, and silk banners inside were likewise taken from religious places in Europe.

Other American barons see themselves as English country lords or French and Italian counts; Hearst, a man of no active religious belief, apparently saw himself as a pope. Life in the 150-room castle was strictly by the master's rules; no one was allowed more than two cocktails; paper napkins were used at the huge dining table, which was set with brand name bottles of ketchup and mustard. Today's visitor will see it all as a clutter of styles, Greco-Roman, Italian and Spanish, much of it uncomfortable and impractical. One of the purest and most beautiful sites is the Neptune Pool, an outdoor re-creation of a Greek temple pool.

Standing by the pool, you wonder about the power of one man to create his own temple, and then you recall that he was spending his millions on these expensive toys at the very heart of the Great Depression, when much of the rest of the world was starving. But as you gaze into the distance, taking in the magnificently beautiful coastline, and the Piedras Blancas, white rock formations that jut up like ancient monuments from the sea, you begin to understand. And you reason that however selfish and greedy the man was in life, at least, his castle, his cathedral, is now public property, where anybody with $10 is free to wander and appreciate the expensive view.

W.A. Swanberg's 1981 book, *Citizen Hearst* remains the best biography of

William Randolph Hearst. For a more personal view of Hearst and San Simeon, Marion Davies' *The Times We Had* is recommended. Both of these are available in paperback in the motels and shops located just south of San Simeon. The best contemporary biography of Hearst is *Hearst: Lord of San Simeon*, by Oliver Carlson and Ernest Sutherland Bates. First published in 1936, this book is now out of print, but available in all California libraries.

Accommodation

Aside from the snackbar in the state-run visitors center, the only commercial enterprise at San Simeon itself is a wonderful old country store across the road from the entrance to San Simeon. Everything else is either owned by the state or the Hearst Corporation. Sebastian's store has been there since 1852. Located just up the road from the state beach and across from the original private docks and warehouses used by Hearst's father, it is crammed with an amazing variety of stuff, complete with a gas pump on the side and a U.S. Post Office at the back. There is also a nice little patio restaurant, serving fresh-caught seafood.

Although there are no lodging or restaurant facilities right at the castle, a fairly tasteful cluster of commercial buildings is located five miles (eight kilometers) south of San Simeon. Needless to say, the motels on the oceanside of the road have the better view, direct beach access, and are more expensive. Three of the better motels are: **The Cavalier Inn**, ✆ (805) 927-4688; **El Rey Inn**, ✆ (805) 927-3998; and the **Green Tree Inn**, ✆ (805) 927-4691.

A word of warning about another commercial development south of here. This is the town of **Cambria** — a living example of why laws are needed to restrict development of scenic and historic properties. At Simeon and all along the coastal highway, you will be bombarded with brochures and other advertisements for Cambria. It is depicted as a "picturesque" village of art galleries and quaint shops; in fact, it is a tacky clutter of the cheapest kinds of tourist traps. A quick

swing through Cambria does make one appreciate the effort to preserve the beautiful coastline north of here.

NORTH TO THE WINE COUNTRY AND THE REDWOOD EMPIRE

THE WINE COUNTRY

Nearly all roads north from San Francisco lead to the gently rolling hills and valleys

that have become famous as The Wine Country. In fact, vineyards and wineries are found throughout California; there is even a winery located right beside the Los Angeles International Airport. Until the late 1800's, the Los Angeles area was the state's major wine producer.

The wine industry dates back to the mission days. The padres planted grapes and made a syrupy sweet concoction for sacramental and personal use, although this wine had little in common with the more refined products that would follow

ABOVE: One of the thousands of Mexican migrant workers who pick the grapes that make the world-famous wines of California.

in later years. As the Gold Rush created a market for livestock and other products, it also gave a boost to the wine industry.

California wine production received an impetus from the experiments of a Hungarian wine maker, Agoston Haraszthy, who went to Europe and brought back hundreds of new varieties of grapes to see if they would prosper in California. Word spread of his experiments, and soon French, Italian, and German wine specialists were moving to the new fields of California. It is a myth that the American vines saved the French vineyards when they were virtually wiped out in the 1870's by a plague of phylloxera, a plant lice that attacks the roots of the vines. However, the prized vinifera grapes in the United States were also killed off by phylloxera. What saved them all was the discovery — in the 1880's — that the native American Labrusca grapes were immune to the lice. These were the plants that grew in such profusion, they caused Leif Eriksson to call the new land, "Vineland". By grafting the finer European vinifera onto the hardier labrusca roots, the wine industry was saved in France — and in California.

The French and other Europeans were involved in California wine-making from the beginning. But in the 1970's, the French government became alarmed at the growing involvement of California in French wine-making and placed heavy restrictions on the percentage of California wine that could be sold as French in France. The snob appeal of French superiority in wine-making was all but destroyed "one crisp May morning in 1976," according to Robert Finnigan in his book, *Essentials of Wine*, when nine of the top French wine experts agreed to a blind test of California wines against French wines. The American wines won hands down, much to the consternation of the judges. The incident was soon being called, "The wine-tasting heard around the world". Something else happened at that time. American taste changed and wine became a favored drink among Americans.

Prohibition had dealt a brutal blow to the vintners of California; some were able to endure the Noble Experiment of 13 years by converting to table grapes, but many went under. In the late 1960's and early 1970's, there was an extraordinary surge in wine consumption in America. And the American palate moved up from ordinary jug wine to the fine Chardonnays and Cabernet-Sauvignons popular in Europe. More than 75 percent of the wine consumed in America is home-grown; more

than 90 percent of that is produced in California. In May 1984, Baron Philippe de Rothschild of France and Robert Mondavi of California held a press conference in San Francisco to announce that the two great wine-makers had joined forces to produce a new red wine. Vineland and California had truly arrived.

While vineyards and wineries are found throughout California, the heaviest concentration is in the three counties north of

OPPOSITE: The vineyards in the Napa Valley north of San Francisco offer a picturesque industry suited to the gently rolling landscape. Paul Draper ABOVE samples the product in the Ridge Winery in Napa Valley.

San Francisco. The Wine Country consists of Napa, Sonoma, and Mendocino counties.

NAPA VALLEY

Napa Valley is the best known of the three, for its wine and for its beautiful surrounding. The narrow valley is one to five miles (one and a half to eight kilometers) wide, and stretches for 40 miles (65 km) along Highway 29 and the parallel route of the Silverado Trail. Napa is an Indian word of

unknown origin, but it has stood for pastoral retreat among Californians for many years. Two early resorts were established at Napa Soda Springs and at Stag's Leap. Many of the wineries are more than a century old, their castle-like buildings and landscaped grounds an inviting attraction even if you don't get to taste the wine.

Here are some of the more interesting wineries in Napa that offer daily tours and winetasting:

The Christian Brothers Mont La Salle Vineyards, 2555 Main Street in St Helena. ℂ (707) 963-0765. A teaching order, the Christian Brothers established schools in Northern California as early as 1855, and sold wine to support their schools. After Prohibition, they expanded into brandy production and bought the large Cresta Blanca winery in St Helena in 1950. Tours are from 10 am to 4:30 pm.

Clos Pegase, 1060 Dunaweal Lane in Calistoga. ℂ (707) 942-4981. Its modern buildings were awarded the San Francisco Museum of Modern Art's top design award. The tasting room is open from 10:30 am to 4:30 pm.

Inglenook Napa Valley, 1991 St Helena Highway in Rutherford. ℂ (707) 967-3359. Inglenook's Napa winery is housed in a century-old stone chateau, and is open for wine tasting and tours from 10 am to 5 pm daily.

Charles Krug Winery, 2800 Main Street in St Helena. ℂ (707) 963-5057. Founded in 1861 by pioneer wine-maker Charles Krug, the winery is a California historical landmark. It is open for tours and tasting from 10 am to 4 pm.

Joseph Mathews Winery, 1711 Main Street in Napa. ℂ (707) 226-1882. Founded in 1878, this is another historic winery, the only stone winery building left in the town of Napa. Tours, tasting, and restaurant are all open from 10 am to 7 pm daily.

SONOMA COUNTY

Sonoma takes its name from an early Indian tribe and is second in wine production only to adjoining Napa County. The town of Sonoma, located on Highway 12 by way of route 116 between Napa and Petaluma, was an important Mexican rancho seat. Here, General Mariano Vallejo built a town plaza and his own adobe Casa Grande, the finest house in northern California. It is also where the "Bear Flag" was raised over the short-lived California Republic. Vallejo's adobe mansion didn't survive, but a later Victorian house he built, has and it is now open to the public in a state historic park.

Sonoma County's most interesting wineries that offer tasting and tours are:

Buena Vista Winery and Vineyards, 18000 Old Winery Road in Sonoma. ℂ (707) 938-1266. Founded in 1857, it is California's oldest winery; its caves and picnic areas are open daily from 10 am to 5 pm.

Chateau Souverain, 400 Souverain Road at Independence Lane and U.S. 101 in Geyserville. ℂ (707) 433-8281. The Chateau Souverain is as famous locally for its award-winning restaurant as for its prized Chardonnay and Cabernet-Sauvignon wines. Open from 10 am to 4 pm, Monday through Thursday, and until 5 pm on Friday, Saturday, and Sunday.

F. Korbel & Brothers, 13250 River Road in Guerneville. ✆ (707) 887-2294. The Korbel Champagne cellars are located in one of the region's most beautiful spots — among the redwoods on the banks of the Russian River. Open daily from 9 am to 5 pm.

Sebastiani Vineyards, 389 Fourth Street East in Sonoma. ✆ (707) 938-5532. Founded by the mission padres in 1825, this huge vineyard was bought by Samuele Sebastiani in 1904, and has been owned by his family ever since. Gift shop and winery are open daily, from 10 am to 4:30 pm.

Smothers Tasting Room, 9575 Highway 12 in Kenwood. ✆ (707) 833-1010. This is where Tom and Dick Smothers went when their **Comedy Hour** got too controversial for CBS Television. Their "Mom's Favorite" red and white wines were an overnight success. The Tasting Room was opened in 1985 to show wines produced from the vineyards on Tom Smothers' ranch in Kenwood. Open daily from 10 am to 4:30 pm.

MENDOCINO COUNTY

The third among the major wine-producing counties, Mendocino is first in many people's minds in scenery. It combines a rugged coastline, the redwood forests, and the valley vineyards in a mix you don't find elsewhere. There are two major rivers cutting through the county: the Eel River that goes through the north, creating the fertile dairying valley by Ferndale; and the Russian River going through the southern part of the county.

The **Russian River** is where San Franciscans go to the beach. Since the ocean beach is often clouded over by fog, many in San Francisco have adopted the sandy banks along the Russian River as their place to get away into the sunshine. The river runs south out of Mendocino county into Sonoma County where it angles west to the ocean. **Guerneville** functions as a kind of inland beach town, and its small restaurants and bars are especially popular with gay men and

THE WINE COUNTRY

women from San Francisco and elsewhere. The coastal town of **Jenner,** another popular beauty spot, is where the Russian River empties into the Pacific.

Two of the Mendocino wineries that offer tours and tasting are: **Parducci Wine Cellars**, 501 Parducci Road in Ukiah, ✆ (707) 462-3828; and the **Weibel Vineyards**, 7051 North State Street in Redwood Valley, ✆ (707) 485-0321. Both are open daily from 10 am to 4 pm.

OPPOSITE: A mechanical grape picker moves through a vineyard in the Napa Valley in the heart of California's wine country.

Mendocino

The town is located on the coast of two of California's most beautiful regions — the wine country and the Redwood Empire. If you arrive for the first time in the beautiful old town with its turn-of-the-century store fronts and rambling wooden country houses, and think you've seen it all before, you probably have. The town has long been favored as a movie location. The *Summer of '41* is just one of many filmed on location here — and nearly all of them are supposedly set on Cape Cod or some coastal village in Maine.

While the name apparently is an Anglicized version of Mendoza, the Spanish viceroy in Mexico for whom Cape Mendocino was named, there is nothing else in Mendocino to recall the Spanish and Mexican presence in California. With so much wood handy, the first settlers built big houses with wide porches and surrounded their flower-filled yards with picket fences, a real oddity in California. The distinctive old water towers that once provided gravity flow into each house have also been preserved. A number of successful artists and writers, such as Alice Walker (author of *The Color Purple*), now call Mendocino home.

While the architecture may evoke New England, the mood in Mendocino is very much like the laid-back, casual style of a southern California beach town. The waters off the rocky coast are popular with surfers. The several fine restaurants are popular with San Franciscans who often drive up for lunch. The **Cafe Beaujolais** offers the best in haute cuisine. Only breakfast and lunch are served and reservations are required. © (707) 937-1259. Most of the old houses have been converted into bed and breakfast inns. The **MacCallum House Inn** was built in 1882 and is one of the coziest. It has a popular bar, the **Grey Whale**, and a restaurant in the main house. MacCallum House is located at 45020 Albion Street; for information write to: P.O. Box 206, Mendocino, CA 95460. © (707) 937-0289. Mendocino Coast Accommodations can provide infor-

mation and reservations for inns, motels, and rental homes in the Mendocino area. © (707) 937-1913.

Followers of Angela Lansbury's popular television series, *Murder, She Wrote,* may recognize the real streets and houses of Mendocino as Jessica's Cabot Cove, Maine. **Blair House** in Mendocino is the home of mystery writer Jessica in the TV series. The 1888 Victorian house has also been converted into an inn, with fireplaces in some of the rooms and a view of the ocean. For more

information on Blair House, © (707) 937-1800.

If all these restored Victorians seem too precious, you can always escape to **Dick's,** a seedy old bar on Main Street, where the town's low life hangs out.

While Mendocino may pass for a New England town, it's still in California. And hot tubs, sauna, and massage are popular here. The **Sweetwater Gardens Hot Tub & Sauna Spa** is located at 955 Ukiah Street, just west of the Café Beaujolais. © (707) 937-4140. North of Mendocino, about halfway to Fort Bragg, is the **Mendocino Tubbs,** promising tranquillity and privacy in the "Serene Gardens of the McCornack

Center for the Healing Arts" in Caspar, CA. The use of hot tubs is $9 an hour; massage is $25 for one hour or $35 for an hour and a half; overnight lodging in cottages with kitchens is available for $50 a night, Sunday through Thursday and $60 a night, Friday and Saturday. ✆ (707) 961-1809.

FERNDALE

If anyone has a complaint about this amazingly well-preserved Victorian village it is

that it's too pretty to be real. No mere restoration, you get the feeling that this place never went through a period of decay, that the owners of these fabulous old gingerbread houses and stores valued them from the start and always took care of them.

Located 260 miles (419 km) north of San Francisco, just south of Eureka, Ferndale is a nice long drive across a fertile valley thick with dairy cattle — and the rich odors that come with livestock. It is far enough away from the highways to set it apart from other restorations you've seen; the houses, again, seem a natural part of the setting. Founded in 1852,

Ferndale was known as the "Cream City" for its dairying industry, which was passed on by an odd mixture of Portuguese, Swiss, Italian, Danish, and German immigrants. These hardy Europeans held on to the farms and saved the area from the new developments that overwhelmed every other American city. There was also Viola McBride, now the town's leading landlady, who started a campaign in the 1940's to buy up and preserve the old stores and houses as they faced destruction.

Ferndale is hardly the sterile restoration it appears from a quick ride-through. Behind the colorful façades are some interesting characters, who give life to the old buildings and color to the town's cultural agenda. Carlos Benneman won his bookstore in a card game at Becker's, a bar next door. A hundred miles from anywhere, you'll find an amazing collection of rare books on sale. Becker's is called "the investment club" by others in town because of the games that go on there. Along with games of chance, it offers delicious *polenta,* a stew made with cornmeal mush. Many of the old family homes that Viola McBride saved have now been converted into popular guesthouses or bed and breakfast inns. Nearly all of the houses are surrounded by lavish gardens of dahlias, fuchsias, and zinnias to match the "butterfat" (as the dairymen call them) houses.

The **Gingerbread Mansion** is one of the most photogenic. It's located at 400 Berding Street, Ferndale, CA 95536. ✆ (707) 786-4000. All rooms have bathrooms, some have fireplaces; rates go from $75 a night to $135, with special mid-week and winter rates. Another showcase Victorian inn is the **Shaw House Inn**, set in an acre (half a hectare) of gardens, at 703 Main Street, Ferndale, CA 95536. ✆ (707) 786-9958.

In Ferndale, you'll find a whole town of Victorian homes and shops; the local dairy farmers called the gingerbread decorations "butterfat", because that's what gave them the money to build these fancy houses.

THE REDWOOD EMPIRE

The redwood is no mere tree, you will quickly learn from Californians. It is the world's tallest tree, and one of the oldest living things on earth. The coastal redwoods *(Sequoia sempervirens)* are found from Big Sur into Oregon; the inland redwoods *(Sequoia gigantea)* are in the Sierra Nevada. The Sierra redwoods live to be 3,200 years old, the coastal trees up to 2,200 years old. The bristle-cone pine lives longer, up to 4,500 years.

The Spaniards, the Russians, and everybody else who beheld the mighty redwoods quickly translated the forests into board feet of lumber. In 1984, redwood logging was a $138-million industry in California. Along with that, however, is a fierce conservation effort that dates back into the mid-1800's. The Sierra Club has been a leader in creating parks and nature preserves; the Save-the-Redwoods League was founded in 1918, and has created more than 135,000 acres (55,000 hectares) of state parks where the redwoods are protected.

Redwood National Park is the largest of the redwood preserves. Located in the extreme northwestern corner of the state, it covers more than 110,000 acres (44,500 hectares) of forestland in Del Norte and Humboldt counties. The logging town of **Crescent City** is the gateway to the park and what has come to be called The Redwood Empire of northern California. The town lies astride U.S. 101, but it is a long, jagged, and tortuous trip up the coast from San Francisco — which leaves the place well off the beaten path and a favored place to those who want to commune with nature and the mighty redwoods.

Actually, there are places quite close to San Francisco where you can walk among the redwoods. **Palo Alto** got its name from the "high tree" a Spanish explorer saw there in 1774. The **Muir Woods** is the closest grove of redwoods to the city, located across the Golden Gate Bridge, but within the Golden Gate National Recreation Area.

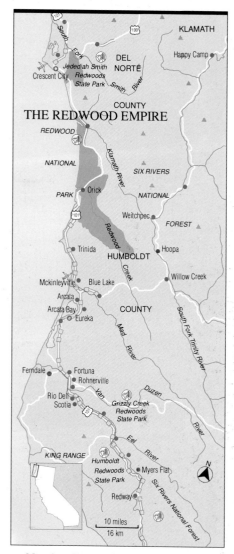

THE REDWOOD EMPIRE

Nearly all of the coastal roads north from San Francisco will take you in among the redwoods. The main roads are California 1, right on the coast, and U.S. 101, further inland. Where these two roads come together at **Leggett** is a good place to begin a trip into the redwoods. Just north of Leggett is the **Richardson Grove State Park**, and from there north, you will find any number of parks and groves; often, the

You do not need to be told you're in the presence of the mighty redwood trees; here is just one of the giants along the "Avenue of the Giants", a stretch of the old U.S. 101 north of San Francisco.

highway grows almost dark as it meanders among the giant trees. A 33 miles (53 km) stretch of an older route 101 has been re-christened "Avenue of the Giants", a some-times garish attempt to profit from the presence of the redwoods. If redwood burl coffee tables and ash trays leave you cold, you may want to avoid this route, though it does take you to some of the more beautiful state redwood preserves. Needless to say, you can't miss the signs on the newer 101 for the Avenue of the Giants, but the route begins at **Sylvandale** and ends at **Stafford.** The best known tourist attraction on the route is the **Shrine Drive Thru Tree** at Myers Flat. This is no state park, but a purely commercial enterprise. Its main draw is the huge tree that has been hollowed out to a width you can drive a car through; there's also a single log so wide you can drive a car on top of it. If you're interested in souvenirs there is a redwood factory where you can buy redwood burl clocks, wall plaques, and jewelry.

FORT ROSS

It was not named for Betsy or anyone else with that English-sounding name. It comes rather from "Rossiya", the last reminder (along with the Russian River) of the Czar's attempt to claim northern Califor-nia. In fact, the practical reason for sending Father Serra's sacred expedition to Cali-fornia in 1770 was because the Russians were known to be hunting and fishing fur-ther and further south from their Aleutian Islands base, and were taking a serious interest in California's northern coast.

Located about 10 miles (16 km) north of present-day Jenner and the mouth of the Russian River (which they called "Slav-ianka", Slav woman), Fort Ross was not established until 1811. The original party included 95 Russians and 80 natives from the Aleutians who helped in the hunting (and destruction) of the vast sea otter herds that then roamed the area. The Russian presence further inspired the young United States Congress to enact the Monroe

Doctrine against foreign incursion into this hemisphere. But with the otter hunted to extinction, the Russians sold their pro-perty and left of their own free will in 1839. At one time, the fort consisted of more than 50 buildings inside a high palisade, includ-ing a wooden onion-domed church with bells cast in St Petersburg. The remaining ruins of the fort were leveled during the 1906 earthquake. The palisade, the church, and several other buildings have been carefully rebuilt on the site. The Fort Ross State Park is open daily, from 10 am to 4:30 pm; there is a $2 parking fee.

FORT BRAGG

Fort Bragg started out in 1857 as an Army post. Eventually abandoned by the mili-tary, it became a busy logging and lumber center. This lumbering past and present is celebrated every year on Labor Day, with the annual Paul Bunyan Days festival in Fort Bragg.

You don't have to be in the area long to understand you're in a company town and the company is Georgia Pacific. Only the government owns more redwoods than this huge paper and lumber conglomerate. Along any of the roads from here north-ward, you'll see the firm's big logging trucks zooming downhill or chugging slowly upwards. At Fort Bragg, it is pos-sible to see a good side of Georgia Pacific. At Highway 1 and Walnut Street is the **Georgia Pacific Nursery**, open to the public free of charge from 8 am to 5 pm, Monday through Friday, from May through October. More than three million redwood and Douglas fir seedlings are grown here to be used in the reforestation of the ancient forests cut by Georgia Pacific. There is a visitors center, an ar-boretum, and tables for picnics.

Georgia Pacific also has a **Logging Museum** at 339 North Main Street in Fort Bragg. The museum is open 8:30 am to 4:30 pm, Wednesday through Sunday. It is located near the town's most famous at-traction, the depot for the western terminus of the California Western Railroad — better known as the "Skunk Train".

The Skunk Train got its name from the first gas engines that powered trains. People used to say that like a skunk, you could smell the train before you could see it. The train was originally a logging railroad, but passenger service started in 1904. A busy schedule of 10 different trips is available during the summer months, which is cut to one daily trip each day from mid-September through mid-June. The entire route is 40 miles (65 km) through rugged redwood country, with two tunnels to go through, and some of the crookedest railroad you'll ever ride on. Most of the cars are the self-powered gas engine skunks; but two diesel-powered locomotives from the old logging days have been restored to use. Willits is the town at the end of the full route; there is a halfway stop at Northspur, where some of the summer trips end for those wanting a shorter ride. The shortest ride is three hours round-trip; the longest is 8½ hours, all the way from Fort Bragg to Willits, and back. The longer trip is $20 for adults and $10 for children; the trip to Northspur is $16 for adults and $8 for children.

EUREKA

Eureka is a refreshing and robust change from the prettiness of Mendocino and Ferndale. You'll sense the difference long before you reach the old logging and sailing town — country music on the radio, logging trucks on the highways. Like Fort Bragg, Eureka is a company town and that company is Georgia Pacific. Logging is still the major industry here, and you can see the smokestacks rising from the lumber mills south of town.

Founded in 1850, during the gold rush in the nearby mountains, Eureka was a violent frontier town in the midst of Wiyot Indian territory. A young Capt. U.S. Grant was among those stationed at the military garrison in 1854. As a young newspaperman in nearby Arcata in 1860, Bret Harte

condemned the white men of Eureka who massacred a village of Indian women and children, while the men were away hunting and fishing. Similar racism broke out in 1885, when the Chinese were run out of Eureka.

The city now recalls a more genteel past that endures in a 10-block **Old Town** along the waterfront. The crown jewel on the city's old section is one of the most beautiful Victorian mansions ever built in America. This is the house built in 1885 for lumber baron William Carson. The

green-and-gold mansion commands a high hill at the end of Second Street. Although it is now a private club, you can see from the sidewalk how the Victorian architect outdid himself in piling one gingerbread on top of another. Further along Second Street is the **Bay Maritime Museum**. © (707) 444-9440.

There are also two beautiful old inns that speak of the elegance and good taste of the town's past. The **Eureka Inn**, located at Seventh and F Streets, first opened in 1922 and soon became northern California's finest hotel. Its celebrity guests included President Hoover, actor John Barrymore, and industrialists John D. Rockefeller Jr. and Cornelius Vanderbilt Jr. The Inn went through a period of decline and decay in the 1950's, but was bought

An engineer on one of the main lines in northern California, now devoted exclusively to hauling timber and other freight; happily the old "Skunk Train" preserves one old line for passenger excursions.

by its present owners in 1960. They have carried out a thorough and ongoing restoration of the hotel and its three restaurants: The Cafe, the Rib Room, and the Rathskeller. For more information, write to the Eureka Inn, Seventh and F Streets, Eureka, CA 95501. ℂ (707) 442-6441.

On a smaller, if cozier and older scale is the **Eagle House**, a Victorian inn dating to 1888. It is the center of much local activity; the **Buon Gusto** bar has good food and a local Dixieland band; the **Eagle House**

Theater is a dinner theater with local productions, and top visiting comedians and musicians. The same owners also run a popular fresh seafood restaurant two blocks away, **The Landing**, located right on the waterfront with a full view of all the activity on the waterfront activity. For more information, write to Eagle House, Second & C Streets, Eureka, CA 95501. ℂ (707) 442-2334, or (800) 522-8686.

ABOVE: Considered the ultimate in American Victoriana, the old Carter Mansion in Eureka still commands an overview of the town as it did when the timber baron built it. Now a private club, the green and gold house features gingerbread on top of gingerbread.

For food that the real loggers might have lived on, try the **Samoa Cookhouse**, now open to the public. Located just across the Samoa Bridge from downtown Eureka, it is the last surviving cookhouse from the old lumber camps in the area. There is a small museum with (heavy) artifacts from the sawmills and lumber camps. The restaurant uses old chairs, long tables, and big food platters passed around family-style. Menu includes heavy meat and potatoes, fried chicken and ham, For more information, ℂ (707) 442-1659.

WEAVERVILLE

A gold-rush town, Weaverville sits astride Highway 299, and calls itself the gateway to the rugged wilderness of northwestern California. From the coastal roads, take 299 through these mountains and get a taste of what the land looked like when the first prospectors came here. In fact, if you look out at some of the cabins along the way, you'll see what present-day prospectors look like. While timber is the major industry in the area, there are still those odd ones looking to get rich finding gold in those hills.

Actually, gold was discovered in the area not long after it was first found at Sutter's mill further south. This led to the area's own gold rush and the quick development of a town called Weaverville. The wooden buildings in the town were prone to fire and finally, more sturdy brick structures were built.

The present-day residents are proud of their little town, and they maintain what is surely the friendliest visitors center located anywhere. Here, you can get information on the national parks in the area, hunting and fishing, and of course, "recreational gold panning". There are also some very educational leaflets that explain the flora and fauna of the area and help identify the many different pines and pine cones you see.

At one time, there was a large Chinese community in Weaverville. A reminder of this period in the town's history is a **Taoist Temple** that has somehow managed to

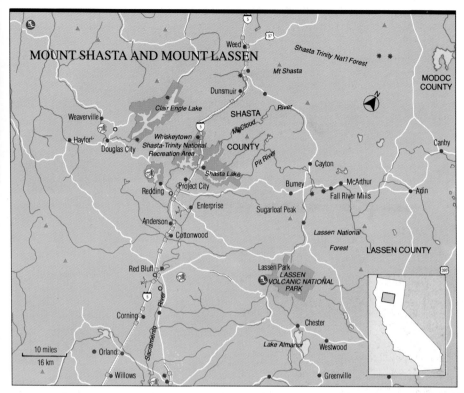

MOUNT SHASTA AND MOUNT LASSEN

survive the Tong wars among the Chinese themselves, and the hostility, and vigilante raids by non-Chinese. The temple is maintained as a state park and like everything else, is located on Highway 299, the town's main street. A quaint little **museum** is also maintained in memory of Jake Jackson, a local boy who started collecting guns and other historical artifacts before World War I. The exhibits here include an 1849 hand pump fire engine which the town bought from San Francisco in 1906. For more information on these sites and anything else about Weaverville and the surrounding area, write to the Trinity County Chamber of Commerce, P.O. Box 517, 317 Main Street, Weaverville, CA 96093. ✆ (916) 623-5211.

MOUNT SHASTA AND MOUNT LASSEN

The two most dramatic volcanic peaks in the Cascade range jut into the central part of northern California from Oregon. Both are at the center of popular national parks.

Mount Shasta is visible from Interstate 5, a magnificent natural wonder, rising to 14,162 ft (4,317 m) and snowcapped well into summer. It is due west of the town of Weed. The town of **Mount Shasta** is located at the southern base of the mountain, right on Interstate 5, and is convenient to both Klamath and Mount Shasta National Parks. There is a road up to the 8,000-ft (2,500-m) level of Mount Shasta, offering a spectacular view of the surrounding mountains and valleys. Facilities for cross-country skiing are located here. For information, write to the Mount Shasta Chamber of Commerce, P.O. Box 201, Mount Shasta, CA 96067. ✆ (916) 926-4865. An 18-hole golf course is located on the north slope of Mount Shasta, beside Lake Shastina; for information, ✆ (916) 938-4385.

There is some evidence that Mount Shasta has been active in the last 300 years. But, until Mount St Helens in Washington erupted in 1980, the only volcanic eruption in historic times within the contiguous

48 states was that of Mount Lassen, about 75 miles (120 km) southeast of Mount Shasta. The 10,457-ft (3,187-m) peak is now the centerpiece of **Mount Lassen Volcanic National Park**, 48 miles (77 km) east of Redding (and Interstate 5) on California Highway 44. In 1907, President Theodore Roosevelt declared Lassen Peak and nearby Cinder Cone national monuments. When the eruptions began in 1914, the entire 165 sq miles (427 sq km) area was set aside as a national park. There are seven campgrounds within the park. At the southwest campground is a ski chalet where ski equipment can be rented or bought. There is also a small lunch counter at the Lassen Chalet. Otherwise, there is no commercial development at all.

An excellent road guide to the park is available for $2 at its northern entrance, right off Highway 44. There are small numbered markers along the roadway, so you can match the color pictures in the guide and the text with what you're seeing. There are stops before all the major spots of geologic interest, but you'll also learn about the wildflowers and trees growing in the park.

The most interesting short hike from the main road is a two-and-aquarter-mile (three-and-a-half-kilometer) walk to the hot springs basin called **Bumpass Hell.** The park has other hot springs and bubbling mudpots, but this is the most spectacular of the active hydrothermal areas, steaming escape valves from the molten lava beds deep beneath the earth's crust. The main "devastated area" gives an awesome demonstration of the power of Nature. More than 70 years after the last eruption in 1917, there is nothing but ash and lava beds as far as you can see. The mud-flow from the eruptions covered the meadows with 20 ft (six meters) of mud and debris. (A local property dispute involving the

OPPOSITE: Horses graze in a meadow beside the steep forested peaks near Mount Lassen at the northern end of the Sierra Nevada range of mountains.

route of a creek was hopelessly confused when the volcanic eruption covered over everything in question.)

The steam you see rising from the various mudpots and hot springs is not the only surface evidence of the unstable ground beneath. An earlier visitors center had to be relocated because of the shifting grounds above and below it. The main — and only — road through the park is constantly being rebuilt in places because of slides.

Address enquiries to Mount Lassen Volcanic National Park, P.O. Box 100, Mineral, CA 96063. © (916) 595-4444.

EAST TO SACRAMENTO AND THE GOLD RUSH COUNTRY

SACRAMENTO

Sacramento became the state capital of California in 1854. Looking at the state from the heavily populated southland of today, one wonders how the capital could ever have been located so far north. However, until water was brought in at the turn of the century, southern California was a sparsely populated desert wasteland, with only a few thousand people living in the pueblos of Los Angeles and San Diego.

Sacramento, moreover, was at the heartland of early California. Gold was first discovered near Sacramento, and this led to the rush on all of "them thar hills" in the surrounding area. The city took its name from the county which, in turn, got its name from the river; presumably there was a religious Spaniard back there somewhere who did intend for something to be named for the Holy Sacrament, or Sacramento. It lies at the confluence of the American and Sacramento rivers, and the rich delta farmlands spreading out around them. Nearly all of the surrounding land was originally owned by John Sutter, a German-born Swiss who came to California in 1839, became a Mexican citizen, and

was given the largest land grant allowed, 11 square leagues or 48,400 acres (19,595 hectares). Sutter set himself up as baron of what he called "Nueva Helvetia", or new Switzerland, forcing Indians to work as serfs on his farms, orchards and vineyards. Everybody but Sutter called it "Sutter's Fort", however, because of a massive fort he built with walls three feet (a meter) thick and 15 ft (4.5 meters) high. It was to this fort that the Donner party was heading and, in fact, it's where the survivors settled.

While you hear little about the miners, their gold quickly enriched the area and brought in of thousands new emigrants, the result being that California never went through the probational period as a territory before becoming a state. Among those who profited immensely were the "Big Four", four storekeepers in Sacramento who would become the richest and most powerful men in the country at that time: Charles Crocker, Mark Hopkins, Collis P. Huntington, and Leland Stanford. No ordinary storekeepers, they also functioned as bankers — making loans, and taking the gold as payment. Starting out with a short-line railroad from Sacramento to Folsom, they would go on to build the first transcontinental railroad. Eventually, they monopolized rail traffic into California, by which time they were called "The Octopus".

You get some idea of the wealth of Sacramento and California compared to the rest of the United States when you consider that the magnificent neo-classical **Capitol** with its 237-ft (72-m) dome was constructed in 1861. At that time, the U.S. Congress could not find the money to complete the dome on the U.S. Capitol or to finish the Washington Monument — both of them weathering away as unfinished nubs as the country faced civil war. The Capitol is set in a 40-acre (16-hectare) park and located on 10th Street and Capitol Mall; public tours of the seven museum rooms and other parts of the building are conducted daily on the hour from 9 am to 5 pm.

A reconstruction of **Sutter's Fort,** and the **State Indian Museum** are located at 27th and L Streets. The museum houses important artifacts and exhibits on the early history of the area. About 20 years ago, the movement to restore "Old Sacramento" began, revitalizing the city's waterfront and downtown areas. A more recent $10-million waterfront redevelopment include the reconstruction of four original buildings that had been destroyed, and a two-block-long **plank wharf,** where a reconstructed paddlewheel riverboat, the *Matthew McKinley,* now takes on passengers.

Although the capital is a true city of nearly 300,000 inhabitants, much of it still recalls a quiet old river port town. There are many elaborate Victorian houses along the tree-lined streets. Most of the older houses are located in the area from Seventh to 16th and E to I Streets. The **Sacramento History Center** at 101 I Street, ℂ (916) 449-2057, is an excellent place to begin a tour of old Sacramento.

Also worth a visit is the fabulous 15-room Victorian **Governor's Mansion** that was home to 13 California governors from 1877 to 1967, when Ronald and Nancy Reagan refused to live in it, calling it a "firetrap", (The later revelations about Nancy's astrologer came as no surprise to old hands in the state capital who remembered Reagan insisted on being sworn in as governor at some odd minutes after midnight — on the advice of an astrologer.) Now open as a museum, the Governor's Mansion is located at 16th and H streets and is open from 10 am to 4 pm. ℂ (916) 323-3047. The **Crocker Art Museum**, in a restored Victorian house at 216 O Street, houses the oldest art museum in the West. Started in 1873, the original collection of European masters has been expanded to include nineteenth-century California artists and modern artists. The museum is open Wednesday through Sunday, from 10 am to 5 pm.

The **California State Historic Railroad Museum**, 125 I street, claims to be the largest interpretive railroad museum in the world, It has 100,000 sq ft (30,00 sq m) of space housing 21 restored locomotives and cars, and 46 exhibits. Admission is $3 for adults, $1 for children The museum is open from 10 am to 5 pm daily. ℂ (916) 448-4466.

Keep in mind that Sacramento is a river delta town and there is still a great deal of life on the river — most of it recreational in recent years. For information on renting houseboats on the Sacramento River, write to **Holiday Flotels,** Delta, 11540 W. Eight Mile Road, Stockton, CA 95208. ℂ (209) 477-9544. A *Guide to Houseboating on the Delta* can also be ordered from Schell Books, P.O. Box 9140, Stockton, CA 95208 for $3.63.

There are many of new and old restaurants to match the charm and sophistication of the revitalized city. The **Rosemount Grill** at 3145 Folsom Boulevard has been a favorite for 73 years. ℂ (916) 455-5387. Among the restored old places is the **Fat City Bar & Café**, 1001 Front Street. ℂ (916) 446-6768. **A.J. Bump's** three locations are favorite hangouts for business and professional people. The menu features steaks and fresh seafood, and there's live entertainment. Locations are: 8055 Freeport Boulevard, ℂ (916) 665-2251; 450 Bercut Drive, ℂ (916) 442-0496; and 228 G Street in Davis, ℂ (916) 758-4290.

The small hotels, and bed and breakfast inns in Sacramento are convenient and tasteful. Two elegant mansions near the Capitol and the convention center are the **Amber House Bed & Breakfast Inn**, 1315 22nd Street, and **Aunt Abigail's Bed & Breakfast Inn**, 2120 G Street. For more information on the Amber House, ✆ (916) 444-8085; for Aunt Abigail's, ✆ (916) 441-5007. The **Hyatt Regency Sacramento** is a new luxury class hotel which claims the largest and best facilities in river city. It is located at 1209 L Street, Sacramento, CA 95814. ✆ (916) 443-1234.

GOLD RUSH COUNTRY

Gold rushes actually took place throughout California — from the hills west of San Diego to Catalina Island, Death Valley, and up into the northwestern redwood forests. But the original rush, the one that captured the imaginations of thousands of people throughout the world, was in the area east and south of Sacramento.

To get to the heart of the old gold country, take U.S. 50 east from Sacramento to the town of **Placerville**, located just south of the spot where the first gold was found at Sutter's mill. Earlier called "Dry Diggins" and "Hangtown", Placerville was an important stop on the stage and, later, the rail lines. Three major industrialists once worked there as young men: railroad man Mark Hopkins, meat packer Philip Armour, and John Studebaker, who worked as a wheelwright in Placerville in preparation for his later career as automaker.

California Highway 49, south from Placerville, will take you into **Calaveras** (Spanish for "skulls") **County** and the heart of the **Mother Lode,** the 120 miles (194 km) stretch where the first major gold mines were found and incorrectly believed to be part of the same vein or lode. Mark Twain lived and wrote in the area; in fact, one of his most popular early stories was entitled *The Celebrated Jumping Frog of Calaveras.* It was set in Angels Camp, just one of the many picturesque towns you'll find in gold rush country today. On the zigzag from Angels Camp to the town of Sonora, you will pass signs to the **State Historic Park of Columbia.** Any questions you may have about the gold rush will be answered in this unusually fine historic park.

Columbia was considered "the gem" of the Mother Lode. From the first strike in 1850 through three decades later, more than $87 million in gold was taken from the Columbia mine. The town matched its new found wealth with blocks of tree-lined streets, and fine brick and stone stores and houses. Twelve full blocks — the entire town — are now preserved in the historic park. The Wells Fargo office, the dry goods store, the Masonic temple, the churches, the private houses, and, of course, the saloons, have all been carefully restored. For a more authentic atmosphere, there are mule-drawn wagons moving about, and a human powered water pump with its own uniformed Columbia Fire Department force. There are also exhibits on Lola Montez and Lotta Crabtree who once entertained here before going on to fame and notoriety in the big cities. Other exhibits describe the life and deeds of the bandits, Black Bart, and Joaquin Murietta, the Mexican hero-bandit whose head was pickled and displayed in a jar for many years after his death.

Further south in Tuolomne (an Indian tribal name pronounced "twallomee") is **Jamestown**, another important gold rush town. Of special interest here is the **Jamestown Railtown State Historical Park**. The old depot is carefully preserved as well as the locomotives, and passenger and freight cars. These are often used in movies but the Jamestown depot's real moment of fame came when it was used as the setting for the popular television series, *Petticoat Junction*.

THE SIERRAS

LAKE TAHOE AND SKI COUNTRY

Your mind runs out of superlatives when you come around a curve in one of the roads over the High Sierras and behold for the first time Lake Tahoe spread out before you. It is the crown jewel of the Sierras, a glistening emerald so breathtakingly beautiful it must be experienced. It is the largest alpine lake in America, 6,228 ft (1,898 m) above sea level, 22 miles (35 km) long, and 12 miles (19 km) wide. There is no water on earth as clear and pure — so clear you can see 120 ft (37 m) beneath the surface.

The lake went through several political names before the state finally settled on Tahoe, which was believed to be the Washo Indian word for lake. Like nearby Squaw Valley, Tahoe is famous as a winter resort for skiing. But in recent years, it has also gained popularity as a summer resort for hiking, boating, and — on the Nevada side — gambling.

Development along the lake is mainly divided up into South Shore and North Shore, although there is an east and west shore as well. The **South Shore** is more crowded, but it is also the oldest, and many beautiful old turn-of-the-century mansions are located here. **Harrah's Lake Tahoe Resort Casino** is located on the Nevada side of the South Shore. It is the most luxurious of the lake's many hotels and casinos. Each of its 540 rooms comes with two full bathrooms, three telephones, and three television sets. The **Summit Restaurant** on Harrah's 18th floor has a panoramic view and the best food of any of the casino restaurants. If you don't like the action at Harrah's, nearby is Harvey's 17-story glass tower and **Caesar's Lake Tahoe**.

Tahoe's **North Shore** isn't so crowded; life is slower here, and the mood is decidedly more cultured than that of the busy casinos to the south. There is a North Tahoe Fine Arts Council which sponsors an annual art fair and regular musical and dramatic presentations. **Captain Jon's** restaurant is one of the area's finest, located right by the docks on the north shore. **Le Petit Pier** has a similar lakeside view and an even more famous cuisine. Founded in 1972 by chef Jean Dufau, it offers an extensive menu of classic French dishes. Captain Jon's is located at 7220 N. Lake Boulevard, Tahoe Vista; ℂ (916) 546-4819; Le Petit Pier is at 7252 N. Lake Boulevard, Tahoe Vista, ℂ (916) 546-4322.

SKIING AT LAKE TAHOE

At **Squaw Valley**, where the 1960 Winter Olympics were held, there are 8,300 acres (3,360 hectares) of skiing. Twenty-seven lifts serve the six peaks. Facilities are located at 6,200 ft (1,890 m) and at 8,200 ft (2,500 m), with excellent lodging and restaurant facilities at the lower elevation. Squaw Valley is located on Highway 89 between Truckee and Tahoe City. For

RIGHT: Skiers ride one of the many chairlifts up to the snow-covered slopes that have made Lake Tahoe one of the most popular winter resorts in California.

information, write to Box 2007, Olympic Valley, CA 95730; © (800) 824-7954. There is a regular shuttle bus service between Squaw Valley and the North Shore of Lake Tahoe.

At **Alpine Meadows**, there are 13 lifts up two mountains. It offers an excellent ski instruction program and is popular with families. Facilities include several restaurants, a lodge, and free shuttle bus service to the North Shore. For information, write to Alpine Meadows, Box 5279, Tahoe City, CA, 95730. © (916) 583-4232 or (800) 822-5959.

Northstar at Tahoe is located on route 267 between Truckee and the North Shore. It is popular for its long gentle runs through beautiful fir forests. For information, write to Northstar at Tahoe, Box 129, Truckee, CA 95734. © (916) 562-1010.

Heavenly Valley, located right on the South Shore of Lake Tahoe, is the largest ski resort in America, with 20 sq miles (52 sq km) of skiable terrain on nine mountains in California and Nevada. There are 25 lifts. An aerial tram goes up to the **Top of the Tram Restaurant**, which has excellent food and awesome views of two states. The Top of the Tram is but one of the many facilities at three lodges at the base of the mountain and four others on the top. For information, write to Heavenly Valley, Box AT, South Lake Tahoe, CA 95705. © (916) 541-1330.

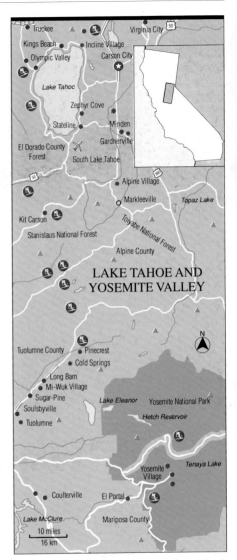

LAKE TAHOE AND YOSEMITE VALLEY

YOSEMITE NATIONAL PARK

The **Yosemite Valley** is one of most dramatically beautiful landscapes on earth and it has held an awesome mystique over Californians from the very first to behold it. A young militiaman among those sent in by the state to remove the Indians from the valley in 1851 thought the tribal name was "yosemity". Apparently, he had heard "Yo-Semite", the word for grizzly bear, which is what the valley has been called since. Artists and adventurers took to the place from the start, and a hotel was built as early as 1859. The state declared the

valley a state park in 1864, a National Park covering the surrounding area was created in 1890; and the present Yosemite National Park of 1,189 sq miles (3,080 sq km) was created in 1905.

The park lies at the heart of the High Sierras and contains the most spectacular landforms and waterfalls created by the earthquakes and glaciers over millions of years. The Yosemite Valley, which gave the park its name, is seven miles (11 km) long and approached from the eastern entrance to the park. Lush and green, it lies in stark contrast to the bare stone walls around it that rise almost straight up to 3,000-4,000 ft (900-1,200 m). Here, wrote the great naturalist John Muir, "God himself seems to be always doing his best."

The best approach to the hotel is from the east; this takes you into the heart of Yosemite Valley where the **National Park Service's Visitor Center** is located and where the main hotels, lodges and campgrounds are.

Yosemite is on the eastern edge of the state and roughly at its geographical center. It's about 200 miles (323 km), and a four-hour drive, from San Francisco; about 300 miles (480 km), and a 7½ hour drive, from Los Angeles. From San Francisco, take Interstate 580 east to Highway 99 south; just below Merced, take Highway 140 east through El Portal and the main entrance to the park. From Los Angeles, take Interstate 5 to Bakersfield, Highway 99 to Merced and 140 on into the park. From the western side, you come into the Tuolmne Meadows entrance from U.S. 395, a scenic route that skirts the eastern edge of the high Sierras.

Accommodation

The most exclusive place to stay in Yosemite is the **Ahawahnee Hotel,** a beautiful 1920's lodge built of heavy timbers, stone, and glass. It is spacious and elegant — to match the splendor of nature all around it. The hotel's 123 rooms, all doubles, rent for $135 during the winter months — November to mid-March — and $149 the rest of the year. One of the hotel's most famous events is the annual Bracebridge dinner at Christmas. The lavish feast was started by the great photographer, Ansel Adams, and his friends in 1927, the year the hotel opened. It is a four-hour-long pageant of song and feasting based on Washington Irving's description of Christmas dinner at Squire Bracebridge's in Yorkshire. The dinner proved so popular that a lottery to pick the participants had to be devised. To be considered, you must pay $100 and get your name in by January 15, a year before the

event. Only 1,750 guests are chosen. For information, write to Reservations Department, Bracebridge Dinner, Yosemite Park & Curry Co., 5410 E. Home Avenue, Fresno, CA.93727 ℂ (209) 252-4848.

For less-elegant quarters but still a magnificent view of Yosemite Falls, there is the **Yosemite Lodge.** The lodge has rooms without bath for as little as $37.75 a night, cabins without bath for $33. **Curry Village** offers hotel rooms ($56), private cabins ($44.75), and canvas tent cabins for

$22.65. The **Wawona Hotel** has rooms for $51.50 without bath, and $64.50 with bath. The **White Wolf Lodge** has regular cabins with bath for $41, and canvas tent cabins for $25.75. Reservations are required, and for the summer months, you need to make reservations several months in advance. A deposit covering one night's stay is required and should be mailed to Yosemite Park and Curry Co. Reservations, 5410 E. Home, Fresno CA 93727. ℂ (209) 252-4848.

Cross country and downhill skiing is available at Yosemite's **Badger Pass.** Cross country guided ski tours to Glacier Point are also available — $90 for an overnight tour, $130 for a three-day tour.

ABOVE: The grand old Ahwahnee Hotel has become almost as important as a cultural center as the natural wonders in Yosemite National Park.

Los Angeles

LOS ANGELES CITY MAP

LAND OF THE LOCUSTS AND THE LOTUS

It took a very talented foreigner to explain the role of Los Angeles in the cultural life of America. In accepting the 1988 Academy Award for best picture, Italian film director Bernardo Bertolucci said: "Los Angeles is the nipple of America."

This odd remark didn't take long to draw the usual howls of derision from the East Coast. NBC's windy weatherman, Willard Scott, said Los Angeles was a nipple all right "because that's where all the boobs are." What Bertolucci meant, of course, was that the city provided nourishment to creative artists, not only in films but also in other areas.

It is easy enough to criticize Los Angeles. The city has the worst air pollution of any place in America. In fact, the word "smog" has become as closely identified with its name as fog once was with London. Hollywood, which brought it glamor and good times, also caused Los Angeles to become known as "Tinseltown", where nothing is permanent, everything is cheap, tacky, and temporary, and dreams are more often of the broken kind.

To many East Coast opinion makers, "La La Land", "El-Lay, El-Lay" is nothing more than the Los Angeles of Nathanael West's classic Hollywood novel, *Day of the Locust*, a surrealistic gathering of hordes of people desperately and hopelessly seeking their dream in Lotus-land.

This attitude fails to reckon with several facts. For one, the movies have not been the major industry in Los Angeles since World War II; the aerospace industry took over, and is still the current leader. With a population of more than three million, the city is now second only to New York in population. It is largest in area, covering 463 sq miles (1,200 sq km), makes it is the largest city in America (New York covers 301 sq miles, or 780 sq km; Dallas, 333 sq miles, or 862 sq km). While the image endures of Los Angeles as the rainbow's end for all those small-town mid-westerners seeking an earthly paradise endures, the facts are now radically different. The 1980 census showed the city to be home to 900,000 blacks, 150,000 Armenians, 115,000 Japanese, 90,000 Chinese, 100,000 Filipinos, 60,000 Koreans, and 30,000 Vietnamese. The Vietnamese are only the latest immigrant group to add to the city's evolving culture. Their children have done so well in the public schools that national studies have been commissioned to figure out why.

As the decade of the 1980s came to a close, sociologists and other observers were taking a second look at Los Angeles as the future of America. On the surface it looked as if little had changed — a police force that functions almost as a Banana Republic army, racism and black slums, violence (17 murders in one recent weekend) to match the city's Wild West beginnings. In spite of all this, the physical and spiritual evidence of Los Angeles' becoming a great American boom town in 1990 is everywhere apparent.

ABOVE: A young girl in Hare Krishna outfit hardly stands out among the colorful throngs on Venice Beach. OVERLEAF: Graffiti and imaginative punk styles make an arresting Hollywood street scene.

It is just possible that the place will finally become a real city, and not merely a bunch of suburbs in search of one.

FROM PUEBLO TO MEGALOPOLIS

However grand the skyline of Los Angeles has become today, it all began around a humble village of mud-adobe huts. The city's name dates to 1769 when a religious expedition of Spaniards, led by Gaspar de Portola, camped by the river on a spot in the heart of present-day Los Angeles. They named the river for the Porciuncula which flowed past St Francis' favorite chapel, the Nuestra Señora la Reina de Los Angeles, the mother church of the Franciscan order. Some accounts say the spot itself was named all that plus *de Porciuncula* for the river. But by the time Governor Felipe de Neve led a band of 44 black, Indian, and Spanish settlers to the spot, it had been shortened to "Pueblo de la Reina de los Angeles". That, in turn, became "Los Angeles", which was the name adopted for the town and the county when California became part of the United States in 1850.

For most of its first hundred years, Los Angeles was little more than a village of a few hundred farmers and ranchers. After Mexican independence, the land was divided up into enormous ranchos. Among the new lords of these domains were dozens of "Yankee dons" who took a Spanish first name, embraced Catholicism, married into the old families, and gained title to their own fiefdoms of hundreds of square miles. Incredibly, some of these families (like the Dominguez-Carson family on Rancho San Pedro, south of Los Angeles) held on to these lands until very recent years. Pio Pico, the last Mexican governor, was a Los Angeles resident who owned 531,263 acres (215,000 hectares) of southern California; his neighbors included the Alvarados, Castros, Peraltas, and Vallejos. The names of these original dons are preserved in Los Angeles street names. By the treaty ending the Mexican War, the Americans agreed to respect the Mexicans' titles to their ranches, but an act of Congress in 1851 allowed them to be broken up.

The world's attention at that time was on the Gold Rush in northern California, which indirectly benefited local residents when the overnight rush of emigrants to San Francisco and Sacramento created an insatiable market for Los Angeles' livestock. But for the next two decades, Los Angeles continued as a dusty little speck on the map. It had such a bad reputation for violence that some said its name should be changed to El Diablo. One contemporary observer noted: "Criminals, murderers, bandits and thieves were hung in accordance with the law or without the law, whichever was most convenient or expedient to the good of the town."

The violence reached its peak in 1871 when a vigilante mob went on a rampage and killed 19 Chinese after a Chinese man had accidentally killed a white man. This shocked the more responsible town fathers into action — especially after the incident made headlines in newspapers and magazines throughout the country. In a very short time, the local sponsors would be vitally concerned about outside opinion as they began the first of many boom periods to sell and develop real estate in the Los Angeles area.

In 1876, the city was connected to the Southern Pacific Railroad in San Francisco. This seemed to open up unlimited opportunities. Even greater markets were visualized in 1885 when the town's own railroad, the Santa Fe, was completed across the country. For a while, competition was so fierce between the two railroads that the passenger fare from Kansas City to Los Angeles was only a dollar.

The town of 12,000 exploded into a city of 50,000 in less than two years. Downtown property went for $1,000 a storefront; 70 miles (113 km) of new developments were laid out from Santa Monica on the oceanfront all the way inland to San

Bernardino. But the bubble burst in 1887. People were fleeing at the rate of 3,000 a month when railroad owners and local businessmen founded the Los Angeles Chamber of Commerce to restore confidence in local investments. The new slogans and publicity campaigns worked, and soon the city's population had doubled again, back to 50,000.

It didn't hurt that this coincided with the discovery of oil in an ordinary front yard by E.L. Doheny and C.A. Canfield. More than 1,400 oil derricks sprang up almost overnight in the area from downtown Los Angeles to Beverly Hills. Until very recent times, you could still see derricks at work in this area. These fields were eventually depleted, but in 1921, huge new oilfields were discovered southwest of the city at Long Beach.

Some competition had existed between Los Angeles and San Diego, but with the arrival of the Santa Fe Railway, the discovery of oil, and the development of an artificial harbor at San Pedro, Los Angeles' commercial supremacy was assured. Water was a serious problem though, since the whole area had less than 10 in (255 mm) of rainfall a year, and was technically a desert. But that, too, was solved by a $22.5 million bond issue to build a viaduct that would transport the entire Owens River 238 miles (148 km) from the High Sierras to Los Angeles.

The millions of dollars allotted for the early water projects gave rise to massive corruption involving some of the town's leading citizens. (Some of the corruption in these projects was used as a backdrop to the action in the movie, *Chinatown*.) For a start, the pipeline reached only the arid San Fernando Valley. The bond issue had stipulated only that the water be brought to the city limits — so the city simply annexed what was then 108,000 acres (43,725 hectares) of desert wasteland and took the city to the water, once again enriching the valley's landowners and speculators.

It was the coincident development of the automobile and moving pictures that really put Los Angeles on the map and

helped it come in to its own as a city. New York and the cities of the East had developed long before the automobile and functioned quite well without it. But Los Angeles was too vast. It thus became the first city that depended on the automobile, the first commuter city.

In the early days, people spoke with admiration of Los Angeles' grand boulevards that stretched from downtown 18 to 40 miles (30 to 65 km) in every direction. The celebrated freeway system did not begin

until 1940, with the construction of the Arroyo Seco Parkway, now part of the Pasadena Freeway. But what was then a blessing has now become a curse. It is a shocking bit of *déjà vu* to experience the freeways now, with their gridlocks and bumper-to-bumper traffic, and then to look at a picture of the original lanes a year after they opened. The word "freeway" was coined by a city planner in 1930 to connote "freedom from grade intersections, and from private entranceways, stores and factories." In Los Angeles, as one author noted, it also

ABOVE: The Hollywood Freeway is a vital link in Los Angeles's massive freeway system, which is best avoided during rush hours.

Los Angeles

meant "the freedom of mobility and personal expression — that captured the hearts and imagination of Angelenos." (Los Angeles now has 26 freeways, with 722 miles (1,164 km) of superhighway. In one of his songs, Burt Bacharach says, "Los Angeles is a great big freeway," and Randy Newman in his anthem to Los Angeles sings: "We were born to ride.")

THE MOVIES

Look for origins wherever you will, but it was the movies that put Los Angeles on the map and made it a place nearly everyone in the world wanted to visit before they died. The 1939 *W.P.A. Guide to California,* says, Los Angeles "is known to the ends of the earth as the mother of Hollywood, that dazzling daughter still sheltered under the family roof." But, as the great mystery writer Raymond Chandler observed in his novel, *The Little Sister,* that relationship was never one of a happy family:

"Real cities have something else, some individual bony structure under the muck. Los Angeles has Hollywood — and hates it. It ought to consider itself damn lucky. Without Hollywood it would be a mail-order city. Everything in the catalogue you could get better somewhere else."

Planned as a Temperance colony during the 1880's boom, Hollywood was just another suburb until 1911, when the first movie studio opened there. Word spread like wildfire, and the town was soon over-run by actors and movie men. More important, the movies themselves became popular and sold. By the end of the 1920's, the movies were becoming Los Angeles' leading industry. With the development of sound film, they became even more important. Escapist entertainment was one of the few businesses making money, and during the height of the Depression Louis B. Mayer was the highest paid American executive of his time.

A garish billboard reflects the changes in Hollywood's once-glamorous Sunset Boulevard.

With the coming of World War II, the movies took second place to the area's booming aerospace industry, a lead it still holds today. Some of America's largest airplane manufacturers had grown up in the Los Angeles area because of the dry, warm climate. As fate would have it, they turned out to be convenient to the air bases backing up the massive air war in the Pacific. Allan Loughead (a name he changed to Lockheed) was a native California aviator who established what would become a major aerospace corporation first at Santa Barbara, and later at Burbank. John K. Northrop was an engineer at Lockheed who founded his own corporation in 1928 that later became part of the Douglas Aircraft Corp. The latter had earlier been founded by Donald Douglas in an old movie studio in 1920. These are just three of the corporations that have remained at the top of the expanding aeronautics and space industry in America.

Like most of the rest of America, Los Angeles coasted through the 1950's, liking Ike and loving Lucy. Having a neat car and being able to go to the beach every day seemed like heaven to every kid in America. Dozens of movies and songs reflected that "California Dreamin' " was a national pastime. Even the social upheaval of the 1960's did not rock the city as it did other places; the University of California, Los Angeles (UCLA) and the University of Southern California (USC) campuses were relatively calm compared to those of Berkeley and Columbia. But in 1964, the *Los Angeles Free Press* became the first of the New Left counterculture publications. "The Freep" had a tremendous impact on young people in The Movement nationwide and had many imitators, including the "straight" or established presses.

Los Angeles was also the scene of the first bloody racial riot of the mid-1960's. It took place, in the Watts section southeast of downtown Los Angeles. During five days of rioting in August 1965, 34 people were killed and more than 1,000 injured. More than $40 million worth of property was damaged. If violence in the ghetto

didn't sink in to the real estate-conscious city, the damage to property did. A state commission investigated and recommended more jobs, better housing, and schools. The most enduring result of the riots was the election of a former policeman, Tom Bradley, as the city's first black mayor in 1973. While Bradley serves as an important symbol to his own people in the ghettos, he has been a lackluster leader and has failed in two attempts to become governor of the state. Bradley was the first step up from the old racism, as many see it, but what many also hope for is that a truly dynamic leader will emerge from the new Los Angeles to lead the city into the 1990's in what promises to be its most prosperous decade ever.

There was a time in the 1960's and 1970's when Hollywood seemed on the verge of becoming a hideous new Skid Row. Drug addicts and hustlers of every description had taken over the streets and many, if not most, of the grand old shops and stores along Hollywood and Sunset Boulevards had either closed down or were just barely making it. The movie industry started to disperse. There were new studios in San Francisco and even as far away as Wilmington, N.C. But Hollywood merchants began a cleanup of their own streets and for every movie studio that left town, another exciting new one took its place.

Once again, Los Angeles and Hollywood have managed to endure, nay prevail. The Academy Awards did not move to a non-union town and every year, millions of people around the world tune in to see a fabulous show and find out just who and what "the Academy" has deemed worthy of its highest awards. If Chicago suffers from a "Second City" inferiority complex to New York, Los Angeles has had to live with something much worse — being regarded as not quite worthy of serious consideration: in a word, tacky. New York's trendy *Spy* magazine said that Los Angeles is where people go "to do everything they're too embarrassed to do in New York."

Ronald Brownstein observed in the January 15, 1989 edition of the *Los Angeles Times Magazine:* "In the national mythology, California, particularly Southern California, has always been on the front line of social trends. If California didn't initiate the postwar move to suburbia, it perfected it. In the early 1960s, the campus and inner-city unrest that eventually engulfed the nation crystallized in Berkeley and Watts. The singles scene that defined the anomie of the 1970s found its purest expression in the beach-front towns of Los Angeles; it was morning again in America here first, with Los Angeles, and then the nation, awaking to a solipsistic vision of sunshine, greed and the perfect biceps.

Along the way, Southern California also came to be seen as the spawning ground for political trends. The professionalization of politics — the creation of a priesthood of political consultants — began here in the mid-1960s. The conservative backlash against the 1960s drew its first blood with the election of Ronald Reagan as governor in 1965. Environmentalism emerged as a powerful political force after the Santa Barbara oil spill in 1969. In the mid-1970s, Gov. Edmund G. (Jerry) Brown sketched the first outlines of a liberalism with limits. And in 1978, crusty Howard Jarvis' Proposition 13 heralded the dawning of the anti-government rebellion that swept Ronald Reagan into the Oval Office two years later. In the 1980s, California has pioneered the impersonal media- and money-based negative politics that now dominates national elections.

All of these trends influenced the nation's life in meaningful ways, but they didn't really challenge the stereotypical view of Los Angeles. Southern California's reputation as the nation's social foundry only reinforced its reputation for obsessively trendy quirkiness... ."

But, as Brownstein went on to explain, many of the changes inspired by Los Angeles were not quirks. Suddenly, new and more serious attention is being paid to Los Angeles. He mentioned several important new books that will be published in the coming year examining Los Angeles' new leadership in American life. For one thing, these authors point out that immigration into Southern California — at a rate of 110,000 a year — during the 1980's may have exceeded the "historic rush of the huddled masses from Europe at the turn of the century." These new immigrants, largely from Asia and Latin America, have established a new mold for American culture: not the mythical "melting pot", but a "collage" of disparate cultures living peacefully side by side.

On a less academic scale, Los Angeles has also arrived in that eastern bastion of trends and culture, New York City. In April of 1989, Bloomingdale's will launch a two-month celebration of California fashions to be preceded by a huge banquet catered by Los Angeles' own Wolfgang Puck. Unable to lure the celebrated chef and restaurant owner to New York, restaurant owners have hired away Puck's own chefs and established dozens of incredibly successful "California-style" cafes and restaurants. One of Puck's former chefs at Spago's in West Hollywood now runs the kitchen at New York's The Melrose. At Manhattan's Big Kahuna, there's California cuisine on the menu and all manner of California surfing gear on the walls.

The editor of New York's *Metropolitan Home* magazine said: "There are so many cultural signals coming from Los Angeles that are changing ways of socializing, of living at home." But if life in Los Angeles and Southern California is now being seriously scrutinized from the ivory towers of Manhattan, can cultural decline be far behind? Not likely. After all, "doing your own thing" was what made life in "La La Land" fun and different, and that's what brought on all the new and serious attention from the East. While the others figure out what it all means, Los Angelenos are likely to go on being themselves, being happy.

BEVERLY HILLS

While Hollywood itself has gone through a rough cycle to match the broken dreams of one of its stars, the nearby Incorporated City of Beverly Hills has remained what it was and always has been: an elegant enclave of the very rich.

Bought by developers from Beverly Farms, Massachusetts in 1906, Beverly Hills was planned from the beginning for large public gardens and huge private estates along curving palm-lined boulevards. The lavish Beverly Hills Hotel, built in 1912, set the tone. And, as can be said of few places in America, that very high tone has somehow endured. By 1920, Beverly Hills had only 674 residents; and the most recent count (1983) showed only 32,700. This city within a city is famous mainly for its beautiful

estates. It is not only the favored home of the movie stars, but also where a number of Texas and Arab oil barons choose to live, alongside Greek shipping tycoons even multimillionaire televangelist Oral Roberts has a home here.

To fashionable women throughout the world, Beverly Hills is not the home of the stars, but the home of Rodeo Drive, one of the most famous shopping streets in the world. You won't come here looking for bargains, by the way, these are some of the most elegant and expensive places to be found anywhere. Nearly all of the shops are in old two- and three-story buildings and you'll find the mood here surprisingly low-key. Many of the restaurants are expensive, but there are just as many with reasonably

Cheerleaders strut in a Los Angles parade.

priced food, affordable to those who also work in Beverly Hills. At the heart of Beverly Hills, where the two great boulevards come together, is the **Beverly-Wilshire Hotel,** one of the grand hotels of the world. In late 1988, the older section of the hotel reopened in unusual fashion after a top-to-bottom renovation. The management let the employees stay in the elegant suites and rooms for a night as a kind of test-run. There were no complaints about the price — or the service. For more information on Beverly Hills, write or call the Beverly Hills Visitors Bureau at 239 S. Beverly Drive, Beverly Hills, CA 90212; ✆ (213) 271-8174, or (800) 345-2210.

DOWNTOWN LOS ANGELES

Not many years ago, people would have laughed at you if you had talked about going downtown for anything. It was, of course, here that the pueblo and then the city of Los Angeles began. But the city quickly spread out and forgot about its place of origin. For years, the City Hall erected during the boom years of the 1920's loomed as the city's tallest building; although it surely gained more fame in the movies as the "Daily Planet" building where Superman worked.

The real estate and stock market bust of 1929 was especially hard on downtown Los Angeles which owed its very existence to wild speculators. In the 1950's and 1960's, the downtown area seemed destined for decay and total abandonment as grand new cities sprang up in the outlying areas. However, in the early 1970's, a spectacular downtown renaissance began, that created a real city where none had existed. The round glass towers of the Westin Bonaventure Hotel were soon dwarfed by other skyscrapers housing offices and condominiums, other hotels, and some of the city's best indoor shopping galleries and malls. There are several new theaters in the downtown area and the construction of the **Museum of Contemporary Art**

downtown enhances the cultural fare in the area. As for older structures, the **Biltmore Hotel** has been restored to its former elegance when it was the host of Hollywood.

Just as Walt Disney constantly reminded his people that "it all began with a mouse," Los Angelenos should remember that their grand modern city began with a tiny pueblo of mud-adobe huts. Remarkably, some of that original pueblo has survived and is preserved a few blocks from all the steel and glass skyscrapers.

The historic district is centered around the old **Plaza,** bounded by Main, Los Angeles and Marchessault Streets near the beginning of Sunset Boulevard. This plaza dates to 1800, when it replaced an earlier town square wiped out in a flood. The restoration of **Olvera Street** just off the plaza began in 1929. In its place was successfully re-created a Mexican market street full of stalls and shops set among the historic old adobe and brick buildings, now serving either as museums or restaurants. Of these, the **Avila Adobe** at 14 Olvera Street dates from the early 1800's, although it is only one wing of an 18-room mansion. **La Golondrina** building at 35 Olvera Street is a two-story brick house built before 1865 as a winery. Across the street from the plaza is **The Plaza Church,** which is also called the Church of Our Lady, the Queen of Angels. The historic structure is still a functioning parish church, and to walk into the enormous dark chapel is to step back into old Mexico. It was built in 1818 to 1822 by "Jose" Chapman, one of the "Yankee dons".

Since it was their city to begin with — and most of them never left — the Mexicans have always represented one of the largest ethnic groups in Los Angeles. Until very recent years, their neighborhoods spread east and south from the original downtown pueblo around Olvera Street. For more than a hundred years, the Chinese have also called downtown Los Angeles home; lately, a Japanese community has also taken shape.

CHINATOWN

Los Angeles' Chinatown may not compare in size or splendor with that of San Francisco, but what is surprising in downtown Los Angeles is that such a large and historic quarter has survived at all. The Chinese had provided much of the labor on the Southern Pacific Railroad and when the tracks reached the end of the line at Los Angeles, many of them settled nearby. Their descendants have managed to hold on to the shops and restaurants in the area — largely because nobody else wanted them.

The heart of Chinatown is the 900 block of North Broadway. These are authentic Chinese places so don't expect too much in the way of decorations and furnishings. Two of the best restaurants are the **Mon Kee** at 679 1-2 Spring Street, © (213) 628-6717; and the **Miriwa,** upstairs at 747 Broadway, © (213) 687-3088. A cozy little bar and restaurant you might miss is the **Yee Mee Loo** at 690 Spring Street, © (213) 624-4539. The dark-paneled bar is a rare place in Los Angeles. Inside, you feel a kind of connection to an earlier time, and in the adjoining clean well-lighted restaurant, the food is good and reasonably priced.

As evidence that Chinatown also evolves and changes along with the rest of Los Angeles, you will begin now to see Vietnamese stores and restaurants operated by refugees from the war in Indochina. One of the best new Vietnamese restaurants is **La Cigale** which offers both French and Oriental cuisine. It is located at 685 N. Spring Street in Chinatown, © (213) 620-1572.

LITTLE TOKYO

Since Japanese residents were put in camps and had their property seized during World War II, Little Tokyo is a fairly recent development. New as it is, is still a fun and exotic place to wander about and sample the sushi and sashimi in the various little restaurants. There are two large shopping complexes within the area. **Japanese Village Plaza** is at 327 E. Second Street, © (213) 620-8861. It is a foreign village within the city, an open square with all kinds of Japanese shops and restaurants around it. **Little Tokyo Square**, 333 S. Alameda Avenue, © (213) 546-5556, is a three-level enclosed shopping center with 40 shops and restaurants, a supermarket, a movie theater, and the **Little Tokyo Bowl** video game parlor.

MUSEUMS

For a long time, East Coast snobs looked down their noses on Los Angeles as a cultural wasteland — or worse, as a garbage heap of tacky stuff nobody would describe as art. But in recent years, a number of art museums have opened and put the city on the map of Culture with a capital C. Beyond that, there are some museums to be found here that you will find no place else.

J. PAUL GETTY MUSEUM

J. Paul Getty was not only the world's richest man, he was also one of the most cantankerous and selfish men who ever lived. Selfish is hardly the word one would use to describe a man who left $2.2 billion, the bulk of his estate, to a public art museum. But even in this final act of seeming generosity to the public, Getty was being spiteful toward his own children. "A curse on the family" was how one biographer described it.

Getty's family members were provided for through various trusts, but the billionaire — in a late codicil to his will — decided to leave nearly all his estate to the J. Paul Getty Museum in Los Angeles. In a sensational kidnapping case played up by the press, he had refused to even consider paying ransom when his grandson and namesake was captured — until the boy's ear sliced off by his abductors, was delivered to him. (J. Paul Getty III never recovered from the trauma.)

The Getty Museum started in Getty's former home in Malibu, a magnificent ranch with a sweeping view of the Pacific. It first opened to the public in 1953. A new wing was added to the house for his burgeoning art collection, but even this became too small.

At first, Getty wanted to build a copy of his huge English country house for the museum in Malibu. An architect talked him out of it, but could not change his mind about reconstructing a fabulous Roman country villa covered by lava when Mount Vesuvius erupted in AD 79. In the study of his English house, Getty pored over plans and spent whole days going over the scale model for the Los Angeles museum. Oddly, however, he never visited it during construction or after it was completed and opened in January 1974.

With the multi-billion bequest on Getty's death in 1976, the museum became the richest art museum in the world. As his biographer Russell Miller wrote in *The House of Getty*, even this last act of philanthropy was tainted: "The Getty Museum has become feared for its wealth and ability to pillage the art market."

The original Getty collection comprised Greek and Roman antiquities, French decorative art, and European paintings from the early fourteenth to the late nineteenth century. Needless to say, the museum's collections have greatly expanded. But fears that this new-rich upstart in California was going to upset the world art market turned out to be unfounded. It just didn't happen. More important, the museum directors wisely decided to spend more of their multimillion dollar annual budget on education and research. In 1985, the Getty Museum purchased a 105-acre (42.5-hectare) tract in the Santa Monica Mountains near the campus of UCLA and began construction of a 450,000 sq ft (41,800 sq m) museum and an advanced study center, complete with a library and the very best facilities for art students and scholars. In 1989, the museum went even further in its public

service outreach — it launched a huge cooperative program to assist the government of China in preserving many of its antiquities. At the rate it is going, the museum may well outlive the man's reputation and the Getty name may come to stand for something besides greed and selfishness.

The J. Paul Getty Museum is located at 17985 Pacific Coast Highway in Malibu, between Sunset Boulevard and Topanga Canyon Boulevard, roughly 25 miles

(40 km) west of downtown Los Angeles. The museum is open from 10 am to 5 pm, Tuesday through Sunday, but is closed on Mondays and New Year's Day, Independence Day, Thanksgiving Day, and Christmas Day. There is no charge for admission; however, parking is very limited and you must make reservations for parking week in advance. The rich neighbors don't allow any parking off

The main courtyard in the J. Paul Getty Museum OPPOSITE is a copy of a Roman country villa destroyed by the eruption of Mount Vesuvius. A BC 503 marble statue of a nude youth in Kouros ABOVE is just one among the fabulous collection of the world's richest art museum.

museum property but there are special racks for bicycles and ample space for motorcycles. For reservations, ✆ (213) 458-2003.

THE GEORGE C. PAGE MUSEUM OF LA BREA DISCOVERIES

The visitor to Los Angeles will find all kind of unusual sights to behold, but in this author's opinion, the most extraordinary are those very carefully preserved at the George C. Page Museum of La Brea Discoveries, 5801 Wilshire Boulevard. Note the address; it is right in the heart of Tinseltown, La La Land, where nothing is permanent and everything is made to be thrown away. One is already amazed to come across anything in Los Angeles that has survived the last hundred years, but here you will find a whole city block still being excavated for relics of the Ice Age. In Hancock Park, which looks like an ordinary city park, you will find what appears to be ornamental ponds. These are actually bubbling tar pits. The Indians and, later, the Spanish and Mexicans had used the tar *(la brea)* to waterproof their baskets, among other things. The first bones were discovered in the pits in 1906, leading to the extraordinary discoveries that are still going on. Allan Hancock was one of those who made it rich off the oil discoveries in the area. His home stood near the park and in 1916, he gave the area of the tar pits to the city for a public park. The George C. Page Museum opened in 1977. The earthquake of 1971 had opened new pockets of oil bubbling up in the park. And in the excavations for the museum building itself, they found a rich treasure of animal skeletons from the Ice Age.

The museum is open from 10 am to 5 pm, Tuesday through Sunday. Admission is $3 for adults, $1.50 for children, and 75 cents for seniors. A tour of the museum begins with a film that explains the prehistory of the area, and how and why so many thousand's of animals were trapped in the tar pits (some had come for water and got stuck, others came to eat them and then got stuck themselves). Whatever the cause, the tar preserved the bones and literally thousands of complete skeletons of dozens of extinct animals. Most notable of these are the huge mastodons and mammoths, but there have also been excavated remains of camels, saber tooth tigers, and other exotic species not found in historic times in North America. In one part of the museum, you can observe the meticulous preservation work going on — tiny insects being pieced together in one section, 30-ft (nine-meter) -high mastodons in another. For more information on the La Brea Pits (or La Brea Tar Pits as they are often redundantly called), ✆ (213) 936-2230.

THE MUSEUM OF CONTEMPORARY ART (MOCA)

MOCA is a grand showcase for a world-class collection of modern art. *Los Angeles Times* columnist Jack Smith describes the building as an "architectural bonbon: red terra-cotta boxes under glass pyramids with a great glass drum on top. It looks like a tiny carved jewel box against the bunch of skyscrapers on Bunker Hill." Others describe the museum building as a "toy box". Aside from the permanent collection, MOCA also features an outstanding schedule of changing exhibits. It is located at 250 Grand Avenue in downtown Los Angeles. For more information, ✆ (213) 626-6222.

The $4 ticket to MOCA will also get you into the old modern art museum in downtown Los Angeles called the **Temporary Contemporary**, it is located in an enormous warehouse building at 152 N. Central Street (at First). The Temporary proved so popular when it opened that it became a permanent fixture and nobody wanted to mess with such a clever name. For more information on the Temporary Contemporary, ✆ (213) 621-2766.

MUSEUM OF NEON ART

Located at 704 Traction Avenue (east of Alameda Street near Little Tokyo) in downtown Los Angeles, this delightful museum features the latest in modern neon design and technology in exhibits such as "Eclectic Electric". Also on exhibit are older forms of neon from theater marquees and other signs. The museum is open from 11 am to 5 pm, Tuesday through Saturday. Admission is $2.50 for adults, children free. In addition to the gallery exhibits, the museum also sponsors occasional bus tours of neon highlights in Los Angeles. There are also classes on neon design and technique. For more information, ✆ (213) 617-0274.

MAX FACTOR MUSEUM

The museum illustrates just one of the many spin-off industries that developed in support of the movie industry. The exhibits display memorabilia collected 75 years in the beauty and make-up business in and out of Hollywood. The museum is at 1666 N. Highland Avenue in Hollywood, and open from 10 am to 4 pm, Monday through Saturday. It is closed on holidays. For more information, ✆ (213) 463-6668.

THE HOLLYWOOD STUDIO MUSEUM

Located in the famous De Mille barn where Hollywood's first feature-length film was shown in 1913. The museum's focus is on the first years of movie-making in Hollywood and can be found at 2100 N. Highland Avenue in Hollywood. It is open from 10 am to 4 pm from Tuesday through Sunday; ✆ (213) 874-2276.

GENE AUTRY'S WESTERN HERITAGE MUSEUM

The newest addition to the city's museum scene, this $5 million facility opened in late 1988 dedicated to the "real and fiction-al" American West. The exhibits consist of historic documents, costumes, firearms, paintings, and art objects such as Frederic Remington sculptures. Included of course are those giants of the silver screen, the great (if imagined) American cowboy, of which businessman Gene Autry was once the greatest. The museum is located in Griffith Park at 4700 Zoo Drive; ✆ (213) 460-5698.

GOLF

Maybe it's because there's so much else to do, or because there are a number of world class golf courses only an hour or two hours away. But whatever the explanation, golf has never developed as a major pastime in Los Angeles. Many of the golf courses in the area are affiliated with private clubs and closed to the public except to reciprocal members of other clubs.

There are several municipal golf courses in Los Angeles and the adjacent towns and cities. The most popular city-run courses in Los Angeles are the two in **Griffith Park** and the **Rancho Golf Course,** which is considered the busiest golf course in the world. The two 18-hole courses at Griffith Park cover the low foothills at the eastern edge of the park, and are named Harding and Wilson for the Presidents. For information on the courses at Griffith Park, ✆ (213) 663-2555; for information on the Rancho Golf Course, located at 10450 W. Pico Boulevard, ✆ (213) 838-7373.

PROFESSIONAL SPORTS

It's not true that the only place Los Angeles seems like one place is when one is looking down from four or five miles up in an airplane. If you happen to catch a winning season with any of the several professional teams located in the Los Angeles area, you'll think you're back in small-town America as a wacky mix of celebrities and plain folk shout their heads off for the home team. Movie star Jack Nicholson, for example, never misses a Lakers basketball game. Long-time cowboy star Gene Autry, of course, owns the California Angels major-league baseball team.

All games of the National Basketball Association's Los Angeles Lakers take place in the **Great Western Forum,** located at Manchester Boulevard and Prairie Avenue in Inglewood. It is reached by way of the Harbor Freeway (Interstate 110) from downtown Los Angeles, and Califor-

nia Highway 42. The Forum is also where the city's National Hockey League team, the Kings, plays its games. In addition to major sporting events, the Forum also stages a wide variety of musical and other stage performances. For general information on the Forum, ℂ (213) 673-1300; for information on the Lakers, ℂ (213) 419-3121; for information on the Kings, ℂ (213) 419-3160.

Sport spectaculars: Major league baseball OPPOSITE, TOP at Dodger Stadium located just off the freeways near the downtown and football OPPOSITE BELOW at Rose Bowl Pasadena: The Washington Redskins triumph over the Miami Dolphins in the 1983 Super Bowl.

The city has not one but two major-league baseball teams. The world champion (in 1988) Los Angeles Dodgers play in **Dodger Stadium,** at the intersection of Interstates 5 and 110 just north of downtown Los Angeles. Dodger Stadium is located at 1000 Elysian Park Avenue, ℂ (213) 224-1400. The **California Angels** have their own stadium in Anaheim, located just off Interstate 5 at 2000 S. State College Boulevard, ℂ (213) 625-1123.

Anaheim Stadium is also where the Los Angeles Rams play their games. The Rams' offices are located at 10271 W. Pico Boulevard. For ticket information, ℂ (213) 277-4700. The city's second National Football League team, the Los Angeles Raiders, plays its games in the **Los Angeles Coliseum** which was built in 1925 and enlarged for the 1932 summer Olympic Games. The Coliseum is located on the campus of the University of Southern California, just off the Harbor Freeway and at the intersection of Vermont Avenue and Martin Luther King Jr. Boulevard. The Raiders' business office is located at 322 Center Street in El Segundo; for ticket information, ℂ (213) 322-5901.

COLLEGE SPORTS

In addition to the Los Angeles Coliseum, which was used in the 1932 and 1984 summer Olympics, there are other athletic facilities built for college sports. Most are located on the USC campus. But across town, in Westwood, is USC's main athletic rival, UCLA (the University of California, Los Angeles), where many of the Olympic events were also staged. For information on athletic events at USC, ℂ (213) 743-2221; for information on UCLA athletics, ℂ (213) 206-6831.

SHOPPING

Beverly Hills is the premiere shopping place in Los Angeles. Along **Rodeo Drive** and its cross streets, you will find nearly all of the world's most famous fashion

designers. In spite of its great wealth, Beverly Hills has managed to keep its shopping district on a low-key village scale — although a very expensive one.

Another shopping area that has "just growed" in recent years is **Melrose Avenue**. While it hasn't replaced Rodeo Drive, it does offer a more casual and picturesque alternative. For many years, it was an ordinary run-down street, running parallel to and in-between Santa Monica Boulevard and Beverly Boulevard near West Hollywood's beloved "blue whale" Design Center. The area started as a middle-class neighborhood of cottages with well-tended yards and gardens. In recent years, the "cottages" have become high-priced homes and the once run-down shops have become quite fashionable. Here you will find an abundance of antique stores, some of the city's finest restaurants, and dozens of unique designer shops that have given "California style" a new and respectable name even in New York. If further proof of the area's new-found fame is needed, it can be found in the name given one of those popular new California restaurants opened in New York City — The Melrose.

But Los Angeles being one vast suburb, the most popular shopping places are the shopping centers, malls, and galleries. Here is a list of some of the city's most glamorous indoor shopping centers:

Beverly Center, 8500 Beverly Boulevard. © (213) 854-0070.

Bonaventure Shopping Gallery (six levels of shops in the Westin Bonaventure Hotel), 404 S. Figueroa Street. © (213) 687-0680.

Broadway Plaza, 750 W. Seventh Street in downtown Los Angeles. © (213) 624-2891.

Century City Shopping Center, 10250 Santa Monica Boulevard. © (213) 553-5300.

The Cooper Building, 860 S. Los Angeles Street downtown. © (213) 622-1139.

Farmers Market and Shopping Village, 6333 W. Third Street, © (213) 933-9211.

Seventh Market Place, Citicorp Plaza at 725 S. Figueroa Street. © (213) 955-7190.

HOTELS

Ambassador Hotel, 3400 Wilshire Boulevard, a Los Angeles landmark known as the place where Bobby Kennedy was killed after giving a speech in his campaign for president in 1968. © (213) 387-7011.

Bel Age Hotel, 1020 N. San Vicente Boulevard, © (213) 854-1111 or (800) 424-4443.

Bel Air Hotel, 701 Stone Canyon Road, is set in beautiful gardens and is truly the most romantic hotel in Los Angeles. © (213) 472-1211.

Beverly Hills Hotel, 9641 W. Sunset Boulevard in Beverly Hills, has spacious grounds like the surrounding estates; home of the famous Polo Lounge. © (213) 275-4282.

Biltmore Hotel, 506 S. Grand Avenue in the heart of downtown Los Angeles, was given a new lease on life in a magnificent restoration that preserves the baronial country house ambience with heavy beams and high ceilings. © (213) 824-1011.

Century Plaza Hotel, Avenue of the Stars and Constellation Boulevard in Century City, was where President Ronald Reagan often stayed while President. One of the first of the glitzy new high-rise hotels built in the New York style. © (213) 277-2000.

Chateau Marmont, 8221 W. Sunset Boulevard, is a rare survivor from Hollywood's more glamorous days. Built in 1927, the elegant main chateau-like hotel and the surrounding cottages are sprawled on a steep hillside up from the old Sunset Strip. It has been a favorite for those who valued personal service and privacy, most notably Greta Garbo and Howard Hughes. Actor Robert de Niro is among the current residents. Here also was where comedic actor John Belushi died from an overdose of drugs. © (213) 656-1010.

Disneyland Hotel, 1150 W. Cerritos Avenue in Anaheim, is the official hotel of Disneyland. It is a 60-acre (24-hectare) resort adjoining the Magic Kingdom with three high-rise towers and a marina playground covering three acres (more than a hectare). The resort complex includes restaurants, entertainment, and shopping facilities. ℂ (714) 778-6600 or (800) 854-6165.

Four Seasons Hotel Los Angeles, 300 S. Doheny Drive, is a luxury hotel located in a quiet residential area at the edge of Beverly Hills. ℂ (213) 273-2222 or (800) 332-3442.

Hyatt On Sunset at 8401 Sunset Boulevard, overlooks Hollywood and Los Angeles from a choice spot near many of the best restaurants in the city. ℂ (213) 656-1234 or (800) 228-9000.

L'Ermitage Hotel, 9291 Burton Way in Beverly Hills, is a luxury hotel offering certain special amenities in keeping with the neighborhood. These include complimentary limousine service within Beverly Hills, overnight shoeshine, morning newspaper, and free caviar and paté during happy hour in the cocktail lounges. ℂ (213) 278-344 or (800) 424-4443.

Loews Santa Monica Beach Hotel, recently opened, is the only hotel in Los Angeles located right on a beach. Near the pier in Santa Monica, it is convenient to the major freeways and Los Angeles International Airport. ℂ (213) 458-6700 or (800) 223-0888.

Mondrian Hotel, 8440 Sunset Boulevard, is ultra-modern in design and services. The 188 suites and public areas are decorated in the very latest in contemporary art. ℂ (213) 650-8999 or (800) 424-4443.

Ojai Valley Inn and Country Club, operated by the Hilton chain, is a world-famous resort hotel located 75 miles (121 km) north of Los Angeles and 14 miles (23 km) inland from the ocean. The resort has its own 18-hole golf course, tennis courts, and riding stables, and is a popular retreat for wealthy Los Angeles residents. ℂ (805) 646-5511 and (800) 422-6524.

Queen Mary Hotel is no less than Her Majesty's ship *Queen Mary*, now berthed at Pier J in Long Beach, easily reached by way of the Harbor Freeway from downtown Los Angeles. The luxury cruise ship now has 365 hotel rooms and 17 suites. ℂ (213) 435-3511.

The Registry Hotel (formerly called The Sheraton Premiere), 555 Universal Terrace Parkway in Universal City, is a luxury hotel especially convenient to the studios and other attractions in the Universal City and Burbank area. ℂ (818) 506-2500 or (800) 356-3360.

The Ritz-Carlton, Laguna Niguel, 33533 Ritz Carlton Drive in Laguna Niguel, is a luxury beachfront resort halfway between Los Angeles and San Diego. It is one of the most beautiful of the new resort complexes, and the oceanfront gardens alone are a major at-

traction. ℂ (714) 240-2000 or (800) 241-3333.

Sheraton Town House, 2961 Wilshire Boulevard, is located near Bullock's on Wilshire and not far from the old Ambassador Hotel, but otherwise it's a fairly quiet neighborhood. It is a comfortable old hotel, a refreshing throwback to days when all hotels had a higher standard of services. ℂ (213) 382-7171.

Stouffer Hotel, 5400 W. Century Boulevard near Los Angeles International Airport, offers an unusually comfortable way to see the city and the airport by night—from a Jacuzzi hot tub on the terrace of your own room. ℂ (213) 216 5858 or (800) 468-3571.

Sunset Marquis Hotel & Villas, 1200 N. Alta Loma Road, just off Sunset Strip and within walking distance of the restaurants and clubs there, has 120 suites, most equipped with kitchens. ℂ (213) 657-1333 or (800) 858-9758.

The Hyatt Hotel Long Beach, is one of a chain of holds much admired for their high standards of elegance.

Westin Bonaventure Hotel at 404 S. Figueroa, set the tone for the city's downtown renaissance, with its round green glass towers rising above old downtown Los Angeles. Unfortunately the hotel is so huge and self-contained it can be a bit overwhelming, and you soon forget you're in sunny California. The Bonaventure is operated by the Westin chain. ✆ (213) 824-1000.

Westwood Marquis Hotel and Gardens, 930 Hilgard Avenue, has 258 elegant suites including a penthouse. Expensive, but amenities include free limousine service in Westwood and Beverly Hills. ✆ (213) 208-8765 or (800) 421-2317.

BED AND BREAKFAST

Los Angeles might seem like the last place you'd expect to find the cozy bed and breakfast places that have become fashionable and profitable throughout the rest of America. But even here, in the heart of the megalopolis, the trend has taken off. Some might even say that here, it is taken to the Los Angeles extreme.

Conversion to bed and breakfast places saved many of the precious few Victorian houses in Los Angeles that had managed to survive the wrecking ball. Many of these have been restored to their 1890's splendor and become so popular you have to get long reservations months in advance. Be advised, "bed and breakfast" does not mean cheap. But the reservations list at the following places suggests that the comforts of (a restored Victorian) home are well worth the money. Here are some of the best in Los Angeles:

Eastlake Inn, a beautifully restored 1887 Victorian house in a National Historic District, is located at 1442 Kellam Avenue, Los Angeles, CA 90026. ✆ (213) 250-1620.

Terrace Manor is a 1902 Tudor manor house, located at 1353 Alvarado Terrace, Los Angeles, CA 90006.

Salisbury House, 2273 W. 20th Street, Los Angeles, CA 90018, ✆ (213) 737-7817.

La Maida House, 11159 La Maida Street, North Hollywood, CA 91601. ✆ (818) 769-3857.

The Venice Beach House is a fabulous 1911 gray shingled house with nine guest rooms just a half-block from the beach and all the craziness that is present-day Venice. It is an elegant restoration, a calm and cozy place after the busy boardwalk. Located at 15 Thirtieth Avenue, Venice, CA 90291. ✆ (213) 823-1966.

For information on other bed and

breakfast places in the Los Angeles area, write to House Guests, Inc., P.O. Box 1185 Huntington Beach, CA 92647. ✆ (714) 891-3736. Telex: RCA 277709.

RESTAURANTS

Because Los Angeles is the sometime home of many of the world's most talented people — a vast clientele of people with the flair to appreciate exciting cuisine and with the money to pay for it — it is also home to some truly extraordinary restaurants. Knowing where to see and be seen while dining out is part of the art and fun of living in Los Angeles.

THE GRAND AND GLITTERING

In this category, expect to pay dearly for what you get. Also, reservations are a must at nearly all of the restaurants listed. And, highly unusual in southern California, you may find that many of them have a dress code requiring jackets and ties for men.

Chasen's, 9039 Beverly Boulevard, at Doheny, is a Hollywood landmark and still a favorite hangout of some of the grand old names in show business. Open for dinner only, 6 pm to 1 am, closed Mondays. ✆ (213) 271-216.

Citrus, 6730 Melrose Avenue, is considered by many to be not just the best French restaurant but the best restaurant of any kind in southern California. The chef, Michel Richard, has become a star in his own right. The place provides a spacious elegant setting where diners can observe state-of-the-art nouvelle cuisine being prepared in the glass-walled kitchen. ✆ (213) 857-0034.

Harry's Bar and American Grill is in the ABC Entertainment Center at 2020 Avenue of the Stars, Plaza Level, in Century City. The interior is a replica of the famous Harry's Bar in Florence, Italy. It is a sophisticated, comfortable place in which to enjoy the best of northern Italian cuisine. Also offered are grilled prime beef, fresh fish, and veal. ✆ (213) 277-2333.

The Ivy, 113 North Robertson Boulevard is popular with Los Angeles' leading celebrities. The antique-filled rooms are comfortable, and the California cuisine is the best of its kind: fresh-baked breads and desserts, an unusual variety of salads, fresh fish, and grilled meats. ✆ (213) 274-8303.

Jimmy's, 201 Moreno Drive in Beverly Hills is a quietly elegant place. Specialties include rack of veal with Morilles. ✆ (213) 879-2394.

Le Chardonnay, 8284 Melrose Avenue, is owned and operated by two of the most respected French restaurateurs in the area.

The main dining room is decorated with art nouveau mirrors, tiles, and woodwork. The Garden Room offers a sunny atrium setting for lunch. The menu here is ranked as one of the best in French haute cuisine in Los Angeles. ✆ (213) 655-8880.

Le Dome, 8720 Sunset Boulevard, caters to international celebrities. The fare is light and dainty, featuring an amazing menu of salads, but what it lacks in substance, it makes up for in quality. The steak tartare is ranked as the very best in Los Angeles. Singer Elton John was among the original owners of Le Dome, and the restaurant and bar have remained a popular hangout for a glittering array of talented young singers and actors. ✆ (213) 659-6919.

L'Orangerie, 903 North La Cienega, is recognized as possibly the best French restaurant in all of California. Open for dinner only seven days a week, from 6:30 — 11 pm. ✆ (213) 652-9770.

Ma Maison, 8555 Beverly Boulevard, is one of Los Angeles' most reputable French restaurants. ✆ (213) 278-5444.

Morton's, 8800 Melrose Avenue in West Hollywood, is popular with the celebrity set because of its simple but predictably superb cuisine. ✆ (213) 276-5205.

Musso & Frank Grill, 6667 Hollywood Boulevard, first opened in 1919, and is Hollywood's oldest restaurant. It retains the style and class synonymous with the old Hollywood Boulevard. And the food is still good, too. Open for breakfast, lunch, and dinner, Monday through Saturday, from 11 am to 11 pm. ✆ (213) 467-7788.

Palm, 9001 Santa Monica Boulevard in West Hollywood, is the West Coast branch of New York's famous restaurant of the same name and features predictably heavy East Coast fare: live lobsters flown in from Nova Scotia, thick steaks, and cheesecakes imported from The Bronx. ✆ (213) 550-8811.

Polo Lounge in the Beverly Hills Hotel, 9641 Sunset Boulevard, Beverly Hills, has

At the Eastlake Inn and other bed and breakfast places in Los Angeles you will find a cozy serenity that may surprise you in the heart of the bustling city.

endured since 1912 as one of the most popular celebrity hangouts in Los Angeles. Lunch is the big meal here, featuring a changing menu of crepes and salads, and a regular menu of delicious sandwiches. ✆ (213) 276-2251.

72 Market Street is the name and address of this restaurant that brought a taste of super-chic Los Angeles into Venice Beach. Actor Dudley Moore is among the star owners, and the modern sculptured interior and highly innovative cuisine both live

by Puck's wife, Barbara Lazaroff. Chinois on Main is located at 2709 Main Street in Santa Monica, and features a menu of Puck's own interpretations of French and Chinese cuisine. Spago's, ✆ (213) 652-4025; Chinois on Main, ✆ (213) 392-9025.

THE MIDDLE GROUND

Alice's Restaurant on the pier at Malibu, 23000 Pacific Coast Highway, is a delightful beachfront restaurant. The menu

up to the star billing usually given this restaurant. ✆ (213) 652-6000.

Spago, 8795 W. Sunset Boulevard, is famous largely because of its imaginative young owner and chef, Wolfgang Puck. Successful as a caterer to the rich and famous at a very young age, Puck has become a rare celebrity in his own right. This is partly because of his ever-changing "California nouvelle cuisine" at Spago, but also because of the man himself, one of seemingly unlimited energy who is incredibly generous with his time and talents for any number of charities. The daring interior designs at Spago and at Puck's newer restaurant in Santa Monica, **Chinois on Main**, were done

features a California mix of salads and seafood, pasta, and some special Mexican dishes. ✆ (213) 456-6646.

The Ginger Man, 369 N. Bedford Drive, is not quite Archie Bunker's Place as seen in the television series, but is more informal than most places in Beverly Hills. It is owned by actors Carroll O'Connor and Patrick O'Neal. The attempt to transplant the very popular New York bar across from Lincoln Center has never quite succeeded, but you can often get a table here when the more trendy places are full. ✆ (213) 273-7585.

Gladstone's 4 Fish, 17300 Pacific Coast Highway in Pacific Palisades, is owned and operated by Bob Morris, one of California's most successful restaurateurs. Located right on the beach, with a magnificent view of the Pacific, it has indoor and outdoor dining areas and a true laid-back beach mood. There are four huge tanks where you can look at the live lobsters and rock crabs. Then you can watch through the glass-walled kitchen as they are tossed into boiling water. In addition to its famous lunches and dinners, Gladstone's also offers a huge fisherman's breakfast of eggs and a half-pound of swordfish or ham. ✆ (213) 454-3474.

Hard Rock Cafe, 8600 Beverly Boulevard, in the Beverly Center, has a pure American menu — hamburgers, veggie burgers, watermelon barbecue sauce. The rock-and-roll memorabilia serve as a backdrop to the young and glamorous clientele. ✆ (213) 276-7605.

Pacific Dining Car, 1310 W. Sixth Street, at the western edge of downtown Los Angeles, has been an old reliable steakhouse in Los Angeles since 1921, with prime beef cut, aged in their own cooler, and cooked over mesquite charcoal. The menu also includes fresh seafood, veal, and lamb dishes. Open 24 hours a day, seven days a week. ✆ (213) 483-6000.

R.J.'s The Rib Joint, 252 North Beverly Drive in Beverly Hills, has the same owner as Gladstone's 4 Fish. This place may be in the heart of posh Beverly Hills but the food is hearty, unpretentious American. A huge Green Grocer salad bar offers fresh vegetables; the menu provides a glutton's paradise with buckets of steamed clams, lobsters, chickens, steaks, and pork or beef ribs cooked over hickory coals and served with delicious barbecue sauces. To round out this all-American feast, there are old-fashioned chocolate and coconut layer cakes a foot high. ✆ (213) 274-7427.

The Ritz Cafe, 9320 W. Pico Boulevard, describes itself as "Distinctly American, Deliciously Southern". The menu, however, is not merely southern, it's pure New Orleans Creole. And that means Louisiana Crayfish boiled in spices, and "blackened" fish in the pan, with a rich cream cheese pecan pie for dessert. The interior decoration is so authentic, bright lights and all, you'll think you are back in the French Quarter. ✆ (213) 550-7737.

THE ETHNIC

CHINESE

Miriwa, 750 N. Hill Street in Chinatown, is a great place for the best in dim sum cuisine, especially at lunchtime on weekends. ✆ (213) 687-3088. (Note that the restaurant is in between blocks and is also listed as 747 Broadway.)

Mon Kee, 679 1/2 Spring Street in Chinatown; hardly elegant decor, but the best in authentic Chinese food. ✆ (213) 628-6717.

ITALIAN

Chianti Ristorante & Cucina, 7383 Melrose Avenue, offers the best example of Italian high cuisine in one of the most luxurious restaurant settings in the city. With a clientele as elegant as the decor, Chianti is one of the more exclusive "in" places in Los Angeles. But it is not all show and show-biz, because the food here is regarded by most critics as the best of Italian cuisine. ✆ (213) 653-8333.

JAPANESE

Teru Sushi, 11940 Ventura Boulevard in Studio City, stands out among the many sushi bars in Los Angeles. Located near the CBS studios, it is so popular that there is nearly always a wait. But the many and varied sushi dishes here are highly praised by those who are serious about Japanese food; some special dishes are found only at Teru Sushi. Never mind what you've heard about Oriental reserve, this is a boisterous and friendly place worth waiting in line for. ✆ (818) 763-6201.

Yamashiro, 1999 N. Sycamore Avenue, is the "hilltop Japanese palace above the

Barney's Beanery in West Hollywood is a rare old neighborhood hangout that has managed to survive in modern Los Angeles.

magic castle in Hollywood Hills." Located on top of a steep hill overlooking old Hollywood, this is the most spectacular place to eat in Los Angeles. This Oriental palace with 12 acres (nearly five hectares) of terraced gardens has a colorful history that includes serving as the home of the rich and powerful "400 Club". It became a public restaurant in 1960. Always famous for the view and the setting, the food is also now highly regarded. ✆ (213) 466-5125.

Yamato 2025 Avenue of the Stars, Century City, is at the Century Plaza Hotel. Western-style dining is available, but most people prefer the classical Japanese style, seated on the floor. The menu is classic Japanese. ✆ (213) 277-1840.

MOROCCAN

Dar Maghreb ("House of Morocco"), 7651 W. Sunset Boulevard, is made to order for all your romantic fantasies of an Arabian palace. You open the door in a plain white building and enter another world, lavishly furnished with bright carpets, cushions, and tiles around a beautiful courtyard fountain. The authentic Moroccan ambience is carried to the table where no silverware is provided, but the fresh bread helps, and wash cloths are provided after sultan-style feasts of couscous, chicken, lamb, seafood, rabbit, and quail. ✆ (213) 876-7651.

THAI

Chan Dara has three locations: 1511 Cahuenga Boulevard, ✆ (213) 464-8585; 310 N. Larchmont Boulevard, ✆ (213) 467-1052; and 11940 W. Pico Boulevard, ✆ (213) 479-4461.

Siamese Princess, 8048 W. Third Street, has a casual neighborhood ambience, but the fine Thai cuisine attracts a clientele from throughout the city. ✆ (213) 653-2643.

NEIGHBORHOOD FAVORITES

Barney's Beanery, 8447 Santa Monica Boulevard, is one of the last of the old neighborhood bars and beaneries. Nearly every table here is poolside — pool meaning billiards in this case, because much of the space in Barney's is taken up by pool tables. There is also a long, narrow bar that has been a cozy neighborhood spot for many years. In addition to chili-beans, Barney's has the usual run of sandwiches and daily plate specials. It's a far cry from haute cuisine, but it's good solid food at low prices and a true neighborly atmosphere that is rare in the sprawling city of Los Angeles. ✆ (213) 654-2287.

El Adobe Cafe, 5536 Melrose Avenue, is one of the few surviving Mexican restaurants that used to be found throughout the city. It was the favorite eating place of Jerry Brown when he was California's governor. The food here is standard Mexican burritos, enchiladas, rice, and beans, but there's plenty of it, and the price is reasonable. ✆ (213) 462-9421.

Philippe, The Original, 1001 N. Alameda Street, is the home of the "French dip" sandwich. Philippe's has been serving sandwiches to Hollywood celebrities and neighborhood folks for 80 years. In addition to the famous roast beef on French roll, the menu also includes fresh pork, cured ham, and lamb sandwiches. ✆ (213) 628-3781.

SIDE TRIPS

PASADENA, CITY OF ROSES

Pasadena has become so identified with the annual Rose Bowl and the extravagant "Tournament of Roses" parade that precedes the football game, that it is difficult to think of one without the other. Located just seven and a half miles (12 km) north of downtown Los Angeles, by way of the Pasadena Freeway (California 110), Pasadena is set in a valley at the foot of the San Gabriel Mountains. Originally called "Indiana Colony" because its first residents came from the state of Indiana, it became known officially as "Pasadena" by a peculiar route. The folk from Indiana couldn't understand enough Spanish to pick a suitable name in the Chippewa language, so one of them wrote a missionary friend among the Chippewa Indians in Mississippi. He wrote back a long phrase that meant "key or crown of the valley" in the Chippewa language. "Pa Sa De Na" was only the last part of that phrase but it sounded good enough.

Pasadena was a turn-of-the-century equivalent of present-day Palm Springs, although its wealthy residents included an unusual number of artists and writers attracted by the scenery, and the year-round balmy climate. The **Pasadena Playhouse,** a dramatic arts school and theater, was founded there in 1916.

The famous Rose Parade was first held on January 1, 1889, when the city was 14 years old. It was a fund-raising event for the local hunt club, and involved a competition for the best decorated horses and carriages — all decked with fresh roses and other flowers. In 1902, the parade was followed by a football game; in 1916 that game became a championship match which, since 1946, has decided the best of the winning teams in the Pacific Coast and Big Ten conferences. The huge stadium with 105,000 seats and no obstructed views was built in 1923, and the game came to be called the Rose Bowl. It's played on New Year's Day, unless that falls on a Sunday, in which case it is played the next day.

The **Tournament of Roses** has become an annual tradition in America. Some people camp out for 48 hours along the parade route to get the best views. More than a million people come to Pasadena to see it in person and more millions watch the parade on network television. The floats — still covered with fresh flowers — cost millions of dollars, and have become another means of advertising for the major corporations. It is a signal honor for high school bands to compete in the band competition, and hundreds of high school and college musicians keep the music going.

In 1978, a local group started the annual "Doo Dah" Parade to make fun of the extravagant Rose Parade. This featured floats decorated in the poorest of taste, drill — or "drool" — teams such as surfers with boards up and down, and, everybody's favorite the businessmen's special. In this one, men in suits and ties perform precision drills with their briefcases up, down, even open and shut. Like so many other spoofs before it, the Doo Dah Parade caught on so well that the city had to persuade its organizers to please not stage it on New Year's Day. And, you guessed it, the Doo Dah Parade can now be seen on network television every Thanksgiving.

The auditorium at Pasadena's Ambassador College is the site of television's annual Emmy Awards and a number of other events.

New Yorkers and others in the East Coast art world raised a howl in the early 1970's when Norton Simon announced that his world-famous collection of sculptures, paintings, and other art objects would be placed in a museum in such an out-of-the-way place as Pasadena. The **Norton Simon Museum** opened in 1975 and has proved a popular Pasadena attraction and a highly successful venture. Casual art lovers and serious students of art can come and appreciate the collection without the hassles of the major inner city museums. Eventually to become part of the University of California, the **Norton Simon Museum of Art** is located at 411 Colorado Boulevard, Pasadena. © (213) 681-2484.

Another Pasadena landmark is the **Henry E. Huntingon Library, Art Gallery and Gardens.** Henry E. Huntington consolidated two of the state's biggest fortunes and kept the money in the family when he married the widow of his uncle, Collis P. Huntington, one of San Francisco's "Big Four". With proceeds from "The Octopus" — as the Southern Pacific Railroad was known — Huntington built a huge mansion on an estate in San Marino, adjacent to Pasadena. He spent his later years building up his library of rare books and his art collection, and overseeing the elaborate botanical gardens that surrounded the mansion. In 1919, he set up a trust with a $10.5 million endowment and deeded his estate and all of his collections for public use. Among the rare books are 12 folios and 37 quartos of Shakespeare, and the manuscript of Benjamin Franklin's autobiography. The most famous of the paintings in his art collection is Gainsborough's *Blue Boy*, which Huntington bought in 1922 for $620,000. With its own distinguished research staff, the Huntington Library has continued to add to the original collections which attract scholars from throughout the world. Likewise, the 200 acres (81 hectares) of botanical gardens have become widely known for their collections of camellias, cacti, and other plants, and for the Japanese-style landscaping. The Huntington Library, Art Gallery and Gardens are located at 1151 Oxford Road, San Marino. ✆ (818) 405-2275.

THE SUPER FUN PARKS

DISNEYLAND

Disneyland was the highlight of Soviet Premier Nikita S. Khrushchev's 1959 tour of the United States. So, it came as no surprise that when a member of the Russian gymnastics team was asked what her "favorite city" was in a visit to the United States, she fired back without a moment's hesitation: "Disneyland,".

In a series of commercials, the Disney theme ("When you wish upon a star") plays softly in the background as the screen focuses on America's athletic champions. "Pitcher Orel Hershiser, you and the Los Angeles Dodgers have just won baseball's World Series. What are you doing to do now?" A big grin comes over Hershiser's face: "I'm going to Disneyland." Likewise, Joe Montana after he and the San Francisco Forty-Niners won the Super Bowl: "I'm going to Disneyland."

Disneyland is no mere fun park at work, this is a powerful American institution that transcends the usual competition in the business and social world.

Before the United States teams went to the 1988 Summer Olympics in Seoul, South Korea, they first went to Disneyland for an all-American send-off only Disneyland could stage. That fact was not wasted on then Vice-President George Bush: he formally began his campaign for president at Disneyland.

Disneyland is not the oldest American theme park, but it has become the "granddaddy" all the same. It is a unique American idea created by the great Walt Disney. "And never forget it all began with a mouse," he would tell his colleagues in his own phenomenally successful movie studios. That mouse was, of course, Mickey, who celebrated his 60th anniversary in 1988, with a year-long celebration at Disneyland.

Disney came to Hollywood from Chicago in 1923, but it was his animated talkie starring Mickey Mouse in 1928 that assured his success. His own studios opened in 1940. Many people have enjoyed similar successes in California, but few have given as much back as Disney. Much of his estate was left to the California Institute of the Arts. In 1989, construction began on a huge new music center in downtown Los Angeles, thanks to a $50 million gift from Disney's widow.

And then, there is Disneyland. First opened on a 160- later 185-acre (65-, later 75-hectare) plot in Anaheim, the park featured four areas: Fantasyland, Adventureland, Frontierland, and Tomorrowland. In this great park, Disney created an America that never was. He has a Main Street that is safe, clean, popular attraction is Space Mountain, which has the area's only enclosed (and sometimes dark) roller coaster ride.

One of the oldest and most popular rides remains the bobsleds off the Matterhorn and the Pirates of the Caribbean, which features some extraordinarily life-like automated and animated swashbucklers. In early 1989, the Magic Kingdom opened a new "Splash Mountain" in the Bear Country area, with a setting based on Disney's classic *Song of the South*.

and fun — as few American streets ever have been. And that is a key to Disney's success and the success of Disneyland. It's not any place as it really is, but as we'd all like it to be. And, after 60 years, who can really separate the original American institutions from those that originated with Walt Disney.

Among the latest attractions in the Magic Kingdom of Disneyland is Star Tours, designed by filmmaker George Lucas. It is the park's most popular current attraction. It takes you, through the very latest in film special effects, on a journey through space. And, incredibly, you never leave your seat and your seat (although it rumbles and shakes a few times) never leaves the ground. Another

In 1988, the Main Street Electrical Parade was brought back by popular demand. This turns the small-town parade into a fanciful Disney extravaganza. Certain popular standbys remain, but Disneyland is constantly changing, with new shows and new rides every year. When you wish upon a star, as Disney's Tinkerbell sang, your dreams will come true. More than two decades after Disney's death, his dreams are still being played out every day at Disneyland. More than 13.5 million

At Knott's Berry Farm OPPOSITE and ABOVE just south of Los Angeles you'll find an all-American theme park, the state's oldest. The log ride is just one of the thrill rides.

people pay to share in those dreams and fantasies every year.

Disneyland is located at 1313 South Harbor Boulevard, just off Interstate 5, in Anaheim; admission (good for all rides) is $21.50 for adults, and $16 for children from three to 12-years. ✆ (714) 999-4000.

KNOTT'S BERRY FARM

Located 20 miles (32 km) southeast of Los Angeles in Buena Park, Knott's Berry

Farm is California's oldest theme park. It started in 1920, when Walter Knott opened a little roadside stand to sell berries from the farm and jams made from them. Like all good American businessmen, Knott saw opportunities to expand. First, he added a Chicken Dinner restaurant that was so popular he built a little Ghost Town to amuse people while they were waiting. By 1946, more than a million dinners a year were being served and sold. The expansion continued with a narrow gauge railroad, a Chapel by the Lake, and a "Freedom Center", which featured a full-scale replica of Independence Hall in Philadelphia.

Now, of course, Knott's Berry Farm has expanded to the point that most people forget it ever was a berry farm. It offers

On the midway at the Los Angeles County Fair you find scenes much as you would at fairs back in Kansas or anywhere in America. OPPOSITE: Youngsters join in the frivolity at the grand Snoopy Parade at Knott's Berry Farm.

165 different rides to the more than four million people who visit the park every year. (You can still get a chicken dinner; 3,338 are sold every day.) The newest ride at Knott's Berry Farm is a white-water rafting trip in the Wild Water Wilderness, three and a half acres (nearly one and a half hectares) of water rides. Voices and signs warn you before getting into the Bigfoot Rapids Ride that "You will get wet; you may get drenched". Six people at a time board the rafts, and are then spun in and out of the rough waters, over falls and rapids. Two of the more popular older rides are the Log Ride, a fast 15-minute trip along a 2,100-ft (640-m) water course; and the Calico Mine, in which you ride an ore car through a (re-created) mine.

Knott's Berry Farm is located at 8039 Beach Boulevard, in Buena Park (just north of Disneyland and Anaheim); admission is good for all rides: $16.95 for adults and $13.95 for children three to 11-years and seniors. ✆ (714) 220-5200.

SIX FLAGS MAGIC MOUNTAIN

It bills itself as the "Rambo of theme parks". It is famous for its thrill rides, many of which are not for young children or faint-hearted adults. Six Flags, latest scare is the Ninja, a kind of upside-down roller coaster. The track is above you, and you ride in a little car that seems to swing free through the air — at 55 miles (89 km) per hour. As the newest and most advertised ride at Magic Mountain, the Ninja often requires a wait of more than an hour.

Meanwhile, you'll find that the park's older roller coasters are still the meanest in the business. The Great American Revolution involves a 360-degree loop; the rightly named Shock Wave propels its standing riders along an awesome steel track, and up and around that same loop; and then there is the Colossus. This is the largest dual-track wooden roller coaster in the world, and the ride begins with a 110-ft (34-m) drop. There are other thrill

rides that twist and spin and hurl you about. Good advice from an experienced thrill rider: never get on a ride until you have watched it go for a full cycle — and know what you're in for.

Six Flags Magic Mountain is located at 26101 Magic Mountain Parkway in Valencia, about 30 minutes' drive north of Los Angeles right on Interstate 5. Admission is $18 for adults and $9 for children under 48 in (1.2 m) in height. © (805) 255-4111.

trail persist from the Santa Barbara days. One-eighth of Reagan's time as president was spent on vacation, most of it in Santa Barbara. Many of the residents are of the old rich "bi-coastal" families, who don't care for the glitter of Los Angeles.

The mission itself was named in honor of a Roman girl who was beheaded by her father because she had embraced Christianity. At a perilous point in their voyage to Mexico, Father Serra and his Franciscan brothers felt they'd been saved by appealing

BEACHES

SANTA BARBARA

This wealthy resort city is known as the Queen of the Missions, having grown up in this century around the old mission. It is also the queen of California's coastal cities. Ronald and Nancy Reagan used to escape the real-world troubles of Washington, while he was president, at a ranch inland from Santa Barbara. They've now retired to the more urban setting of Bel Air, but the images of the President chopping wood, clearing brush, and riding out on the

to Santa Barbara. And she was so honored by the tenth of the 21 missions. An earlier mission building was destroyed by the earthquake of 1812, but the present stone structure has endured since its construction in 1815 and 1833. With its impressive twin-towered façade, the church became known for its architecture; it was also built on a rise and used as a landmark and beacon by ships at sea for many years. Located at East Los Olivos and Upper Laguna Streets, the mission now includes a large monastery and seminary. Although it is a parish church, the mission is open to the public 9 am to 5 pm Monday through Saturday, and 1 to 5 pm on Sundays. © (805) 682-4713.

Municipal buildings aren't usually on anybody's list of places to see. But the **Santa Barbara County Courthouse** is an exception. Part of a vast reconstruction effort after a 1925 earthquake, it looks for all the world like a Spanish castle — with carved doors and elaborate tilework throughout. At the top of the 70-ft (21-m) clock tower, there is an observation deck with a splendid 360-degree view of the seaside city and the mountains beyond. Another part of the post-1925 reconstruction is De la Guerra Plaza and El Paseo, an area of shops and restaurants built around the de la Guerra home, part of which dates to 1827.

The oldest and most popular festival in Santa Barbara is the annual **Old Spanish Days Fiesta,** in early August. The festival involves four days of equestrian parades, costume parties, and nightly shows in the sunken gardens at the courthouse. For more information on Santa Barbara, write to the Santa Barbara Conference and Visitors Bureau, P.O. Box 299, Santa Barbara, CA 93102; ✆ (805) 965-3021. The bureau, located at 1330 State Street, also offers free guided tours of the downtown area.

The tranquillity of Santa Barbara would eventually be disturbed by the construction of offshore oil drilling rigs in the Santa Barbara Channel. Started in 1958, the oil drilling here would by 1988 be producing 375 million of the 435 million barrels of oil produced annually from California. The drilling would disturb the normally laid-back, conservative city even more when a massive spill from one of the rigs killed wildlife throughout the area, and fouled beaches for miles. This led to one of the state's first major battles over the environment — and Santa Barbara becoming a environment center for environmentalist action. The Nature Conservancy is one of the country's most active environmental groups. At its headquarters on **Stearns Wharf,** and on the group's nature preserve on Santa Cruz Island, you can see exhibits on the environment.

Next door to the Nature Conservancy is the **Santa Barbara Museum of Natural History's Sea Center,** with aquarium exhibits and a huge model of a gray whale. For information, ✆ (805) 962-0885.

VENTURA

A shortened version of San Buenaventura, Ventura was the name given to the ninth of the Franciscan missions, the last founded by Father Serra himself. Some say the original name was too long for the railroad schedules; others that the mail was getting sent to San Bernardino. Whatever the

origins of the name, Ventura became an important port city for the nearby agricultural areas. In more recent times, the food-processing plants have given way to oil refineries.

The main mission church was restored in 1929 and in 1957. While much of the structure is a reconstruction, the rafters, tile, and Indian paintings in the sanctuary are from the original. There is a small admission fee, and it is open to the public from

OPPOSITE: The Malibu Pier offers prime fishing positions and a quiet escape from the bustle of nearby Los Angeles. ABOVE: Some of the best shows in Los Angeles are staged by amateurs on the boardwalk at Venice Beach.

10 am to 5 pm, Monday through Saturday, and 10 am to 4 pm on Sundays.

The five other buildings that were part of the original mission complex have been excavated and a small interpretive museum displays the artifacts found there. The Mission Archaeological Dig is at 113 East Main Street, and is open from 10 am to 5 pm Tuesday through Sunday.

Channel Islands National Park

Offshore from Ventura, the park's headquarters and visitors' center are at 1901 Spinnaker Drive, Ventura Harbor. There are films, exhibits, and lectures explaining the life and history of the Channel Islands. The visitors' center is open from 8 am to 5:30 pm, Sunday through Thursday, and from 8 am to 7 pm, Friday and Saturday.

The five islands that make up the national park are almost entirely dedicated to nature preserves now. All are open to the public. There are also regular boat trips to all of the islands from Ventura. **Santa Cruz** is the largest of the islands, a two- or two-and-one-half hour boat ride from Ventura, depending on which part of the island you land at. Until the Nature Conservancy acquired an interest in the island in 1978, most of it was in a private cattle ranch. The Conservancy now tends its part of the island as a nature preserve within the National Park; the **Scorpion Ranch** at the east end of the island continues as a private ranch, but visitors are welcome to explore the old ranch buildings and the surrounding countryside on guided tours.

At the other end of Santa Cruz is **Christy Ranch,** a renovated 1864 adobe house, where meals are served to visitors on airplane tours from Camarillo airport. The 96 sq miles (249 sq km) island has a varied landscape of two rugged mountain ranges with a fertile valley in between, and a coastline of high cliffs, broad beaches, and secluded coves. The wildlife here has taken some interesting turns; eight plant species grow here and nowhere else, the scrub jay bird is much larger than its counterpart on

the mainland, the fox on the island much smaller.

Island Adventures operates the facilities at Scorpion Ranch and the nearby **Smuggler's Cove,** a popular place for fishermen. At Scorpion Ranch, you must bring your own food; prices start at $100 per person, which includes boat transportation. At Smuggler's Cove, the rates are $300 to $350 for a three-day visit, but that includes meals and air transportation. For more information, write to Island Adventures, 907 Daly Road, Ojai, CA 92023; ✆ (805) 646-2513. For information on trips to Christy Ranch, write to Channel Islands Adventures, 305 Durley Street, Camarillo, CA 93101; ✆ (805) 987-1678. The Nature Conservancy offers guided tours of Santa Cruz through the Island Packers boat tours.

There are campgrounds on the other islands: San Miguel, Anacapa, Santa Rosa, and Santa Barbara. However, visitors should check well in advance with park rangers at the Channel Islands headquarters in Ventura to be sure space is available and to make reservations. In addition to the special Nature Conservancy tours, the Island Packers has regular boats to all of the islands. For information on any of the tours, write to Island Packers, 1867 Spinnaker Drive, Ventura, CA 93001; ✆ (805) 642-1393.

MALIBU AND PACIFIC PALISADES

These resorts can be likened to what Beverly Hills and Bel Air were to the Hollywood community of the 1920's. Instead of their own city, however, new stars are seeking isolation. Many houses are built on cliffs so that there are no neighbors back and front and no view of those on either side. Up there on the mountaintops above the Pacific Highway, are the homes of Barbra Streisand, Bob Dylan, and other world-famous stars. Those are in the multimillion-dollar range; for the million dollar or so beach cottages, look below the road. Here you'll find the home of *Dallas'*

J.R. Ewing/the actor Larry Hagman and other stars of television and the movies.

Malibu is an Indian name of unknown origin. The 22 miles (35-km) stretch of beachfront was part of a huge ranch for many years. It was subdivided in the 1920's into lots for movie stars and other wealthy people. J. Paul Getty bought a large tract overlooking the ocean for his retirement home. The Getty art museum was originally located in a wing of his Malibu house, which he eventually shunned for a country house in England, where he retired to and died. But Getty's body was brought back for burial in a family mausoleum on the Malibu ranch property. The new J. Paul Getty Museum (see also page 117) is located nearby.

SANTA MONICA

The "Bay City" of Raymond Chandler's novels is Santa Monica. It is also where English author Christopher Isherwood chose to spend the last half of his life. If you take Wilshire Boulevard in downtown Los Angeles, and stay on it for 25 miles (40 km), you will reach a dead-end at the oceanfront in Santa Monica. You can also take the Wilshire Boulevard bus, and not have to worry about the driving. Of course, the Santa Monica Freeway (Interstate 10 west) is a lot quicker and the way local people would go. But that won't take you through Beverly Hills.

In spite of its recent affluence, Santa Monica still has much of that lazy beach town spirit Chandler described. The mood here is friendly and slow. The famous pier at Santa Monica was brutally battered by the storms of the winter of 1982 and 1983 — and 300 ft (91 m) of fishing pier with restaurants and shops toppled like matchsticks and floated out to sea. The remaining pier is still popular with fishermen. The old carousel has been restored to a glittering new condition it probably never knew. Right beside the pier is a famous old California landmark, **Big Joe's** hamburger and hot dog stand. You can rent bicycles and skateboards next door — and there is a wide sidewalk along which you will see that grand parade of California beach life. Keep walking south along that sidewalk, and you'll come to Venice Beach.

VENICE BEACH

Venice Beach shows the extreme of side beach life in California. It is some sort of throwback to Greenwich Village of the sixties, San Francisco of the fifties and

Venice, well, for several decades. Here you will find all the bizarre characters California is famous for. The sidewalks and the wide beaches are often body-to-body, a kind of massive outdoor disco with sounds blaring from a thousand different directions. Along the sidewalks, vendors set up food stands and shops selling everything from bad art to good sunglasses. One part of the beach is favored by gay sunbathers, another by girl-watchers. You won't need a map to tell you which is which, and it's no problem here if you don't think you fit in. In Venice, nobody fits and everybody fits. At the edge of an old city recreation area, a "muscle beach" has survived — a small outdoor gymnasium for the hard-core bodybuilder. There is even a small bleacher where you can sit and watch; but the bodybuilding is tame entertainment here and there is seldom much of an audience.

California seals bask in the sun on a buoy off Santa Monica Beach.

The best shows are the spontaneous ones along the sidewalk itself. Many of the performers are regulars, and they come with their own billboards, full of clippings and reviews of their shows. One regular is a sword-swallower. Every sort of juggler and magician can be found here, too. The ones who draw the most crowds are the young gymnasts on skateboards. It is absolutely amazing the kinds of stunts some of them can do on a skateboard.

of oceanfront tidelands in 1904. Abbot dredged canals and constructed a little city in the Venetian style, complete with gondolas and gondoliers. His idea was to create a cultural center patterned on the Chatauqua forums of the East Coast. Sarah Bernhardt appeared in a production of *Camille* at his Venice pier, but that was Venice's grandest moment. The little city of the arts never quite lived up to the plan. Some say that the decadence is part of Venice's current charm, because some of

A small warning should be sufficient for anyone moving about in these crowds. The city now has frequent police patrols to curb the criminal element among the beach crowd. However, that element is still there, and it is a foolish tourist who wanders about with large amounts of cash or with loose wallets or pocketbooks.

There is little evidence of it today, but here and there, you do see the arched windows or colonnade of an old building that has survived from the original grand plan of a new Venice by Santa Monica Bay. This was part of a scheme by a developer named Abbot Kinney, a wealthy cigarette heir who bought 160 acres (65 hectares)

that original spirit of the arts has endured. It is also where some of Los Angeles' most interesting artists and writers live.

REDONDO BEACH

Redondo Beach has the distinction of being the first place in California where the great sport of surfing was ever seen. The year was 1907. Railroad tycoon Henry E. Huntington had brought George Freeth from Hawaii to stage exhibitions with his long heavy wooden surfboard, riding the waves into the beachfront property Huntington was trying to develop and sell. Perhaps because of the bulky boards, the sport didn't catch on for many years. When a Californian named Bob Simmons developed a "board" made of lightweight synthetic material in the early 1950's, it was an overnight sensation. Surfing became the sport of young Californians, with theme songs provided by the Beach Boys, starting with *Surfin' USA* in 1961.

Needless to say, the developments succeeded, and the area from Santa Monica south is now one of the most intensively developed coastal areas in the world. If the busy crowds are too much for you, however, you can always drive a few miles and still find a secluded spot.

PALOS VERDES PENINSULA

Some spectacular views and even some isolated coves, where sunbathers feel free enough to dispense with bathing suits, are offered here. Once part of a Sepulveda family rancho, much of the peninsula was developed into large estates in the 1920's. Although privately owned, the areas around the public beaches are protected as nature preserves by the residents. Signs warn you not to disturb any of the wildlife you find in the tidal pools or along the beaches. The most interesting architectural site on the peninsula is the Wayfarer's Chapel, a modern design of redwood beams and glass by Lloyd Wright, son of Frank Lloyd Wright.

SAN PEDRO

This man-made harbor literally put Los Angeles on the map. Although 25 miles (40 km) away from downtown Los Angeles, it is still within the city limits. The harbor was part of the deal to make Los Angeles the western terminus of the Santa Fe Railroad. With the nearby shipbuilding and military installations at Wilmington, Terminal Island, and Long Beach, it has become one of the largest and busiest deepwater ports in the world. Two museums explain the area's marine and maritime history. The **Cabrillo Marine**

Museum, located at 3720 Stephen White Drive, and is open 9 am to 5 pm every day; ✆ (213) 548-7562. It has aquarium exhibits and ship model displays; it also sponsors whale-watching cruises in the winter months. The **Los Angeles Maritime Museum** is located at Berth 84 at the end of Sixth Street. The exhibits here focus on the history of the San Pedro harbor; there is also a 16-ft (five-meter) scale model of the *RMS Titanic*. Museum hours are 9 am to 4 pm Monday through Friday

and 12:30 to 4 pm Saturday and Sunday. For more information, ✆ (213) 548-7618.

At the south end of the Harbor Freeway, you'll find a new shopping area, the **Port O' Call Village,** a re-creation of a nineteenth century port village with 65 shops and restaurants. ✆ (213) 831-0287.

San Pedro is also the departure point for trips to Santa Catalina Island. Cruises to Catalina depart from the Catalina Terminal under the Vincent Thomas Bridge.

Muscle men OPPOSITE work out in the open air gymnasium that has given this part of Venice the name, "Muscle Beach". ABOVE RIGHT: Venice is a great place for bikers or walkers taking in one of California's liveliest and most bizarre scenes.

LONG BEACH

Just what the name says, Long Beach is nearly five and a half miles (nine kilometers) of beach, 500 ft (150 m) wide. Founded as a beach resort in 1897, it is now the second largest incorporated area in Los Angeles County. It has also become an important military port, and a commercial center for oil refineries and food-processing plants. The city was virtually leveled by an earthquake in

one of the most luxurious cruise ships ever built, the premier ship of Cunard White Star Fleet. In a major municipal investment, the city bought the ship and transformed it into a hotel, restaurant, convention center, and museum. The investment has paid off handsomely; the *Queen Mary* is now a very popular hotel and tourist attraction. There are regular tours from 10 am to 6 pm everyday; admission is $6 for adults, $4 for children. For information. © (213) 435-4747.

1933. This quake was thought to be just as severe as the big one that hit San Francisco in 1906 but it occurred on a much smaller fault line. It killed 120 people, and damaged $50 million worth of property. As in San Francisco, the people rallied to rebuild on the same ground, and Long Beach is now one of Southern California's most prosperous communities. In recent years, it has become a major convention center with many attractions to keep visitors busy.

The **Municipal Beach** that gave the city its name remains the main draw. At the west end of the beach is a more recent attraction, the *Queen Mary,* docked at Pier J. When it was launched in 1934, the *Queen Mary* was

Also at Pier J is the "Spruce Goose", the nickname given to one of Howard Hughes' more spectacular failures. This enormous wooden plane was flown only once, by Hughes himself. His idea of a lightweight transport plane failed and the plane lay abandoned in storage, until the City of Long Beach decided to make a tourist attraction out of it. It is housed in a free-standing aluminum dome, which also houses a collection of Hughes memorabilia. There is an admission charge of $6 for adults, $4 for children, it is open from 10 am to 6 pm daily.

Pier J is also the site for a complex of shops and restaurants called **London Towne**. The whole complex is reached by way of Queen's Way Bridge or Long Beach Freeway; just follow the signs.

Two historic sites in Long Beach — **Rancho Los Alamitos** and **Rancho Los Cerritos** — preserve the memory of the rancho period of California. Both were once owned by the Bixby family — brothers and cousins who came from Maine, and succeeded as sheep and cattle ranchers in various parts of California. The family became even richer when vast oil reserves at Signal Hill were discovered on Bixby ranch property. Rancho Los Alamitos is located at 6400 Bixby HIll Road. There is no admission fee. A guided tour will take you to the main adobe house, the blacksmith shop, the barns, and the extensive gardens. For more information, © (213) 431-2511. Rancho Los Cerritos at 4600 Virginia Road is a 10-room adobe and redwood ranch house with Italian-style gardens. It is open to the public free of charge. Both historic sites are open from 1 to 5 pm, Wednesday through Sunday. For more information on Los Cerritos. © (213) 424-9423.

HUNTINGTON BEACH

This beach resort community is located 40 miles (65 km) south of Los Angeles by way of Interstate 405 and California 39. Although it is a major producer of oil, its city and state beaches are popular for swimming and surfing. Huntington is considered the best surfing area in California, and attracts many of the world's greatest surfers. The International Surfing Championships are held here. For information on Huntington City Beach, © (714) 536-5511; for Huntington State Beach, © (714) 536-3053.

NEWPORT BEACH

Located 50 miles (80 km) south of downtown Los Angeles by way of Interstate Highways 405 and 5, and California Highway 55, Newport Beach is a self-styled "American riviera", has some of the world's most expensive residential real estate and is the preferred home of California's wealthiest

people for at least part of the year. It boasts a six miles (10 km) -long beach and a harbor that is considered the premier dock for private yachts and pleasure boats in southern California. Most of the tourist attractions are found on the **Balboa Peninsula,** a six miles (10 km) -long finger of land that protects the harbor. Built in 1905, the **Balboa Pavilion,** at 400 Main Street, is a fabulous Victorian survivor. Here, you can board cruises of the harbor and also excursion boats to Catalina Island.

About two miles (three kilometers) from the pavilion, on the ocean side of the peninsula, is the **Newport Pier,** a reconstruction of an older pier destroyed by a hurricane in the 1930's. On one side of the pier is an open-air market selling fish caught by the "dory fishing flect", a fleet of small fishing boats that have been hauling in their catch here since the 1890's.

The *H.M.S. Queen Mary* OPPOSITE was given new life when the grand old cruise ship was bought by the city of Long Beach and converted into a floating hotel and restaurant. ABOVE: Volleyball is an endless game on California's beaches, seen here at Hermosa Beach south of Los Angeles.

LAGUNA BEACH

A picturesque beach town is Laguna Beach, about five miles (eight kilometers) south of Newport Beach. The setting of steep cliffs and hills rising straight up from the beaches has long made it a favorite spot of artists and writers. The beaches are just as popular with the more athletic surfers and swimmers. The mood here is festive year-round, among the owners and visitors of the quaint antique

shops and artists' galleries. A winter festival of parades, art exhibits, and other events is held from mid-February to early March. Staged in July and August, the **Sawdust Festival** is a major arts and crafts show. But the most famous of Long Beach's festivals is the **Festival of Arts and Pageant of the Masters**. It showcases works by local artists and includes a much-awaited stage show when Laguna Beach residents pose in tableaux recreating famous paintings. The festival is held in the Irvine Bowl in July and August. Depending on the show, tickets range from $6 to $25, and reservations are required. For more information, © (714) 494-1147.

SAN JUAN CAPISTRANO

San Juan Capistrano is one of California's most famous mission sites. The song, *When the Swallows Come Back to Capistrano,* brought it fame and made it the most visited of the old missions. According to legend, the swallows returned to the mission every St Joseph's Day, March 19, and nested in the ruins.

Founded in 1775, San Juan Capistrano was the seventh mission established in California and, for a time one of the most prosperous. It had a magnificent church that rose like a cathedral over the barren landscape, but this was destroyed by an earthquake in 1812. The story went that, the service had just ended when the first quake hit; the people, who were outside the building ran back inside to pray and many were crushed when the walls and roof collapsed in the aftershocks. The mission site is just off Interstate 5; in fact, you can see what looks like a mission church from the highway. This church, though, is a fairly recent construction in the Spanish style, not a replica, and not part of the historic complex.

San Juan Capistrano's ruins are still quite impressive, but they are marred by the ubiquitous signs appealing for money. One of these promises a mass in the old Serra Chapel (a restored part of the original mission), "for you and every member of your family, living or dead." The historical exhibits are amateurish and inadequate. You can buy a packet of seed for the birds, generally pigeons and sparrows, but don't come expecting to see the swallows of the song.

Spreading out from the mission is a pleasant little town with several homely cafés right across the street from the historic complex. Just south of the town, the 70-80 miles (110-130 km) of beaches of San Diego County begin; these include federal, state, and local preserves, and several boardwalk areas.

SAN CLEMENTE

Right on the southern border of Orange County is San Clemente, a wealthy beach resort, developed in the 1920's, that took the "pseudo-Spanish" style to the extreme. There are no streets or avenues here, only *avenidas* and *caminitas*. The town's main claim to fame was the brief period when President Richard Nixon's beachfront house, "Casa Pacifica", served as the "Western White House". When he resigned in disgrace in the wake of Watergate, Nixon chose to retire to New York and New Jersey, and Casa Pacifica was sold to the highest bidder, a local developer. The gardens are occasionally opened to the public, but the property is otherwise private and closed to the public.

CATALINA: THE ISLAND OF ROMANCE

If California is a place where others escape to, Catalina Island is one of the most romantic spots where Californians have traditionally gone to get away from it all.

From Al Jolson to the Beach Boys, singers have kept the romance of Avalon and Catalina alive. Located southeast of the Santa Barbara or Channel Islands, the Catalinas consist of four separate islands. Santa Barbara is the smallest and northernmost of these and is part of the Channel Islands National Monument. San Nicolas Island, the farthest from shore, is famous as a nature preserve. It is also known for the legendary Indian woman who lived alone on the island for 28 years after her people were relocated to the mainland in 1835. The southernmost of the Catalinas is 22 miles (35-km) -long San Clemente Island. It is used by the U.S. Navy for bombing practice and other kinds of training. All three of these islands are uninhabited.

When most people speak of Catalina, they are referring to Santa Catalina, the largest of the four and the only one developed as a tourist resort. Some 22 miles (35 km) long and eight miles

(13 km) across at its widest point, Santa Catalina is 26 miles (42 km) from Los Angeles' San Pedro harbor. It was only in 1919, when the Chicago chewing gum magnate William Wrigley Jr. bought the island, that it began to take on an international reputation as a vacation spot. Wrigley developed the pebble beaches, hidden coves, and canyons in the style they deserved. The Mediterranean-style village of Avalon rose at the heart of the beautiful crescent-shaped Avalon Bay. And, at the

heart of Avalon sat a fabulous $2 million casino, a huge round white building with a red tile roof that stands as a prominent reminder of grander days on Santa Catalina.

The casino building has been a museum for several years now, its raucous past described and illustrated in guides and various exhibits. Much of the magnificent art deco interior has been preserved. You can still see the murals in the Avalon Ballroom, where the best of the big bands

The old casino building at Avalon on Catalina Island endures as a fabulous art deco jewel; it was once the playground of Hollywood's most glamorous stars.

once played and glamorous world celebrities danced. Mrs Wrigley made sure the sea motif was carried out in the specially designed furniture — the couches shaped like waves, the chairs like sea shells. Completed in 1929, the casino was a success in spite of the Depression. Wrigley also built the first movie theater equipped for sound pictures in this building. It became not only just a favorite place for tourists to preview the latest movies, but also for film moguls and stars from Hollywood to see their latest works in such elegant surroundings.

Catalina has remained pretty much unspoiled to this day. Wrigley understood and appreciated the natural beauty of the island and set aside more than 85 percent of the land in a nature conservancy that is off limits to developers.

Getting There

Catalina Express offers a regular schedule of cruise boats to and from the island from early morning to late at night. Boats leave from Berth 95 at San Pedro. From Los Angeles, take the Harbor Freeway (Route 110) to San Pedro and then take the Harbor Boulevard off ramp. "Catalina" signs will then lead you to the Catalina Express parking areas. U.S. Coast Guard regulations apply to passengers on all boats to Catalina. Those wishing to take camping gear should check in advance to be sure it is allowed. In general, take only light luggage since you will have to carry everything yourself. Special rates for groups of 20 or more are available; individual fares are $12.50 each way for adults; $10.50 each way for seniors; $7.50 each way for children. For more information, write Catalina Express, P.O. Box 1391, San Pedro, CA 90733; or call (213) 519-1212 or (800) 257-2227. Reservations are advised; check in 45 minutes before sailing time.

Accommodation

Since hotel and restaurant accommodation is limited, it is wise to make reservations well in advance. The Catalina Island Chamber of Commerce provides informa-tion and reservations for all facilities on the island. For more information, write the Catalina Island Chamber of Commerce, P.O. Box 217, Avalon, CA 90704; or ✆ (213) 510-1520 or (800) 428-2566.

Resort prices prevail in Catalina. Two of the most spectacular views of Avalon Bay are available from two private mansions that have been converted into hotels. The Wrigley mansion is now the **Inn on Mount Ada**, with furnishings re-creating the Georgian mansion built in 1921. ✆ (213) 510-2030. The most popular author of the Old West, Zane Grey, lived and wrote for many years from another beautiful perch overlooking Avalon Bay. In contrast to the Chippendale elegance of the Wrigley mansion, Grey's spacious quarters reflected his rustic subject matter. The **Zane Grey Pueblo Hotel** offers a high-beamed lodge setting decorated with memorabilia from the Old West and a view to match the Wrigleys'. ✆ (213) 510-0966.

Tours

Two companies offer a variety of tours around the islands. For nature lovers, the Catalina Islands are a kind of "American Galapagos", with huge areas of the natural environment preserved. Catalina Safari Tours has regular field trips into the most exotic parts of the islands and can provide lodging at the **Banning House Lodge**, a Catalina landmark built in 1910. ✆ (213) 510-0303.

A busier and more varied schedule of tours — both on land and out to sea — is offered by **Santa Catalina Island Company**. ✆ (213) 510-2000.

The annual Kite Festival is just one many events that give Venice Beach the liveliest reputation of all California beaches.

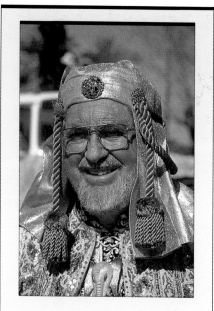

The Deserts: Palm Springs and Death Valley

PALM SPRINGS

Americans have created the best of several worlds in this opulent desert oasis. The climate is dry and warm in the daytime year-round, yet nearly always cool at night. But all the creature comforts of modern American living, including air-conditioning and swimming pools, can be found here.

At every turn, you see the lush green golf courses bordered by the rugged gray mountains or the burnt-brown desert sands. **Golf** is Palm Springs' reason for being. In the **Coachella Valley** in and around the city, there are more than 70 golf courses serving what is essentially a cluster of small towns. Palm Springs has a population of only 30,500, but more than two million people visit this playground of the rich and famous every year. In addition to the 70 golf courses, it has more than 600 tennis courts and 7,000 swimming pools.

It was golf that brought President Dwight Eisenhower to Palm Springs as a regular visitor and President Gerald Ford as a permanent resident. Bob Hope and many entertainment celebrities have long considered the desert city their home. In 1987, singer Sonny Bono was elected mayor of Palm Springs. The Bob Hope Chrysler Classic and the Nabisco Dinah Shore Ladies Professional Golf Association Major Championships are only two of the more than 100 golf tournaments staged here every year.

Although Palm Springs was described as a spa as early as the 1890's because of the *agua caliente* or hot springs, located there, it was only in the late 1920's that it became a favorite weekend and winter retreat of Hollywood celebrities. The 1939 *W.P.A. Guide to California* speaks of it with light disdain as an extension of the (then) glamorous Hollywood Boulevard. But, as such things often develop, the "extension" in the desert has remained glamorous while the original boulevard has decayed. Although decidedly Republican and conservative in character, the mood here has always been unusually tolerant of different kinds of lifestyle. Palm Springs now includes several other towns along Interstate 10: Desert Hot Springs, Cathedral City, Rancho Mirage, Palm Desert, Indian Wells, La Quinta, Indio, and Coachella.

The Cahuilla Indians still control 32,000 acres (13,000 hectares) in the heart of the valley, granted to them as a reservation in 1876. This includes 6,700 acres (2,700 hectares) inside Palm Springs' city limits and four incredibly beautiful canyons that are

listed on the National Register of Historic Places. The 15 mile (24 km) -long **Palm Canyon** is the most famous of these, possibly because it served as the setting for "Shangri-La" in the classic movie, *Lost Horizon*. A paved pathway leads down into the canyon where you'll find an abundance of the Washingtonia palm, the only one of 2,100 palms now growing in California that is indigenous to the place.

The Aerial Tramway OPPOSITE near Palm Springs is one of the area's major attractions and offers some spectacular views from the San Jacinto Mountains. ABOVE: Mules and horses can be rented by the hour for old-fashioned excursions into the canyons near Palm Springs.

The most popular single attraction in Palm Springs is the **Aerial Tramway**. From the floor of Chino Canyon, just off Highway 111, about 15 minutes from downtown Palm Springs, the tramway takes you 6,000 ft (18,30 m) up to the top of 8,516-ft (2600-m) Mount San Jacinto. You are warned to wear a jacket for the trip because the mountaintop is usually 40°F (22°C) colder than the desert floor. The **Alpine Restaurant** serves tramway riders from this spectacular viewpoint. You can even buy a "Ride 'n' Dine" ticket with the meal costing an extra $4. The basic tram fare is $12.95 for adults and $7.95 for children. The tram ride takes you into the **Mount San Jacinto State Park**, which adjoins the **San Jacinto Wilderness Area**. There are 54 miles (87 km) of hiking trails in the rugged 14,000-acre (5,700-hectare) park, offering a cool retreat in summer and a snowy wonderland in winter. The cross-country skiing is excellent and there is a complete ski shop at the **Nordic Ski Center** which offers instruction and equipment rentals. Every January, snow

Hiking trails are open in all of the canyons, with horseback riding available in some areas. As moviegoers two generations ago were stunned by the beauty of the enchanted scenes in *Lost Horizon*, the modern traveler will similarly be lost in amazing array of flora and fauna along the creeks and waterfalls in these canyons. For more information on the canyons, write to Tribal Council Office, 960 E. Tahquitz Way #106, Palm Springs, CA 92262; ✆ (619) 325-5673.

A few miles east of Palm Springs, near Indian Wells, lies **The Living Desert**, a 1,200-acre (486-hectare) park where desert animal and plant life are preserved. Exhibits, shows, and guided tours are available.

The **Palm Springs Desert Museum** is a modern complex housing natural science exhibits and art collections. It includes a performing arts center with a 450-seat auditorium, the **Annenburg Theater**, where classical music, ballet, drama, and film retrospectives are staged throughout the year.

ABOVE: A Navajo Indian Girl appears in native dress at the Indio Date Festival. RIGHT AND OPPOSITE: Elaborate costumes for beautiful women and their Arabian horses are the norm at the Indio Date Festival.

permitting, the Moosehead Championship Sled Dog Races are held in the park.

One of the most unusual events in the Coachella Valley is the annual **Date Festival** at **Indio**. The festival commemorates the successful transplanting of Middle Eastern date palms — still an important commercial crop — to the valley. Among the more exotic entertainment featured during the festival is camel racing.

For information about this festival and other activities in the Coachella Valley, use the 24-hour hotline. It will give you the time and place of all events for the day: ℂ (619) 322-4636. Enquires on Palm Springs should be addressed to The Greater Palm Springs Convention and Visitors Bureau, Airport Park Plaza, 255 N. El Cielo Road, Palm Springs, CA 92262; ℂ(619) 327-8411; or Desert Resorts Convention & Visitors Bureau, Fred

Waring Building, 44-100 Monterey Avenue, Palm Desert, CA 92260, & (619) 568-1886.

SHOPPING

In and around Palm Springs, there are many expensive specialty shops that you would expect to find in resort areas. But the new **Desert Fashion Plaza** brings them all together in one cool modern shopping center right in the heart of town. Entrances are located off Palm Canyon, Tahquitz, and Museum Drives. There is ample parking in the center. The center, which houses more than 60 shops and restaurants, adjoins the area's premiere hotel, Maxim's de Paris Suite Hotel. Among the fashion stores you'll find here are I. Magnin, Saks Fifth Avenue, Gucci, Champs-Elysees, Genevieve, Isis, Katrina, Laura Ashley, Mondi International, Optica, Rodier/Paris, Sabina Children's Fashion, Silverwoods, and Stuards for Men.

RESTAURANTS

Despite of the glamor associated with Palm Springs, its restaurants have never quite measured up to their counterparts in Los Angeles. Still, the quality is well above what you would find in towns of a similar size and in most cities in America. Here are some of the best:

Banducci's Bit of Italy, 1260 Palm Canyon Drive, ✆ (619) 325-2537;

Dar Maghreb, 42-300 Bob Hope Drive, Rancho Mirage, ✆ (619) 568-9486;
Melvyn's Restaurant, Ingleside Inn, 200 W. Ramon Road, ✆ (619) 325-2323;
Michael's Bistro, 70065 Highway 111, Rancho Mirage, ✆ (619) 328-5650;
Rusty Pelican, 72191 Highway 111, Palm Desert, ✆ (619) 346-8065.

HOTELS

At the top of the list of luxurious hotels is Pièrre Cardin's **Maxim's de Paris Suite Hotel**, located right on Palm Canyon Drive at the western end of the Desert Fashion Plaza.

Since a good many of the local residents and visitors to Palm Springs make their living off their looks, there are several very fine health and fitness spas in the area. Most of the resort hotels have their own spas, Maxim's included. One of the more interesting places is the **Spa Hotel** and **Mineral Springs** which was built on the site of the original hot springs and is leased from the Indian tribe. Other hotels with spa facilities are: the **Oasis Hotel and Water Resort**, **Marriott Desert Princess**, **Palm Springs Plaza, Ritz-Carlton, Stouffer Indian Wells Resort, La Mancha Private Club and Villas, Wyndham Palm Springs Hotel, Palm Springs Marquis**, the **Racquet Club of Palm Springs,** and the **Hyatt Grand Champions**.

GOLF

Many of the golf courses in Palm Springs are private clubs, but most have reciprocal arrangements with other clubs that enable members to use facilities elsewhere. Clubs are either open to the public or "semiprivate", meaning you don't have to be a member to play there. Expect to pay resort prices, especially at the more famous golf courses. Four truly outstanding world-class golf courses are located at La Quinta, northeast of downtown Palm Springs, on Highway 111. The oldest of these is the **La Quinta Hotel Golf Club's Dune Course**, at 50-200 Avenida Vista Bonita, ✆ (619) 345-2549. La Quinta's Citrus Course was opened in 1987, is at 50-503 Jefferson Street. ✆ (619) 564-7620. Fees for both courses are $75 for visitors, $60 for hotel guests, and $50 for a guest of a club member. Two other famous Palm Springs courses, designed by Pete Dye and Jack Nicklaus, were opened in 1986–1987. These are the **PGA-West Resort Courses**, at 65-900 PGA Boulevard in La Quinta, ✆ (619) 564-7170. Fees for the stadium course at PGA-West are $125 for visitors, $60 for guests of members. For the **Nicklaus Course**, fees are $75 for visitors, $60 for guests of members.

Two municipal courses deserve special mention because their fees are so much less than those at the resorts. Fees are $16 at **Palm Springs Municipal Golf Course**, 1895 Golf Club Drive, ℭ (619) 328-1005; $9 at the **Indio Municipal Golf Course** at 83-040 Avenue 42 in Indio, ℭ (619) 347-9156.

BALLOON FLIGHTS

One of the most adventurous ways to sightsee in the desert is by hot air balloon. It is a very popular pastime in Palm Springs and there are several places where you can book passage on a balloon ride: **Desert Balloon Charters**, P.O. Box 2713, Palm Desert, CA 92261, ℭ (619) 346-8575; **Fantasy Balloon Flights** in Palm Springs, ℭ (619) 568-0997; **Rise & Float Balloon Tours**, P.O. Box 36, Palm Springs, CA 92263, ℭ (619) 341-2686; and **Sunrise Balloons**, 82-550 Airport Boulevard, Thermal, CA 92274, ℭ (619) 346-7591.

HORSEBACK RIDING

The desert area offers some extraordinary riding trails and guides. Organized rides can be arranged easily through the following stables, both located in Palm Springs: **Smoke Tree Stables**, ℭ (619) 327-1372; and **Vandenburg Stables**, ℭ (619) 328-4560.

DEATH VALLEY

Like the premature reports of Mark Twain's death, the reputation of Death Valley has always been an exaggeration of the facts. In truth, only one person died among the passengers of that first wagon train that gave the place its sinister name — and that was the only death recorded in Death Valley for the entire trek West during the Gold Rush.

It takes a firsthand view of Death Valley to begin to understand the awesome mystique that has grown up around the name. When you come across the rugged mountains on either side of the valley nowadays, you will want to stop at the frequent view-ing points because of the overwhelming beauty of the place. But that beauty is best appreciated from the safety and comfort of an air-conditioned car or bus. To those first settlers, it must have seemed the very landscape of Hell — the hottest, driest, most barren place any of them had ever imagined outside the Bible's *Book of Revelations*. Their sentiment is clearly reflected in the names that had evolved for various points in the valley: Dante's View, Devil's Cornfield, Devil's Hole, Hell's Gate.

Death Valley extends for 140 miles (225 km) in Inyo County in eastern California, along the border of Nevada. In 1933, the federal government created the Death Valley National Monument. The protected area now extends across the border into Nevada. The valley floor ranges from four to 16 miles (six to 26 km) wide. Even in the hottest time of summer, there is a trickle of water in Salt Creek which oozes across the valley. The lowest point in the valley and

Boris Becker OPPOSITE shows off his champion form at Palm Springs' Grand Champions tennis tournament. ABOVE: Hikers are dwarfed by the Arches, just one of the many weird formations you'll find in Death Valley.

in America is at **Badwater,** 282 ft (86 m) below sea level, and only a 90-minute drive from **Mount Whitney** in the Sierra Nevadas, the highest point in the contiguous 48 states.

Few deaths were recorded in the early days of Death Valley because most settlers knew how to steer clear of it. However, as the mines began to peter out in California, prospectors began to spread out, looking for all kinds of minerals they could sell. There were some small strikes of silver and gold in the valley, but what put the place on the map was

wheels seven feet (two meters) in diameter, the mules were able to get a load of 36½ tons (including a 1,200-gallon, or 4,545-liter, water tank) across the desert. Twenty-Mule Team Borax became a popular American trademark and stories from those days provided material for *Death Valley Days,* a weekly television series that ran from 1952 to 1972. As historian James D. Hart has noted, it was that series that "helped make Ronald Reagan widely admired and assisted him toward later political success."

the discovery of borax there in 1880. Borax is used in the manufacture of glass and in glazes for ceramics and porcelain enamel. The boron minerals (or borates) come from hot springs and vapors of volcanic rocks. The seeping groundwater from the ancient lakebeds that covered much of Death Valley created rich veins of the minerals. When the lakes evaporated and formed the weird landscape of salt and sand, the borates became accessible.

The only problem was how to get the stuff 165 miles (265 km) to the nearest railroad once it had been mined. Enter the famous 20-mule teams. Using enormous specially designed wagons 16 ft (five meters) long with

TOURING DEATH VALLEY

Among the most colorful and enduring prospectors was **Death Valley Scotty,** whose elaborate castle is now a major tourist attraction at the north end of the valley. Walter Perry Scott was a flamboyant con man whose exploits caught the fancy of a Chicago millionaire named Albert Johnson. Scotty was ostensibly prospecting in Death Valley, but obviously both men were also taken with the place or they wouldn't have spent all that time and money erecting such a fabulous retreat under such difficult conditions. Since Scotty himself lived until 1953, there are dozens of fresh tales by and about him you will hear on the guided tours of **Scotty's Castle**. Now owned and operated by the National Park Service, the castle is open year-round and there are regular tours from 9 am to 5 pm at a fee of $4 for adults and $2 for seniors and children. There is also a snack bar and gift shop at the castle. Of vital importance, one of three gas stations in Death Valley is located here.

There is no regular public transportation in and out of the valley even today. Gray Line Tours offers overnight packages from Las Vegas. The valley lies parallel to the California–Nevada state line, U.S. Highway 395 in California, and U.S. 95 in Nevada. Highway 395 is an extraordinarily beautiful scenic route — through the Owens Valley, along the eastern wall of the high Sierras. At the intersection of 395 and California 136, there is a visitors' center fully stocked with maps and guidebooks and staff people to answer any questions about a trip to Death Valley. Outside, on the center's patio, there is a viewing platform for Mount Whitney, located just across U.S. 395. Highway 136 connects with California 190 which takes you on across the Panamint Valley and the rugged Panamint Mountains which form the western wall of Death Valley. The highways are well-maintained, but they are narrow and zigzag in places — with no guardrails and sheer drops of several thousand feet in parts.

Technically, Death Valley is not a valley, but a fault scarp, or *graben*, like many of the other California deserts. The spectacularly sharp and jagged mountains are the result of fairly recent — in geologic terms — uplifting and faulting in the earth's crust. The extraordinary fact about Death Valley is that the fault scarp is almost as deep as it is high — at the lowest point, 282 ft (86 m) below sea level, it is still 8,000 ft (2,440 m) down to bedrock.

Once over the high mountain wall and into the valley itself, **Stovepipe Wells** is the first sign of civilization you will come to. Here, there is a general store and gas station open year-round, plus a motel and restaurant open during the peak-season winter months.

From Stovepipe Wells, you can look out over an amazing stretch of sand dunes 300 miles (480 km) from the ocean.

The tourist center of Death Valley is at **Furnace Creek**, a natural oasis fed by fresh groundwater. There is a modern — and blessedly air-conditioned — visitors' center maintained by the National Park Service. Any tour of the valley should begin here. Huge maps and exhibits explain all the myths and realities of the valley, even the truth about old Scotty and just what Borax is now used for.

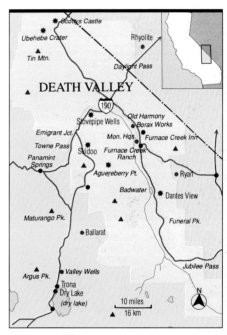

Right behind the visitors' center, you may be utterly amazed to come on a glistening emerald green 18-hole golf course, a startling contrast to the barren desert around it. The golf course is part of the main commercial tourist complex built by Pacific Borax, the corporation which still owns nearly all mineral rights to and much of the real estate in Death Valley. The **Furnace Creek Ranch** is the less expensive of the two places built by Pacific Borax; it is also open year-round.

OPPOSITE: It took specially designed wagons to haul the borax across the treacherous deserts and some of them are on show at the Pacific Borax Museum.

In addition to reasonably priced motel rooms, there is also a cafeteria, gift shop, gas station, post office, tennis courts, swimming pool, and the golf course. The **Borax Museum** is also located in the Furnace Creek Ranch compound. Here you can see the huge wagons and stagecoaches that were all that once linked the valley with the outside world.

Up the hill from Furnace Creek is the **Furnace Creek Inn,** a luxury-class hotel also built by Pacific Borax. The Inn is only

viewing points where you can look back on the broad sweep of the valley. From there, you cross over the Amargosa Range of mountains and take to U.S. 95 to Las Vegas or, at Death Valley Junction, you can take California Highway 127 south to Interstate Highway 15 to Los Angeles and San Diego.

Death Valley Junction has all the appearances of a ghost town, although officially it has a population of six. During the winter season, it also has the **Amargosa**

open during winter months. The hotel complex features a swimming pool, tennis courts, and an exotic "oasis garden". There are two dining rooms, one formal and one more casual. For reservations at either the Furnace Creek Inn or Ranch, ✆ (619) 786-2345 or (800) 528-6367.

During the winter season, sightseeing tour buses leave at regular intervals from Furnace Creek. However, if you only have a day to see Death Valley, you can see much of it from your own car, driving through California Highway 190 that takes from three to four hours. From Furnace Creek, the highway passes by **Zabriskie Point,** one of the most popular

Opera House, a wonderful throwback to the days when performers would amble into town and put on a show. The interior of the tiny opera house is covered with elaborate murals. At center stage performs Marta Becket, a New York ballerina in her sixties who somehow landed here and created her own fantasy production starring herself. You can see Madame Marta's grand performances every Friday, Saturday, and Monday night during the winter season. Transportation is available from Furnace Creek.

Exploring Death Valley by Ruth Kirk, the wife of a Death Valley park ranger, is an excellent guide to the valley. It describes "both the harshness and the beauty" of the valley which, as a resident for three years, the author came to love "in spite of its desolation, or perhaps because of it." The book sells for $5.95 plus postage through the Death Valley Natural History Association, P.O. Box 188, Death Valley, CA 92328. This association has an extensive list of more than 150 books and guides about the valley, including children's books, posters, maps, and photographs that can be ordered from the same address.

of the public campgrounds in the valley are open year-round. Even the most experienced campers should check first with the National Park Service, Death Valley National Monument, Death Valley, CA 92328; © (619) 786-2331. The Park Service advises visitors to avoid the holiday weekends during the winter months when park facilities are filled to overflowing. Conditions vary at each of the nine campgrounds since they are located at from 196 ft (60 m) below sea level to

CAMPING IN DEATH VALLEY

Keep in mind that Death Valley is one of the hottest and driest places on earth, and that until very recent times it was virtually inaccessible by automobile. The warnings you see posted about travel into Death Valley should be taken very seriously. Be sure you have plenty of gas in the car and bottled water for yourself. If you should run out of gas or have car trouble of any sort, it could take hours for help to arrive and it will be expensive when it does arrive. Californians generally avoid desert travel in the summer months. Only three

8,200 ft (2,500 m) above. There is a fee of $4 or $5 at five campgrounds, no charge at four of them. Water and flush toilets are available at six campgrounds, but three have no water at all. It is best to plan ahead and to heed all warnings once you get there.

Death Valley attracted men as eccentric as its strange landscape. OPPOSITE LEFT: Scotty's Castle at the north end of the Valley is the elaborate monument to a colorful con man. OPPOSITE RIGHT: Calico is a picturesque ghost town now, all that's left of another dream of striking it rich in Death Valley gone bust. ABOVE: Golden Canyon reflects the "harshness and the beauty" that draws thousands of visitors to Death Valley every year.

San Diego and Environs

If the three major cities of California are thought of as sisters, then San Diego is the plain one who married a sailor and much to everybody's amazement lived to be as prosperous as her more glamorous relations.

With a population of 1.5 million, San Diego is the seventh largest city in America. Several of the giants in the aerospace industry are located here. The city is surrounded by military bases employing the very latest in modern naval and air technology. The area's "high tech" or computer based industries rank second only to the famed "Silicon Valley" in Northern California.

Nature has blessed San Diego with the best of all of California's natural wonders in terms of beaches, mountains and deserts. Located in the extreme southwest corner of the United States, the city has the Pacific Ocean for its western boundary and its southern city limit is the international border with Mexico. The huge natural harbor and bay are protected on the north by a picturesque peninsula rising to a 1,000 ft (300 m) headland at Point Loma; to the West, the bay is protected by a barrier of sand stretching from Mexico to the bay entrance at Point Loma, providing a beautiful playground of beaches and a training ground for the omnipresent military forces. The San Diego Zoo and Wild Animal Park are world famous among animal lovers; Sea World — where you can watch killer whales perform like dolphins — is one of the country's most popular tourist attractions.

And yet, the city still suffers from an inferiority complex that seems baseless in light of its current place in the sun. Any mention of San Diego in the national media will be reprinted in the local newspapers. A San Francisco columnist scoffed that San Diego was a great place if you liked to look at gray ships. In 1972, the Nixon administration, in a last-minute decision, decided to move the Republican National Convention from San Diego to Miami. In a delightful moment of over-reaction and reverse snobbery, the city declared itself America's Finest City.

T-shirts and bumper stickers carrying the slogans: "There is No Life East of Interstate 5" and "Another Ho-Hum Day in Paradise" also began to appear. That Republican rejection also spawned the annual City Fest, a week of neighborhood street fairs and parties in summer when the city celebrates itself.

This was only the latest in a long history of snubs and broken promises. And, if San Diego seems insecure in dealing with the outside world, it is not without reason. In

most places in America, you find some sort of "history trail" that leads to places where famous people have slept or historic events taken place. In San Diego, there was a "trivia trail" — but then that too was torn down for another motel and restaurant complex.

WHERE CALIFORNIA BEGAN

San Diego rightly claims to be the place where modern California began. The first Spanish explorers stopped here in 1542 — and kept on going. Another 60 years went by before the next ones came and named the place. But they also sailed on north looking for the fabled northern passage to

OPPOSITE: San Diego's entire western boundary is the Pacific Ocean and there's every sort of beach to satisfy any lover of sand and sun. ABOVE: San Diego's changing skyline reflects the new growth in population which have made it the country's sixth largest city.

the Atlantic. Still another 167 years went by before the Spaniards came to stay, with Father Serra founding the first of the California missions at San Diego. This would be destroyed in an Indian attack in a matter of months. Relocated 6 miles (10 km) up the valley, the mission was attacked and destroyed again in 1775.

On Presidio Hill, there are many monuments to the Mormon Battalion that marched across the mountains and deserts to the aid of San Diego in the Mexican War; in fact, the war was over by the time they got here. The Gold Rush brought wealth and settlers into northern California, but nothing to San Diego. When Alonzo Horton — now celebrated as the father of modern San Diego — arrived with dreams of building a new city, he was laughed at because another man from San Francisco had already tried and failed. Horton witnessed a brief boom when the town's population went from 3,000 to 30,000, but the bust that followed was devastating. He ended his days on a hundred dollars a month, "rent" the city paid for land he'd donated as a park.

By the late 1800's, the battle between developers of Los Angeles and San Diego had become fierce. One map of southern California produced by Los Angeles did not show San Diego at all. San Diegans were optimistic that their promise would be fulfilled when the new transcontinental railroad ended on their bay. But Los Angeles came up with a man-made harbor, a terminal building, and a booty of $600,000 — and got the railroad. Not least of all, there was oil in Los Angeles, but none in San Diego.

Some of the first motion pictures were shot in San Diego, but soon the film companies all settled in Hollywood. By 1911, the spirit of San Diego had become understandably depressed; the town was also suffering the worst drought in memory. The desperate town officials brought in a rainmaker to do his magic. There followed a devastating deluge — the worst rains in history caused floods that completely wiped out the main bridge and highway into town. The rainmaker pressed for his fee, San Diego said sure — if he'd also pay for the millions of dollars worth of damage the rains had caused. Like so many other tragicomedies in California's history, the experience provided the plot for a movie called *The Rainmaker.*

With the completion of the Panama Canal, San Diego officials once again saw a chance for renewal and growth. The city would be the first major United States port reached by ships from the canal. But San Francisco also saw its opportunity to attract business. It staged an exposition that was declared the official one and attracted all the foreign exhibits.

Undeterred, San Diego went ahead with its own world-class exposition, the smallest town ever to do so. It proved to be a major success and a turning point in San Diego's history. San Francisco's fair was constructed in the "classical" or "beaux arts" style. The San Diego exposition, on the other hand, was a much less pretentious affair, drawing on California's Spanish heritage. A classic photograph of 1915 shows the Victorian brick turrets of the old train station on Broadway downtown being torn down beside the new Santa Fe depot. It was rebuilt in the new streamlined "mission style". Even the San Diego police station would be built in the new style — with tiled roofs, a bell tower, and low colonnades.

San Diego may have missed out on the gold, the oil, the movies, and the railroads, but visitors to the 1915 exposition didn't seem to notice. They liked the year-round warm dry climate and discovered a place where (if water could be found) just about anything would grow. The scenery was also beautiful — deserts, mountains, sandy beaches, and rugged sea cliffs.

Among those who visited the exposition were the U.S. Secretary of the Navy and his young assistant, the future President Franklin D. Roosevelt. They saw the potential for the huge natural harbor and the wide open spaces surrounding the town. As one writer observed, "the

---

OPPOSITE: Surfboard and bikini are all a pretty girl needs for a fun day on the beaches near San Diego.

military finally appreciated what the locals never had." During World War I, the exposition buildings were converted into barracks and the San Diego harbor became an important U.S. Navy port. In the ensuing years, the vast undeveloped lands around San Diego would be put to use for training and target practice. They needed a bombing range; San Diego gave them a whole county.

Today, the city has one of the heaviest concentrations of military personnel in the world. Locals joke that when the big one comes (meaning war, not earthquake) they won't have to worry and wait; they'll be among the first targets hit. Nearly one in ten employed San Diegans works either for the military or for a Defense Department contractor.

With the fuel crisis of the 1970's, San Diego became one of the golden places at the end of the fabled "Sun Belt". Nearly every list of ideal places to live in America put San Diego near the top. Indeed, it has many of the advantages and few of the disadvantages of a big city. The freeways are still free of the rush-hour gridlocks that take place in Los Angeles twice a day. You can never find a convenient place to park in San Francisco; parking is seldom a problem anywhere in San Diego.

Still, the jokes prevail. When the San Diego Padres faced the Chicago Cubs in the 1984 Baseball World Series, one Chicago reporter scoffed that San Diego was where "admirals retire and grow roses". Another Chicago report listed among its sports statistics: "Most mayors under indictment: San Diego — 2." The Wall Street Journal has called it the "flimflam capital of America" because one petty scandal seems to replace another.

It should be noted that the World Series is played in the fall when it's still warm in Chicago. By the time of the midwinter Super Bowl of the National Football League in San Diego in 1988, no complaints were heard from sportswriters or anyone else. Long after the game was over, you could still see them wandering about

town and the beaches in short sleeves and new tans.

There have always been an eccentric few — most notably that "damned old crank", newspaper tycoon E.W. Scripps — who loved the place as it was. But, by and large, city officials have chafed at being described as "an obscure port town". This attitude was best described by San Diego Tribune editor Neil Morgan in a 1976 book, Yesterday's San Diego: "San Diego is a success story — but a story of success evolving from failures, for San Diego today is the result of unrealized dreams of greatness. From the beginning, San Diego seemed a more logical setting than Los Angeles or San Francisco for a great metropolis. Our founders and boosters sought desperately to be big and we have still, somehow, not entirely succeeded."

What city officials at the time didn't seem to understand was that "being big" was not what everyone wanted. There were thousands of us who came here by accident, fell in love with the climate and the scenery, and loved the small-town atmosphere of the place. In 1987 alone, there were 75,000 new residents in San Diego.

There is evidence that the city is beginning to appreciate itself. A new "cultural czar" took office in 1988. She took one look at San Diego and loved its cultural potential. First off, she said, there ought to be a tattoo festival. For decades, city officials had systematically tried to destroy the "port town" image. First they closed down the massage parlors and honky tonks the sailors frequented, and then they forced out the "card shops" where the old-timers had been playing poker since before San Diego became a city. "If they go after the tattoo parlors, we'll know it's time to leave," mourned one old sailor. But now the city's new head of arts and culture is saying that all this is part of what makes San Diego a special place.

Although San Diego's politics have long been characterized as backward, if not downright reactionary, the city now has a progressive young mayor by the name of

Maureen O'Connor. In 1988, O'Connor led a delegation on a tour of the Soviet Union and came back with plans for a major cultural exhibit in San Diego in 1989 to feature Russian theater, dance, and many art objects never before seen outside the U.S.S.R. With her upbeat emphasis on the arts, O'Connor has brought her own version of *perestroika* into this once obscure port town.

DOWNTOWN AND AROUND

Like most American cities, San Diego abandoned its downtown area for the suburbs in the 1960's. Even the city's only daily newspaper moved out to a new building beside the new freeways and shopping malls. But unlike other cities, San Diego did not use its Urban Renewal money to destroy and rebuild the old buildings. As landscape architect Ian McHarg said in his book, *In Design With Nature*, "poverty exercises a great restraint on vulgarity and wealth is its fuel." Much of the downtown Gaslamp quarter was saved because it just wasn't worth tearing down. Now, the Gaslamp and the rest of downtown are the center of an exciting renewal and many of those shops that fled in the sixties are now moving back. **Horton Plaza** (covered under Shopping) is at the center of this revival, but around it is the **Gaslamp Quarter,** a fabulous collection of 1890's and early 1900's storefronts, bars, restaurants, and hotels.

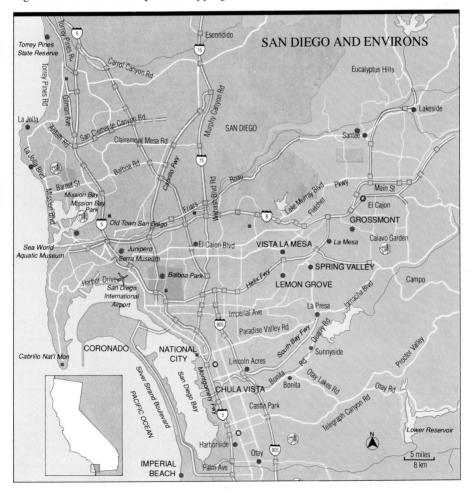

SAN DIEGO AND ENVIRONS

SHELTER ISLAND AND HARBOR ISLAND

They seem a natural part of the landscape now, but these two islands are, in fact, only 20 and 30 years old. Built from soil dredged from the shipping channel, both are connected by wide causeways to the mainland, and so are not real islands at all. **Shelter Island**, the first to be built, is highly commercial. It is the sailing and sport fishing center of San Diego. There is a nice park along the bay front, but the rest of the island is cluttered with restaurants, hotels, and docks for the numerous boats being sold or using the many facilities available here. The **Marlin Club** at 2445 Shelter Island Drive, ℭ (619) 222-2502, has the main sport fishing dock and is open to the public. The fishing season is from June 15 through November. Another place to book passage on one of the fishing trips or just to watch the fishermen unloading their catch is **H&M Sportfishing Landings** at 2803 Emerson Street across from Shelter Island, ℭ (619) 222-1144.

Harbor Island is directly across from Lindbergh Field, the San Diego airport. Businessmen find the hotels and restaurants here convenient. **Tom Ham's Lighthouse** at the western end was the first establishment on the island and, although the food is unpredictable, it is a popular San Diego landmark (the lighthouse is real, Coast Guard-approved). At the other end of the island, the **Reuben E. Lee** floating riverboat restaurant is docked. The food here is not recommended, but its panoramic view of San Diego and the bay is the best there is.

THE EMBARCADERO AND SEAPORT VILLAGE

Like most working ports, San Diego has only recently begun to regard its waterfront as a beauty spot which tourists might like to visit. By 1989, work had almost been completed on a beautifully landscaped park stretching from Harbor Island for 4 miles (6.5 km)

RIGHT: The placid bay and the modern glass buildings of new San Diego reflect the setting sun.

along the Embarcadero and around Seaport Village. Paved walkways, plantings, and benches all along the way allow you to rest and enjoy the view. There are still two working piers — at the end of B Street and G Street, for tuna boats and other fishermen on the waterfront. Once a major industry, tuna fishing has been crippled by foreign competition and the last of the local canneries is now closed. However, you can still see some of the magnificent multimillion-dollar tuna boats which, for all their practical uses, feature lines as sleek as anything you'll see on the most expensive of yachts. At the end of Broadway is another public pier where a different Navy or Coast Guard vessel is on display every weekend.

The waterfront has been largely given over to tourism. The **San Diego Maritime Museum** offers a floating display of several aspects of maritime history. The *Star of India* is a tall sailing ship first commissioned in 1867 and restored in 1961. A ticket to tour this ship also entitles you to visit the exhibits on the old ferryboat *Berkeley* and the steam yacht *Medea.*

The city's most popular seafood restaurant, **Anthony's,** is located at 1360 N. Harbor Drive, built on pilings right over the water. This is just one of 14 facilities operated by the same family in San Diego. They include family restaurants, "Fishette" fast-food facilities, and fresh fish markets. There is always a line of people waiting to be seated but the fish is caught fresh daily (tons of it), and the food and service are predictably good and reasonably priced. © (619) 232-5103.

A new addition to the Embarcadero is the cruise ship terminal, where the major cruise lines now stop on their way from San Francisco and Los Angeles to the Mexican Riviera. The most famous of these is the "Love Boat" (in reality the *Viking Princess)* used in the television series of the same name. For information on Royal Viking cruises, © (800) 862-1133. Also docking at the cruise terminal is the *Ensenada Express.* The round-trip daily fare to Ensenada is $59. For information, © (619) 232-2109.

Just south of the terminal are two major harbor cruise facilities. Harbor Excursions offers one-and two-hour tours of the bay in open tour boats throughout the day; dinner cruises at 7 and 9:30 pm on Fridays and Saturdays. The ticket booth is located at 1050 N. Harbor Drive at the foot of Broadway or you can, © (619) 234-4111 for more information.

The most interesting cruises are offered by Invader Cruises on three historic ships. The 151-ft (46-m) sailing schooner *Invader* was built in 1905; the 110-ft (33-m) riverboat *San Diego Showboat* was built in 1942 as a survey vessel on the Sacramento River; and the 135-ft (41-m) motor yacht *Diplomat* was built in 1930 for a founder of the Standard Oil Corporation. All three ships provide daytime cruises of the bay and dinner cruises at night. The *Invader* ticket booth is located at 1066 N. Harbor Drive. The ships are docked behind it. For more information, © (619) 234-8687. In late December, January, and February, the harbor tour boats all become "whale watchers" with daily schedules outside the harbor to watch the great gray whales swimming past.

Seaport Village might seem a New England fishing village plonked out of place and time in San Diego. In fact, most of the early houses in San Diego were designed and built of pre-cut timbers from New England. The lighthouse at the center of Seaport Village is a replica of a real lighthouse in Washington State. First opened in 1980, Seaport Village consists of a cluster of shops and restaurants right on the waterfront, among tropical flowers and foliage, surrounded by a real boardwalk. There are four major restaurants, 13 fast-food places, and 65 shops that offer everything from handmade Christmas ornaments to pewter miniatures. At the center of the village is a restored 1900 carousel. There are regular performances by musicians and jugglers in the gazebos and open plazas, and the village's own brass band performs at the slightest excuse for a celebration, whether it be Father's Day, Irving Berlin's birthday, or Christmas.

Papagayo is the most elegant and best of the four seafood restaurants. An award-winning menu features imaginative dishes that are changed daily. ✆ (619) 232-581. Just as expensive, but with unpredictable food and service, is the **Harbor House,** a beautiful two-story board and batten structure with huge windows overlooking the bay. ✆ (619) 232-114₺. The **San Diego Pier Cafe** is a picturesque little place built on pilings out over the water. The menu here is on a much lower scale than what you'll find at Papagayo, but the prices are also much lower. ✆ (619) 239-3968. The fourth restaurant is the **Jolly Roger**, one of a chain of restaurants in Hawaii and California with a menu of sandwiches and salads.

At the south end of Seaport Village is the entrance to the **Embarcadero Marina Park,** one of the busiest picnic and kite-flying spots. The America's Cup Village was located here during the September 1988 race; it was the best place from which to view the two boats going and coming to the race course out at sea. The two arms of the park surround the marina in front of the San Diego Marriott and the new civic center. Grassy lawns across low hills overlook the water and curving walkways. The south arm of the park (reached by way of the boardwalk or from Fifth or Eighth Avenues off Harbor Drive) also has a fishing pier, basketball courts, and a workout course along the jogging path. In 1988, the two American catamarans — both called *Stars and Stripes* — built for the America's Cup challenge race with New Zealand were docked here beside the old San Diego Rowing Club. Now a **Chart House Restaurant,** the old board and batten rowing club is the only true historic building on the waterfront. Its wide porches and sunny dining areas evoke the best of an enduring and unpretentious port town. Located at 525 E. Harbor Drive, ✆ (619) 233-7391, this is one of six Chart House restaurants in San Diego.

BALBOA PARK

Of the great city parks in America, only New York's Central Park is older than San Diego's

Balboa Park. In 1867, when 1,400 acres (567 hectares) was set aside for a park here, San Diego was a dusty little village of fewer than 3,000 residents. The town fathers reasoned that the barren hillsides and canyons weren't fit for development. Besides, they were keeping a practical eye on the property. The famous Olmstead Company was sent packing home to Boston with the idea of a woodland retreat in the middle of the city. San Diegans felt the land should be used. Part of it was a city dump until well into the 1970's. At present, the park is cut through by two four-lane highways; the southern portion is a golf course, and one hillside contains the newest and most expensive military hospital in the world.

The real turning point for the park was the 1915 Panama Exposition. That's when "the park" became Balboa Park. It was also the time when the Spanish or mission style of architecture took hold here and spread throughout America. When former president Theodore Roosevelt visited the ornate buildings at the exposition, he said he hoped the city would preserve them, for beauty was not only worthwhile for its own sake but could also be good for business. The original exposition was extended for a second year, through 1916. Then, in 1935, when other cities were staging expositions to revive their economies after the Depression, San Diego spruced up the old buildings, added several new exhibits, and staged another successful exposition. Chicago's World's Fair had Sally Rand doing her exotic dances, but San Diego had a whole colony of male and female nudists on view in a "Utopian community" in the park. During World Wars I and II, the buildings were converted to military use. In recent years, they have become a unique cultural center, a vision of old Spain in the heart of the city. There are now 12 museums, two large restaurants, and two theaters in the exposition buildings.

Outdoor concerts and plays are staged throughout the year at two of the old exhibition sites. The magnificent **Organ Pavilion,** built at a cost of more than $100,000 in 1915, was recently restored. There is a regular program of free organ concerts before this classic colonnade. Built as part of the Ford exhibit for the 1935 exhibition, the **Starlight Theater** is an amphitheater offering a regular season of musicals and other performances. For ticket information on the Starlight Theater, ✆ (619) 544-7827.

The park grounds include a magnificent rose garden, a large desert garden, and the ecently restored palm canyon. But the most famous attraction to grow out of the 1915 exposition is the San Diego Zoo, located behind the older buildings.

THE SAN DIEGO ZOO AND WILD ANIMAL PARK

For many years, San Diego was known as "the place with the great zoo". The **San Diego Zoo** was perhaps the only thing in San Diego that was bigger and better than its counterparts in Los Angeles and San Francisco. First opened as part of the 1915 exposition in Balboa Park, it was one of the first American zoos to take animals out of their cages and put them in their own environments. The zoo quickly became the pride of the city. While it has a world-wide reputation for its scientific work, the San Diego Zoo also loves to put on a good show. Its chief founder was a lover of circus animals and his successors have carried on the tradition of animal performers.

Just one of the 2,400 non-human residents of San Diego's spacious Wild Animal Park. OPPOSITE: Killer whale and human rider perform at San Diego's famed Sea World.

More than three million people visit the original zoo in Balboa Park every year. It covers 100 acres (40 hectares) of once barren hillsides that have been transformed into a tropical garden of 6,000 flowers and trees every bit as rare and exotic as the 3,200 animals who live there. If the inner city zoo is too crowded for you, visit the **Wild Animal Park** where the 2,400 animals have more than 1,800 acres (730 hectares) in which to wander.

Located in the beautiful San Pasqual Valley, the park is 30 miles (50 km) north of downtown San Diego. It can be reached by way of Highway 163 and Interstate 15, turning at Via Rancho Parkway at Escondido. From Los Angeles, take Interstate 5 to Oceanside, then Highway 78 east to Interstate 15, and then south to Via Rancho Parkway where signs lead the way. The main feature of the park is the "Wgasa Bush Line Monorail", a 50-minute train ride through the park. For the more daring, there is the Kilimanjaro hiking trail. By special arrangement, ✆ (619) 747-8702, you can also book places on photo caravans in open trucks that drive right up to the animals. As with the original zoo, there are open stages here for animal performances. (The trainer for the bird shows once worked with Alfred Hitchcock in the movie, *The Birds*.) Admission to the San Diego Zoo or Wild Animal Park is $8.50 for adults, $2.50 for children from three to 15 years old. Children under the age of three are admitted free.

MISSION BAY PARK

Locals claim that Mission Bay Park's 4,600 acres (1,862 hectares) and 27 miles (44 km) of shoreline make it the country's largest public aquatic park. But that apart, it is also one of the most pleasant places in the city to get away for a few minutes or a few hours. There are ample facilities available for recreation — boats and jet skis for rent and tennis at the nearby hotels. The more laid-back can have a leisurely stroll along the man-made lagoon or bay in beautifully landscaped lawns, while joggers can take to

the miles of paved walkways. The lawns are available for picnics, kite-flying, and sun-bathing.

Fiesta Island, a dredged-up blob of sand with a dirt road encircling it, is located at the south end of the park. Although there's no development of any kind here, it has become so popular as a party place for the young set that the city had to clamp down with rigid rules against overnight visitors. Every August, thousands of people crowd the tiny island for the Over-the-Line softball tournament. It's a simple game of hitting a softball over a line, but the game is hardly the thing here. Bikini-watching is what it's all about, and the team names all reflect this in graphic detail on their T-shirts. Local legend has it that ABC's *Wide World of Sports* wanted to show the Over-the-Line tournament on network television but canceled out when San Diegans refused to clean up the language on those shirts. The TV people didn't understand that this kind of fun was the first rule of the game. Fiesta Island is also the favorite local place of jet skiers. You can pull your truck, van, or buggie right on to the beach, unload, and spend the day skiing and stretching out in the sun.

Mission Bay Park is the scene of many special events throughout the year. For information on the waterskiing and hydroplane contests, call Boat and Ski Club, ✆ (619) 276-0830.

SEA WORLD

Located on 135 acres (55 hectares) on Mission Bay, Sea World is without question the city's major tourist attraction and most successful commercial venture. First opened in March 1964 by four UCLA fraternity brothers, it was bought by the publishing and entertainment conglomerate Harcourt Brace Jovanovich in 1976. The small aquatic park has become an enormous entertainment center, with a paid attendance ($19.95 for adults; $14.95 for children and seniors) of nearly four million in 1987.

Sea World has four aquariums, two rides, 30 educational exhibits, and seven extra-ordinary shows. The most popular and dangerous of the shows involves Shamu and his killer whale friends performing in a six–million-gallon saltwater tank before a 5,000-seat stadium. The whale shows were briefly suspended after trainers were injured in three separate accidents. However, shows resumed in 1988 even as these trainers brought suit against Sea World. In smaller stadiums, you can see dolphins and pilot whales in one show, sea lions and otters in another, and human divers in a "Muscle Beach" show.

The largest of the aquariums is a 400,000-gallon (1.5-million-liter) tank that holds the largest live shark display in the world. You're not encouraged to go near the sharks, but there is a "petting pool" where visitors can feed and pet the whales and dolphins. One of the newer exhibits is the multimillion-dollar Penguin Encounter, the most extensive collection of penguins in captivity. Asked to participate in the opening of this facility, French naturalist Jacques Cousteau replied that he did not go anywhere where animals were "enslaved or imprisoned". Obviously, the many millions who are dazzled daily by the shows at Sea World do not share his view.

Sea World is located at 1720 South Shores Road, ✆ (619) 222-6363.

OLD TOWN AND PRESIDIO PARK

The modern state of California began in this unpretentious little settlement at the foot of Presidio Hill. Located along Interstate 5, Old Town is now largely a commercial area. Traces of its Spanish-American origins have been incorporated into the modern shops, restaurants, and hotels. Mexican food reigns supreme here, but there are other fine restaurants (covered under restaurants P.179). The most popular Mexican place is the **Old Town Mexican Cafe** at 2489 San Diego Avenue. The **Casa Bandini** is a bit more expensive, but it is also located in the finest of the old adobe

A playful mural decorates the exterior of the Metropolitan Hotel, one of San Diego's award-winning new single room occupancy hotels for lower-income people.

houses, complete with balconies and an open patio.

The big week in Old Town is that preceding Cinco de Mayo (May 5), a minor holiday in Mexico but, thanks to beer company promotions, celebrated (incorrectly) as Mexican Independence Day in the United States. This is when the Mexican *charros* (cowboys) take over the old corral and prance about in their silver-studded saddles. Adjoining the corral is a full-sized working blacksmith shop and other facilities in keeping with a nineteenth-century stable. There are also historic buildings — a newspaper shop, a schoolhouse, and a tiny chapel.

Just up from the Old Town Historic Park is **Heritage Park**, where seven Victorian houses were moved after facing destruction in other parts of the city. As in the older park, the houses here have been put to commercial use as art galleries, gift shops, and restaurants.

Further up the hill is **Presidio Park**, one of San Diego's most beautiful scenic spots. It marks the site of the original Spanish mission and fort. The mission was later moved 6 miles (10 km) up the valley. But in 1925, a mission-style museum was erected on the site. The **Serra Museum** is such an imposing landmark that it has long been mistakenly photographed as the San Diego Mission. The hilltop park with the sweeping meadowlike lawns is a favorite picnic spot and backdrop for weddings. Maintained by the San Diego Historical Society, the museum provides an excellent introduction to San Diego's Mexican and Spanish past.

La Jolla

Although La Jolla (pronounced La Hoya) is within the city limits of San Diego, it has a separate zip code and a decidedly separate identity. Until fairly recent times, it was a tiny fishing village inhabited by a few artists and writers living in little beach cottages. Luckily, it was also where the two eccentric sisters of newspaper tycoon E.W. Scripps made their home. The sisters lived almost a full century and watched over their private domain with a loving eye and a ready umbrella. The barren landscape was just fine to one sister who thought trees were nasty. Ellen Browning Scripps' many philanthropies include the La Jolla Museum of Contemporary Art (expanded from her home), the Scripps Institute of Oceanography, the Scripps Clinic, and many others. But her most enduring gift was the waterfront itself which, along with Torrey Pines State Park, she bought and presented to the state and city as public preserves.

In recent years, La Jolla has become a kind of Palm Beach west, another resort enclave of the very rich. Some say the hillsides overlooking La Jolla and the ocean contain the most expensive residential property in America. Still, some of the spirit of the artists' colony and fishing village endures. It is unpretentious and the mood in the expensive shops and restaurants is as casual as the rest of southern California. Jaywalking laws that are rigidly enforced in downtown San Diego are ignored in La Jolla; the narrow roads zigzag to such an extent that you're generally safe from the traffic of Mercedes Benzes and Rolls-Royces.

Two bookstores in La Jolla deserve special mention. **John Coles Book Shop**, 780 Prospect Street, ✆ (619) 454-4766, is one of the best new book stores in southern California where frequent book and author parties are held. For used books and a true literary ambience, there is **D.G. Wills Books**, 7527 La Jolla Boulevard, ✆ (619) 456-1800. Dennis Wills left a government job in Washington and opened his dream shop, crammed from floor to ceiling with good old books. Some sort of literary discussion or formal reading is scheduled every week.

Del Mar Racetrack

If the beautiful old Del Mar Racetrack looks like an idealized movie set of a California track, that's because its origins are pure Hollywood. Built by singer Bing Crosby and actor Pat O'Brien in 1937, the buildings are in Spanish or Mexican style with stucco walls and tiled roofs. A favorite haunt of the

Hollywood set is the nearby resort village of Del Mar. It is also home to many big names in music and acting. Singer and composer Burt Bacharach says he always invites Neil Diamond to visit and sing to his horses before they race at Del Mar. The racing season runs for 43 days starting in late July. In 1987, off-track betting for the other California tracks was installed at the Del Mar track. For information, call the Del Mar Thoroughbred Club ✆ (619) 755-1141 or (619) 481-1207.

More popular than the racing is the annual **Del Mar Fair**, staged at the racetrack for three weeks in late June and early July. It is a small-scale version of an old-time state fair, complete with livestock and agricultural exhibits. Two huge exhibition buildings are packed with hucksters selling all the latest gadgets. The fair also features an extraordinary display of flowers and gardens from the major nurseries in southern California.

MISSIONS: SAN DIEGO DE ALCALA AND SAN LUIS REY

Founded in 1769 by Father Serra himself, **San Diego de Alcala** was the first of the chain of missions that would eventually stretch 750 miles (1,210 km) into northern California. Originally located on Presidio Hill above present-day Old Town, the mission was moved in 1774 to its present site 6 miles (10 km) up Mission Valley. Destroyed by an Indian attack in 1775, it was rebuilt in 1780 only to be destroyed again by an earthquake in 1803. After secularization, the buildings were abandoned to ruin for a hundred years. Reconstruction began in 1931. A parish church for many years now, San Diego de Alcala is located north of Interstate 8 and east of Interstate 15 in the city's busy Mission Valley.

Not so well known, but more interesting historically, is the mission **San Luis Rey de Francia**, the 18th of the 21 missions. The largest of all the mission churches was completed here in 1815. It proved to be the most successful, with more Indian converts, and more cattle and sheep than any of the other missions. The buildings here were also saved from ruin when the mission was reopened as a seminary in 1893. Located in the town of San Luis Rey, just off State Highway 76, the mission is five miles (eight kilometers) inland from Oceanside.

CULTURAL LIFE

San Diego's cultural development still has a long way to go. There is a San Diego Symphony, but its financial problems make more news than its music. There is an opera company and a local ballet, but nothing to compare with the companies in San Francisco and Los Angeles. For years, the touring companies of Broadway plays took such a long time to reach San Diego that the plays became more an experience in nostalgia than current American theater.

Recently, however, theater has earned San Diego a prominent place in the national spotlight. Three of the plays nominated for Tony awards on Broadway in 1988 started out in San Diego. Several of the actors honored have also appeared in San Diego within the past year. This is largely due to the award-winning directors at the **La Jolla Playhouse** on the campus of the University of California, San Diego, and the **Old Globe Theater** in Balboa Park. Also heartening is the news that the **San Diego Repertory Theater** has opened its new theaters in Horton Plaza. Two other local groups also offer a wide variety of traditional and experimental theater: the **Gaslamp Theater** downtown and the **Bowery Theater.**

Ticket information for theater events can be obtained by calling the following numbers: La Jolla Playhouse ✆ (619) 534-3960; Old Globe Theater ✆ (619) 239-2255; San Diego Repertory Theater, ✆ (619) 235-8025; Gaslamp Quarter Theater, ✆ (619) 234-9583; and the Bowery Theater, ✆ (619) 232-4088.

In recent years, two of the most popular stand-up comedy showcases in New York and Los Angeles have opened venues in San Diego. The shows, which feature some of the biggest names in the business, have proved successful. The Comedy Store is located at 916 Pearl Street, in La Jolla, ✆ (619) 454-

9176, and Improvisation is at 832 Garnet Avenue in Pacific Beach, ☏ (619) 483-4520.

NIGHTLIFE

The best source for what's happening in San Diego's nightlife is the *San Diego Reader*, a weekly tabloid-sized newspaper published every Thursday and distributed free throughout the city. No other publication has such extensive and high-quality reviews of everything — restaurants, music, dance, comedy,

and what wildflowers are blooming in the mountains. The *Reader* offers an especially good guide to the local music scene which is constantly changing.

Popular Music

The most popular clubs for rock and pop music are:

Bacchanal, 8022 Clairemont Mesa Boulevard. ☏ (619) 560-8000.

Rio's, 4258 W. Pt. Loma Boulevard. ☏ (619) 225-9559.

Belly Up, 143 South Cedros Avenue, Solana Beach. ☏ (619) 481-9022.

Humphrey's Concerts by the Bay, 2241 Shelter Island Drive. ☏ (619) 224-9438.

The Old Pacific Beach Cafe, 4287 Mission Boulevard. ☏ (619) 270-7522.

Concerts

Almost every weekend, concerts are held at the **Nautilus Amphitheater** at Sea World and, less frequently, at the **San Diego Wild Animal Park.** Tickets for any of these can be obtained from Ticketmaster at record stores, box offices, and department stores throughout the city. ☏ (619) 298-5070 or (619) 278-8497 to charge to major credit cards.

Bars

When San Diegans go for a night on the town, they usually go to the smaller bars that feature live music. In downtown proper, several new places have opened in recent years. For the coat-and-tie professional set, there is the **B Street Cafe** and — on a somewhat more casual note — **Croce's.** Owned and operated by singer Jim Croce's widow, Croce's is located at the corner of Fifth Avenue and F Street, and offers a rare sophisticated experience in elegant dining and easy listening jazz. Around the corner is **Patrick's II,** a tiny bar that has become an institution in downtown San Diego's nightlife. Owned and operated by Larry and Tina Matranga, Patrick's is one of the few places that has managed to hold on to the old crowd from the Gaslamp while attracting a new and younger set of San Diegans. There's jazz every Wednesday and Thursday; other nights it's blues, boogie, and old-time rock 'n' roll.

On the beaches, the bar scene is more changeable than that downtown. The **Belly-Up** in Solana Beach is up there at the top of everybody's list of music bars in San Diego. In Pacific Beach there is the **Old Pacific Beach Cafe** and, for a somewhat older crowd, the **Old Ox.**

San Diego is a much more working class place than Los Angeles or San Francisco and after work is a busy time in the bars. There are free taco bars in several places at happy hours. The popular El Toritos and Carlos Murphys bars also feature a variety of Margaritas (strawberry, watermelon, you name it) served in fishbowl-sized goblets.

SHOPPING

If you're looking for the large department store malls, you'll find them off Friar's Road and Interstate 8 in Mission Valley. If you want elegant shops such as Saks Fifth Avenue and Bonwit Teller's, go to downtown La Jolla and Coronado. For arts and crafts, especially of Mexican origin, try the shops in Old Town.

But if you're looking for an exciting blend of all these, you'll find it in the new **Horton Plaza** in the heart of downtown San Diego. Many of the stores that left the city for suburban malls have now moved back to this open-air, multistory shopping center.

Completed in 1985, Horton Plaza shocked downtown San Diego back into life. The new shopping center had a most unlikely adviser involved in its design — science fiction writer, Ray Bradbury. He said it's time developers thought of cities as theater and looked more to Disneyland for inspiration. He encouraged architect Jon Jerde to go ahead with his whimsical and unconventional design, to make it a "fun park", something that would "give us a reason to leave our homes."

The result is a mad blend of walkways and stairs, and clashing colors of banners and pennants and storefronts more like Coney Island than Fifth Avenue. Once lavishly praised by the architectural critic of the *New York Times*, Horton Plaza has been around long enough now to be ridiculed as "comic opera architecture". But whatever it is, Horton Plaza works. It is a fun place to wander through, with jugglers or musicians usually performing in the various open spaces. For New Year's Eve and other special events such as the Super Bowl, the entire place is turned into a gigantic discotheque with a cover charge of $20.

The complex includes three movie theaters and two innovative underground stages for the San Diego Repertory Theater. Four major department stores and 115 specialty shops feature carved wooden toys, books, kites, crystal, safari clothing, fresh vegetables, breads, and much more. There are two restaurants — the Panda for Chinese cuisine and the Harbor House for pizza and American fare — and 33 unusually imaginative fast-food shops. In general, the fast-food places offer better food at cheaper prices than the restaurants. There are several open-air spaces provided with tables and chairs where you can enjoy your lunch and take in the activities on the lower levels.

RESTAURANTS

Recommending restaurants in San Diego can be a hazardous business. While the city has much to recommend it, great restaurants have never been a reason to visit San Diego. Dozens of promising restaurants in seemingly choice locations in the Gaslamp and downtown areas have opened and closed. A prime location in La Jolla has become known

Colorful stacks of pottery in all shapes and sizes OPPOSITE are available along the roads in Baja California at very reasonable prices. ABOVE: Horton Plaza in the heart of downtown San Diego is a colorful place to shop or lunch, or wander about.

as "death row" because so many restaurants have died there. Still, the best and most enduring restaurants are located in La Jolla. That's because, as Willie Sutton used to say when explaining why he robbed banks, that's where the money is. Here are some of the best:

Gustaf Anders, 2182 Avenida de la Playa, is San Diego's best and most expensive restaurant. It offers an award-winning variety of Scandinavian and California cuisine, and the lunch and dinner menus change every day. ℂ (619) 459-4499.

George's at the Cove, 1250 Prospect Street, is a landmark in the heart of La Jolla, famous for its view of the cove. Its fresh seafood menu is changed according to what's available and fresh. ℂ (619) 454-4244.

Shores Restaurant Sea Lodge, in La Jolla Shores at 8110 Camino del Oro, is built right on the water and offers a fresh seafood bar of oysters, clams, shrimp, lobster, and the Mexican specialty *ceviche*. ℂ (619) 456-0600.

Rusty Pelican, 4340 La Jolla Village Drive, is noted for its spectacular landscaping (featuring a waterfall and multilevel walkways) and interior design. It can get raucous during happy hour, when the singles crowd takes over. The menu features fresh seafood served with sourdough bread and a healthy spinach salad. ℂ (619) 587-1886.

La Jolla has no franchise on great cuisine; there are many fine restaurants in some unexpected parts of the city. One of the most consistently praised is **The Belgian Lion**, 2265 Bacon Street in Ocean Beach. The specialties here are elegant Belgian and French preparations of duck and veal with all the trimmings, plus fresh desserts. ℂ (619) 223-2700.

In Old Town, the **Cafe Pacifica**, 2414 San Diego Avenue, has established itself as the city's premier seafood restaurant. The menu nearly always includes fresh sea bass and salmon but is changed daily according to the catch. ℂ (619) 291-6666.

The **Pacifica Grill**, 1202 Kettner Boulevard, is owned and operated by the same people who run Cafe Pacifica. ℂ (619) 696-9226.

In downtown San Diego, new cafes and restaurants seem to be opening every day. Most of these cater to the working lunch crowd, but several have caught on as nightspots and dinner places. **Dobson's**, 956 Broadway Circle near Horton Plaza, is a tiny place, but it offers the best French cuisine in San Diego, and a classy bar that has become a favorite hangout of expensive lawyers after work. **La Gran Tapa**, 611 B Street, has the same owner as Dobson's. It has much more space and a Spanish menu featuring the bite-sized *tapas* found in Spain. ℂ (619) 231-6771 for Dobson's and ℂ(619) 234-8272 for La Gran Tapa.

One of the liveliest of the new places downtown is the **B Street Cafe and Bar** where you'll find a young professional crowd enjoying the live jazz and an American chop house menu. Under the same roof and management is the **East Room,** a quieter setting for gourmet dining on lamb, veal, duck, and fresh fish. ℂ (619) 236-1707.

In the heart of the Gaslamp is a sophisticated cafe and jazz bar reminiscent of those found on Upper East Side New York. This is **Croce's,** owned and operated by the widow of singer Jim Croce. It is located at the corner of Fifth Avenue and F Street. The menu is expensive for San Diego, but with daily "Russian Jewish specials", it is also unique. ℂ (619) 233-4355.

More characteristic of San Diego are the small neighborhood cafes where the atmosphere is warm and homey and the food is often of a surprisingly high quality. Three of the best are:

Drowsy Maggie's, 3089 University Avenue. ℂ (619) 298-8584.

Crest Cafe, in the heart of Hillcrest, 425 Robinson Avenue. ℂ (619) 295-2510.

The **Big Kitchen**, 3003 Grape Street. ℂ (619) 234-5789. Whoopi Goldberg is the most famous of those who once worked and hung out at the Big Kitchen.

Of course, San Diego's **Chicken Pie Shop**, 3801 Fifth Avenue, in Hillcrest, takes the budget meal right off the charts.

For only $2.75 you can get a full dinner, complete with soup or salad and dessert. It's plain old-fashioned fare but you can't beat the price and you can take home the chicken pies for 90 cents each, hot or frozen. ✆ (619) 295-0156.

Alberto's, the best fast-food Mexican place in town, is at 16 locations: Broadway and Ninth (downtown), 6101 University Avenue, 549 25th Street, 4532 Bonita Road (Bonita), 4125 Convoy, 4909 El Cajon Boulevard, 9272 Miramar Road, 3030 Plaza Bonita Road (National City), 13095 Poway Road (Poway), 1480 Rosecrans, 3753 Voltaire, 409 Washington, 1340 N. Second Street (El Cajon), 3446 University Avenue, 8667 Fanita Drive (Santee), and 4918 Newport Avenue.

B Street Cafe, 425 West B Street, California cuisine and live jazz. ✆ (619) 236-1707.

Boll Weevil, best hamburgers in town, at eight locations: 1000 Prospect Street (La Jolla), 1956 Bacon Street, 4425 Convoy Street, 2732 Midway Drive, 7070 Miramar Road, 5826 Mission Gorge Road, Pacific Highway at Elm Street, 9535 Shelter Island Drive.

Cafe Pacifica, 2414 San Diego Avenue, seafood. ✆ (619) 291-6666.

Casa de Bandini, 2660 Calhoun Street, Old Town. ✆ (619) 297-8211.

Celadon, 3628 Fifth Avenue, Thai. ✆ (619) 295-8800.

Chart House San Diego Rowing Club, 525 E. Harbor Drive (Fifth Avenue behind the new convention center). ✆ (619) 233-7391.

China Camp and Fat City, 2137 Pacific Highway, Szechuan cuisine, pink art deco exterior, "goldrush decor" inside. ✆ (619) 232-0686, 232-1367.

Dobson's, 956 Broadway Circle. ✆ (619) 696-0398.

Kansas City Barbecue, 610 W. Market Street. ✆ (619) 231-9680.

La Gran Tapa, 611 B Street. ✆ (619) 234-8272.

Little Joe's, 750 Fifth Avenue, Gaslamp, best pizza and Italian sausage dishes, free delivery. ✆ (619) 234-1320.

Lubach's, 2101 N. Harbor Drive, German food, San Diego landmark. ✆ (619) 232-5129.

Top O' the Cove, 1216 Prospect Street, La Jolla. ✆ (619) 454-7779.

HOTELS

By 1989, San Diego had experienced a hotel boom that dramatically changed its downtown skyline. The most prominent of these are the two green glass towers of the **Marriott Hotel** and **Marina** on Harbor Drive, in between the new convention center and Seaport Village. The 25-story towers are angled away from the waterfront so that nearly all 1,355 rooms have a view of the bay. Hotel facilities include four restaurants and bars and a nicely landscaped pool area on the ground level. The hotel also operates the marina, with slips for 446 yachts. Several excursion boats also operate out of the marina. On the boardwalk, you can rent bicycles for your own excursion along the boardwalk and embarcadero.

The 15-story, $58-million **Omni San Diego Hotel**, with its purple, orange, and pink arches and colonnades, forms a colorful west wall to Horton Plaza shopping center. Although located in the heart of downtown, the hotel also has an outdoor swimming pool and lighted tennis courts. The hotel's Festival restaurant is an elegant dining place and its City Colors bar is a lively addition to the city's nightlife.

Two other new downtown hotels built by the Ramada Inn and Embassy Suites chains were also opened in 1988. And plans have been approved for a 41-story Hyatt Regency with 871 rooms on the waterfront, to be completed in 1991.

For many years, the **Little America Westgate Hotel**, 1055 Second Avenue, was the lone bastion of luxury in the abandoned downtown area. *Esquire* magazine once listed it as one of the three best hotels in the world. Now outshone by all the flashier newcomers, the Westgate is still a favorite among lawyers (who can walk to the nearby courthouses) and others who like the location. All of the 223 rooms in the 20-story hotel are decorated differently, and the bathrooms feature Italian marble with brass and gold fixtures. On the top floors are luxurious suites of two and three bedrooms with a panoramic view of the bay. The hotel's Le Fontainebleau Room has managed to stay at the top of the list of elegant dining places in town.

Also downtown are two older hotels which reopened in recent years. The **U.S. Grant** was beautifully restored and reopened in December 1985. A San Diego landmark since it first opened in 1910, the hotel has been

area, it is a magnificent Victorian mansion with nine rooms decorated to match the stained-glass windows and exterior turrets. The place has become so popular, it is necessary to book four to five months in advance.

Of course, the grande dame of all San Diego hotels is the **Del Coronado,** located across the bay on the oceanfront at Coronado. In 1980, "The Del" celebrated its 100th anniversary with a lavish multimillion-dollar party. One of America's largest wooden structures, it is worth a visit for its rich history

on shaky financial ground lately, and there is some question about its future. There is classical chamber music in the lobby during happy hour, and the richly paneled Grant Grill is once again a popular meeting place in downtown San Diego.

A few blocks south is the **Horton Grand Hotel**, a reconstruction of two old hotels. It is richly decorated with Victorian furnishings and draperies. On the street level is the Ida Bailey (a colorful madame who once worked the area) bar and restaurant. One other Victorian place deserves mention — the **Britt House,** a luxury version of the increasingly popular bed and breakfast places. Located at 406 Maple Street, north of the downtown

and the beautiful woodwork of its exterior balconies, the interior paneling, and enormous vaulted ceilings. The new luxury hotel at Disney World in Florida is almost a replica of the old Del's exterior. Unfortunately, the hotel's newer additions are quite ordinary and do not have the original's ambience.

Not quite as old, but with a settled unpretentious charm all its own, is **La Valencia Hotel** in the heart of downtown La Jolla. With only 150 rooms, it has remained one of the best of the old resort hotels where personal service is important. No place in La Jolla offers a better view of the coves below or the cliffs to the north and south. The hotel's Sky Room has a view and elegant ambience unmatched anywhere in San Diego. The streetside Whaling Bar has no view but it has endured as a grand old watering hole.

On Mission Bay, there are two hotels favored for their proximity to the beautiful bay park. These are the **San Diego Hilton** and the **Hyatt Islandia**. The Hilton is built in a low village-like tropical setting, with tennis courts, pool, and boating facilities on the bay. The Hyatt Islandia is a 17-story tower whose rooms provide a view of the bay and the ocean beyond.

La Costa Hotel and Spa is the most famous resort in the San Diego area. Located inland from Carlsbad, about 10 minutes' drive from the ocean and 45 minutes north from San Diego. It is a small city in itself, with facilities that include a championship golf course, tennis courts, swimming pools, and the most elaborate spa in the country. Spa services start with a skin and figure analysis and then go on to luxurious treatments involving herbal wraps, massage, and whirlpool, steam, and sauna baths. The hotel complex also features a conference center. Five restaurants serve guests at the hotel and spa. Nothing here is for the budget tourist; it is a playground for the super-rich.

Britt House 1887, 406 Maple Street. ✆ (619) 234-2926.

Del Coronado, 1500 Orange Avenue, Coronado. ✆ (619) 435-6611.

Glorietta Bay Inn, Orange Avenue and Glorietta Bay Boulevard, Coronado. ✆ (619) 435-3101.

Hilton Hotel San Diego, 1775 East Mission Bay Drive. ✆ (619) 276-4010.

Horton Grand, 311 Island Avenue. ✆ (619) 544-1886.

Hyatt Islandia, 1441 Quivira Road. ✆ (619) 224-1234.

Inn at Rancho Santa Fe, Linea del Cielo, Rancho Santa Fe. ✆ (619) 756-1131.

Julian Gold Rush Hotel (Inn), 2032 Main Street, Julian. ✆ (619) 765-0201.

La Costa Resort Hotel and Spa, Costa del Mar Road, Carlsbad. ✆ (619) 438-9111.

La Jolla Shores Inn, 5390 La Jolla Boulevard, La Jolla. ✆ (619) 454-0175.

La Valencia Hotel, 1132 Prospect Street, La Jolla. ✆ (619) 454-0771.

Ramada Inn Old Town, 2435 Jefferston Street. ✆ (619) 260-8500.

Rancho Bernardo Inn, 17550 Bernardo Oaks Drive, Rancho Bernardo. & (619) 277-2146.

San Diego Marriott and Marina, 333 W. Harbor Drive. ✆ (619) 234-1500.

Summer House Inn, 7955 La Jolla Shores Drive. ✆ (619) 459-0261.

U.S. Grant Hotel, 326 Broadway. ✆ (619) 232-3121.

Westgate, 1055 Second Avenue. ✆ (619) 238-1818.

GOLF

With more than 70 golf courses in the immediate area, tourist officials say San Diego can easily claim to have more golfing opportunities per visitor than any other major tourist city in America. A complete list of the

OPPOSITE and ABOVE: The Hotel Del Coronado on the beach across the bay from San Diego is the grande dame of all Southern California hotels; a year-long celebration in 1988 honored its first 100 years.

golf courses can be obtained from the San Diego Convention and Visitors Bureau at 1200 Third Avenue, San Diego, CA 92101. *©* (619) 232-3101. Here are some of the more interesting courses:

Torrey Pines Municipal Golf Course. The area's most famous because of the Shearson Lehman Andy Williams Open Tournament held here every year, and the most beautiful because of its location above the steep cliffs behind Black's Beach. Every green has a full view of the ocean. The 36-hole championship course is at 11480 N. Torrey Pines Road, La Jolla, CA 92037. *©* (619) 453-0380.

Balboa Park Golf Course. Convenient to downtown, the 18-hole and nine-hole starter courses cover the southern part of Balboa Park. *©* (619) 232-2470 for the 18-hole course; *©* (619) 232-2717 for the nine-hole course.

Mission Bay Golf Course. Clubhouse and Sandtrap Restaurant and Lounge are at 2702 North Mission Bay Drive in Pacific Beach. *©* (619) 273-1221 for the golf course; *©* (619) 274-3314 for the restaurant.

Coronado City Golf Course. The only public golf course on Coronado. Located at 2000 Visalia Row, Coronado. *©* (619) 435-3121.

Rancho Bernardo Inn Golf Course. 17550 Bernardo Oaks Drive in the heart of the new affluent community of Rancho Bernardo, 25 miles (40 km) north of San Diego on Interstate 15. *©* (619) 277-2146.

PROFESSIONAL SPORTS

Oddly, San Diego's only winning professional team is also the one with the most precarious financial standing. In 1989, it looked as if the Champion Soccers might be defeated in the bankruptcy courts, but a last-minute move saved the American indoor soccer champions for another season. Tickets for soccer games and all other professional sports can be obtained from the major ticket agencies, Ticketron, *©* 268-9686 or Ticketmaster,

© 298-5070, or at the gate. Soccer games are played in the San Diego Sports Arena.

As for baseball and football, the San Diego Padres and the San Diego Chargers are generally regarded with the affection (and sometimes disdain) Americans reserve for bad-luck teams. Both teams play in Jack Murphy Stadium, which has a 24-hour recorded message on events scheduled at the stadium: *©* (619) 281-1330. The Stadium is located at 9449 Friars Road in Mission Valley. For information on the Padres, *©* (619) 283-7294; on the Chargers, *©* (619) 280-2111.

SIDE TRIPS

THE BEACHES

With the Pacific Ocean as its western boundary, San Diego County has more than 70 miles (112 km) of coastline with every sort of beach nature and/or man could produce. The main coastal highway is Interstate 5, which follows roughly the route of the old Pacific Highway.

Once you head south, leaving San Juan Capistrano and San Clemente in Orange County, there is a steady view of the beaches and the ocean for several miles. Somewhere on your left (or to the east), you will see a sign marking the site of the U.S. Marine Corps' Camp Pendleton. The sign says: "Preserving California's Precious Resources".

San Onofre

Even the most devout pacifist in San Diego looks fondly on Camp Pendleton as a vital buffer zone. Without it, San Diego would long ago have been swallowed up in the urban sprawl of Los Angeles. With 18 miles (29 km) of beachfront and spreading 20 miles (32 km) across the mountains inland, Camp Pendleton carries out its preparations for war in a remarkably picturesque setting. At one of the most beautiful viewing

OPPOSITE: Golfers enjoy the clean air and mountain views at Lone Pine in the beautiful Owens Valley east of the High Sierras.

points or rest stops, you will frequently see Marines on the beach below engaged in practice on offshore targets. Everywhere north and south are miles and miles of unspoiled beaches.

If the Marine Corps presence isn't ominous enough, you'll also find a huge nuclear generating plant built right on the beach at San Onofre State Park. That, however, is the only modern obstruction you'll find. San Onofre is a favorite camping spot for those looking for wide beaches and dunes, and the space to be alone with them.

From here southward, there is a succession of state and local beaches, most of them with picnic facilities, lifeguards, and restroom and shower facilities.

Oceanside is the town closest to the Marine base, and the military has an overwhelming presence here. There is also a popular fishing pier and a harbor for small boats.

South Carlsbad and Ponto State Beach

The South Carlsbad and Ponto State beaches offer a 10 miles (16 km) stretch of beaches below high bluffs. If you're looking for the California life the Beach Boys sang about in the 1960's, you'll find that Leucadia and Encinitas have preserved much of that youthful beachtown spirit intact. **Moonlight State Beach** is where the boys and girls are in daylight hours; at dusk they'll be sipping suds and swinging at the same old rock 'n' roll bars their mamas and papas hung out in a generation before them. Two of the older bars that have endured are the **Daley Double Saloon** and **Bobby G's.**

Solana Beach

The most popular music bar is the **Belly Up Tavern**, a few miles south of Leucadia and Encinitas and 21 miles (38 km) north of San Diego at Solana Beach. The Belly Up brings in world-class acts for a price, but its cover charge is nowhere near the price, you'd pay to hear the same groups on the East Coast.

Just south of Solana Beach is Del Mar, still a favorite retreat for the glitterati of Hollywood and other parts, who started coming here when Bing Crosby and Pat O'Brien opened the Del Mar Race Track and the adjoining lands for exclusive home development. The city beaches at the end of 17th Street in Del Mar are a great place for people watching, but parking is a real problem.

Torrey Pines State Park

From Solana Beach you only have to drive a few more minutes south and you'll find plenty of parking plus one of the most beautiful cliffside beaches in California, at Torrey Pines State Park. There are two large parking lots with an all-day fee of $3. Park either by the flat beaches at the base of the cliffs, or on top. This incredibly steep drive, part of the original coastal highway, was a famous obstacle on the early road races held here. At the top, a small museum explains the Torrey Pine that is found only here and on one of the channel islands, and the other flora and fauna (including rattlesnakes) that live in the nature preserve. Several nature trails wind in and around the rugged bluffs. Two steep but nicely graded (with handrails) trails lead down to the beach.

Black's Beach

Once on the beach, walk south and you'll find yourself on San Diego's most notorious beach, Black's Beach. The name comes from the family that once owned it, not from the fact that it is frequented by nudists. Sheer sandstone cliffs rise more than a thousand feet behind the beach. (You'll often see the clifftops lined with people at the Torrey Pines Golf Course peering down through binoculars.) For many years, the main access to the beach was over and down these cliffs. Nearly every year, someone is seriously injured or killed by slipping off these trails. Rescue workers do respond to calls for help, but otherwise, visiting Black's Beach is strictly at your own risk; there are no lifeguards and no aid stations of any kind there. For two years, however, one lone beach-lover devoted his days to restoring the old steps and walkways that had been destroyed in storms. It's still not a climb for the faint of heart, but it's much safer than sliding down the cliff. There are no signs, but this safe walkway is located to the left — or due south — of the old Glider Port, which was closed in 1988 due to insurance problems.

Just south of Black's Beach is the pier of the world-famous Scripps Institution of Oceanography, a marine research center affiliated with the University of California and located here since 1903. The Vaughan is the Marine Room restaurant, an elegant and expensive place, where the view is so close to the sea that the waves often slap right up against the floor-to-ceiling windows.

The Cove at La Jolla

Some locals still cling to the belief that La Jolla is a misspelling of the Spanish word for jewel, "La Hoya". Most likely, it is a correct spelling of the word for "hollow". Over the years, the angry Pacific has hollowed out the sandstone cliffs below La Jolla. Early this

Aquarium–Museum can be found here. Its indoor and outdoor exhibits are open free to the public.

Up on the bluffs above Black's Beach is another well-known institution, the Salk Institute founded by Nobel Prize winner Jonas Salk. Unfortunately, it is not open to the public.

La Jolla Shores

The next beach south is La Jolla Shores, a popular spot for the wealthy residents of the hills in and around La Jolla. The country club here is for members only, but the restaurants and shops around it are open to the public. On the beach itself are picnic facilities, lifeguards, and restrooms. Also on the beach century, there was even a monumental natural arch out in the water, but that has long since crumbled into the waves. At the Cave Curio Shop in La Jolla, you can climb down some steep stairs and come out in the middle of one of these hollow caves. Offshore is a state underwater park where snorkelers and divers can enjoy the spectacular underwater scenery.

Much of downtown La Jolla has been overdeveloped with no regard for the setting. But, thanks to one or two local philanthropists, the waterfront has been preserved as a public park. A walkway takes you around the edges

Pacific and Mission beaches are the fun spots for San Diego's younger set.

of the cliffs to two tiny beaches: **The Cove**, and **The Children's Beach**, which is built inside a man-made cove. Both of these are staffed with lifeguards. To the south, here, you can see the waters pound right up against the cliffs. Sea lions play and sun themselves on the rocks here.

Windansea and the Pumphouse Gang

Below the bluffs at Neptune Place in La Jolla is a spot called Windansea which, in Andy Warhol's phrase, was "famous for ten

popular among San Diego's young and in-crowd. Tans may be unfashionable else-where and *Beach Blanket Bingo* a dated film from the past, but here you'll find greasy suntans, volleyball, and "Life is a Beach" on every ragged T-shirt. The most popular spot for lunch, beer, and live music at Pacific Beach is the Old Pacific Beach Cafe at 4287 Mission Boulevard.

Mission Beach

Further down Mission Beach, the activity

minutes" as the setting of pop-journalist Tom Wolfe's Pumphouse Gang. No swimming is allowed in the treacherous waters here but it is legendary as a surfing spot, reserved for only the best of the local surfers. Windansea's sur-fers remain an elite group that doesn't take kindly to new members, but there's no reason why you can't watch from the safety of the bluffs.

Pacific Beach

Pacific Beach and Mission Beach are next on the beach roads south. You have to wind up and around La Jolla Boulevard to reach Mission Beach Boulevard, which runs paral-lel to the beach. These two are the most

swirls around the edge of the old Belmont Amusement Park, its long abandoned old roller-coaster a much beloved landmark. Although the neighbors fought it to the bitter end, the city allowed private devel-opers to tear down the long-abandoned buildings in the park and replace them with a modern complex of shops and res-taurants. But the old "Plunge" swimming pool was saved as the centerpiece for an enormous new fitness center. Despite the controversy, the **New Belmont** is sure to succeed because it is the only place right on the boardwalk with a full view of the busy beach. The **Coaster Saloon**, across from the old park and a half-block from the boardwalk, is the busiest and friendliest spot here; a favorite of pro football players among many others. **South Mission Beach** is a quieter place favored by San Diego's young and upwardly mobile. The beach ends here with a long jetty of concrete boulders that protect the entrance to Mission Bay aquatic park.

Ocean Beach

To get to Ocean Beach, take Mission Bay Boulevard inland to Sea World Drive, then turn right or south. "O.B" has developed its own kind of community in recent years, a laid-back California beach version of New York's Greenwich Village in the 1950's. It's no longer the low-rent district it once was, but there are still plenty of reasonably priced arts and crafts shops and very good small cafes and restaurants, including what is generally regarded as the best of San Diego's many Mexican restaurants.

Sunset Cliffs

Sunset Cliffs Boulevard will take you still further south along the beach from Ocean Beach, but the beaches here are not recommended. The sandstone cliffs here are highly unstable, the slides sometimes take parts of the narrow roadway down with them. There is one long beach called the Pescadero Street Beach, but it is accessible only at low tide from Orchard Street, not from its namesake above the cliffs. The dangers aside, the cliffs do offer a spectacular view of the sunset — as well as some of the best surf fishing. Beyond Sunset Cliffs is Point Loma, the long jut of headland that protects the entrance to San Diego Bay.

Point Loma

Military installations still cover much of Point Loma. The Navy's "boot camp", or basic training base, is located on the bay side toward San Diego. Further out on the point is a Navy submarine base. On the crest of the ridgeline out to the point is a national military cemetery, with miles and miles of simple stones engraved with the name, rank, and military group of the dead. The memorial park overlooks the bay on one side, the ocean on the other. Just before you get to Cabrillo National Historical Monument, a road (marked "Tide Pools") veers off to the right down to the waterfront. This is a nature preserve, but you can walk out on to the rocks and observe the wide variety of sea life caught in the tidal pools. Closed to the public but clearly visible from the nature preserve are the picturesque old clapboard buildings of the Coast Guard Station. They stand beside the light, right on the waterfront, that currently marks the entrance to San Diego Harbor.

Back up on top of the actual Point Loma, there is a parking fee of $2, but you can drive through without charge. A small museum explains the role of Juan Rodriguez Cabrillo, the Portuguese sea captain (of a Spanish ship) who was the first European to land here in 1542. Here also you'll find the rugged old lighthouse. First constructed in 1855, it is one of the oldest United States government buildings in California.

Point Loma offers the most spectacular view of San Diego — south and well into Mexico, and north beyond La Jolla. And, in January, it is a favorite place from which to view the gray whales making their southward migration.

Coronado

Across the bay entrance from Point Loma is North Island, the site of a naval air station. The barrier peninsula that extends north from Mexico is now a solid stretch of sand, but it was broken up into islands in the past. The Spanish named it as one of the Coronados Islands further south in present-day Mexico. Coronado Beach runs from just south of the Navy station to well below the Del Coronado Hotel. This is a nice beach convenient to the hotels of Coronado, but again, just a few miles more and you are on the Silver Strand, one of

A true California girl rides a jet ski OPPOSITE as if it were a wind stallion, on Mission Bay off Fiesta Island, San Diego.

California's most beautiful unspoiled beaches.

The Silver Strand

The Silver Strand is a state beach staffed with parking lot attendants and lifeguards. It has picnic and restroom facilities. If you fancy a walk along powdery sands for miles and miles without a hotel or any kind of development, then this is your spot. The only problem here, and at the more developed **Imperial Beach** just south of the Silver Strand, is that the whole area is sometimes polluted by sewer spillage from nearby Tijuana. However, United States and Mexican officials have spent a great deal of time and money to end the spillage and such pollution may soon be a thing of the past.

On your map, you may be intrigued by the Border Fields State Park. This is a wildlife preserve right on the border, designed mainly as a buffer against illegal immigration. There is very little to see here. As you are so close, you might as well cross the border at Tijuana and explore the beautiful beaches of Baja.

THE DESERTS

Interstate 8 leads up and over the high mountains that kept the railroads out of San Diego for many years. Once across the mountains, there is little to see except farmland and low desert as the road moves along the Mexican border to Arizona. The border towns of **Calexico** and **Mexicali** are twentieth-century products of an American entrepreneur and not worth a stopover.

However, if you leave Interstate 8 at Highway 79 and go north past Cuyamaca Lake, then east on Highway 78, you will head straight into **Anza-Borrego Desert State Park** and some of the most beautiful desert scenery in California. Covering 470,000 acres (190,000 hectares), it is California's largest state park. It was named for Juan Bautista de Anza, the Spanish military leader who first traversed it in 1774, and for the bighorn sheep (borrego). At first glance, the landscape may seem barren, but in fact there are more than 600 species of plants and 350 kinds of vertebrate animals found here.

In general, locals avoid the deserts in June, July, and August when the daily temperatures rise well above 38°C (100°F). Two spas have sprung up, one at the northeast edge of the park, the other well into the heart of it on private property. The older of these is **Warner Springs.** This area is often ignored in favor of the more popular spots, but it has some excellent campgrounds and hiking trails leading into the nearby mountains. Warner Springs is on Highway 79 north of Santa Ysabel and Julian.

The busiest desert spa near San Diego is at **Borrego Springs.** Even though its developers had envisioned it as a Palm Springs south, Borrego Springs has remained a small town on the Borrego Valley floor surrounded by steep mountain ranges. In addition to **La Casa del Zorro,** the luxury hotel resort owned by the Copley newspaper interests, Borrego Springs has several motels, apartments, and condominiums available for short-term rental. Nearby are trailer parks and campgrounds. There are tennis courts and three public golf courses open to the public.

Camping facilities in the park include the modern facilities of the **Borrego Palm Canyon**. You can also camp in **Coyote Canyon, Pegleg Smith Monument**, or **Borrego Sink** where it's just you and nature. Information on the campgrounds, the town, or the park can be obtained from the Chamber of Commerce, P.O. Box 66, Borrego Springs, CA 92004. ✆ (619) 767-5555. During peak-season winter months, facilities are often crowded or full. Visitors can make reservations for the campgrounds through Ticketron. ✆ 1-(800) 952-5580.

A volunteer organization, the Anza-Borrego Desert Natural History Association, operates a Visitors' Center built right into a hillside so as not to disturb the landscape. Located near the Park Headquarters on Palm Canyon Drive, the center is open from 9 am to 5 pm daily from October through May, and from 10 am to 3 pm on Saturdays and Sundays only in

June, July, August, and September. Staffed by true desert lovers, it offers an excellent slide program on desert geology, and plant and animal life.

Ocotillo Wells, a state park, is located right on Highway 78. It has a store selling picnic supplies, and an adjoining trailer park. Most appealing are its wide open spaces and the freedom to drive right on if you have a vehicle that can do it. This is one of the state parks open to off-road or all-terrain vehicles, but if you stray out of bounds into one of the nature preserves, a park ranger or private citizen will warn you back to the approved area. It is a strange, mysterious landscape, with sandy flats along wide dry riverbeds, and trails leading across the dunes up on to the mesas. When you stand on the edge of one of nature's own tabletops and watch the sun cast its shadow over the battered landscape, you begin to understand the mysticism of the Indians who once roamed the place.

Precautions for Desert Travel
1. Stick to the well-marked trails.
2. Carry a good supply of water at all times.
3. Avoid hiking in the heat of the day.

A personal note about the "dunes" at Ocotillo Wells from one who did a triple somersault on a three-wheeler off the top of one. It turned out that the dune was only sand piled up on one side, with a brutally rough cliff revealed on the other side.

Glamis
A bit of literary whimsy must have moved someone in 1887 to reach back to Macbeth's castle for a name for a desolate and isolated desert post office. Located on Highway 78 about 65 miles (105 km) east of Ocotillo Wells, Glamis is in the heart of the vast sandhills that cover southeastern California to the Colorado River border with Arizona. It remains a tiny red dot on the map, but no longer is it isolated. The most popular of all the off-road–all-terrain parks in the state, it is packed with young people and their noisy engines during the winter months. Since the sale of three-wheelers has already been banned and

their use likely to be prohibited, you might think the crowds would thin down. But the true off-roaders merely switched to four-wheelers, not nearly so daring or dangerous, but almost as much fun on the dunes. On weekends in the peak season, the dunes here are reminiscent of the Hollywood Freeway. But if you're young and looking for the action that has replaced surfing in California, this is where you'll find it — a huge raucous beach blanket party 200 miles (320 km) from the surf.

The Salton Sea
In 1905, the forces of nature and man combined to form the Salton Sea, a body of water 30 miles (48 km) long and eight to 14 miles (13 to 22 km) wide that lies 235 ft (72 m) below sea level in the middle of the desert southeast of Palm Springs and northeast of San Diego. In ancient times, the entire eastern part of California was under the sea. Then, as recently as 500 years ago, the area was covered by a vast freshwater lake.

The lake was created by the unpredictable meanderings of the "Red Bull", on the Colorado River. During a flood in 1905, the river burst through irrigation ditches and poured into the Imperial Valley, filling the dry bed of the Salton Sink once again. The river was eventually tamed, most notably by the Hoover Dam, but the Salton Sea remained.

With no outlets, the water gradually changed from fresh to salty. Faced with the challenge, the state's Department of Fish and Game decided to transfer ocean fish into the landlocked sea. The success of this effort has made Salton Sea what it is today — a favorite fishing ground for tourists and local enthusiasts. There is a state recreation area on the eastern shore, and numerous marinas and camping areas along the rest of the waterfront. To reach the Salton Sea from Palm Springs, take Interstate 10 east to Indio, then take S86 south. From San Diego, take Interstate 8 east to El Centro and S86 north. From Julian and Anza-Borrego, take S78 east and S86 north.

South
of the
Border

FIRST of all, a few words of warning about Mexico. You will hear many stories about the dangers foreign travelers are exposed to in Mexico. Some of these tales may be exaggerated, but enough of them are true that travelers should take heed and be prepared. In 1984, because numerous American tourists were being victimized, the U.S. State Department took the highly unusual step of issuing a warning against travel to Mexico. That same year, Tijuana was declared off limits to U.S. Marines because of many reports of servicemen being shaken down by police in Mexico. During the Easter holidays of 1988, which coincided with the spring break at American colleges, the Tijuana police re-assigned all motorcycle police from the downtown area in an effort to reassure tourists who were worried about police intimidation.

Having written that warning, I should add that I have been a regular visitor to Tijuana for several years, and I have never once been harassed there by the police or anyone else. A small amount of preparation and common sense is all that is needed to save you a lot of grief later on. Women shouldn't carry loose handbags or pocketbooks that can be snatched easily. Avoid carrying large amounts of cash or keeping all your papers and money in one place. It helps to keep in mind the desperate state of the economy in Mexico, especially when compared to its very rich neighbor to the north. A San Diego policeman is paid more for one day's work than a Tijuana policeman earns in a whole month. Recently, the country's leaders have taken steps to ensure the safety of tourists. A new commission set up by the Mexican government and the Chamber of Commerce to investigate claims of police harassment was responsible for the action taken against the erring motorcycle cops in 1988. In the first month, two Tijuana policemen were given five-year jail sentences for extorting $50 from tourists and three other officers were suspended without pay. Since then, the new commission says reports of harassment have dropped to zero. The number to call if you are harassed is, © 1-(706) 682-4175.

LA FRONTERA

In most countries that share a border, the change in cultures and (except for communist/capitalist neighbors) in economies is fairly gradual. But the border between the United States and Mexico provides one of the most dramatic crossings this side of the Berlin Wall. A line on a map and a wire fence are all that separate one of the richest from one of the poorest countries in the

world. The cultural differences are just as marked. Since Tijuana has become the jumping-off — or more correctly, the crawling-under — point for Mexicans and other Central Americans, it has become home to a whole mix of Hispanic and Indian cultures. While it is true that most people in the tourist shops speak some English, the average person in the street speaks no English at all.

OPPOSITE: Statue of a jai alai player stands in front of Tijuana's grand Jai-Alai Palace or *fronton.*
ABOVE: One of the army of Border Patrol agents assigned to the frontier between Mexico and the United States rides a three-wheeler all-terrain vehicle, now outlawed for sale in the United States.

Mexico's poor people ask tourists for money, but they always offer something in exchange—a penny box of Chiclets chewing gum, a simple braided bracelet, or a happy song. Tennessee Williams once described courage as behaving with dignity in a humiliating situation. That is perhaps the best description for the desperately poor population of Mexico. They are an innately polite people, with manners that have long gone out of style in more sophisticated places. And if you treat them with simple good manners and respect, you will find them the most pleasant compadres. They are also fiercely proud. A serious insult to their pride will produce a violent reaction. Most of all, they are a happy people. Despite the terrible plight of their country, they can still laugh and sing. Even young children can sing all the words to the haunting melodies of the past, a rich blend of Latin, Aztec, and Mayan cultures.

The contrast in cultures is matched by a dramatic change in the landscape, from the lush tropical palms and eucalyptus in San Diego to the stark barren hillsides around Tijuana. Of course, the rest of Southern California was also dry and arid before water was pumped in, allowing the exotic plants to grow.

The contrasts you find in upper California are even greater in lower or Baja California. "Baja" brings to mind two radically different images. The first is of the overcrowded and raucous border towns that have provided an escape for Americans since Prohibition banned drinking in the United States in 1920. The other Baja is one of the world's last wild and inaccessible spots, until very recently reserved only for the most rugged adventurers.

"Baja California is a wonderful example of how much bad roads can do for a country," wrote John Wood Krutch in *Baja California and the Geography of Hope* (Sierra Club, 1967). "Nature gave to Baja nearly all of the beauties possible in a dry, warm climate — towering mountains, flowery desert flats, blue water, bird-rich islands, and scores of great, curving beaches as fine as the best anywhere in the world. All of this has remained very nearly inviolate just because very little of what we call progress has marred it. Baja has never needed protection because the land protected itself."

Krutch's words ceased to be true almost before they could be published. The Trans-Baja highway was already under construction at the time. The first part was a four-lane toll road from Tijuana to Ensenada. The final link, a two-lane highway south from Ensenada to Cabo San Lucas, was completed in 1973.

The Baja peninsula is twice as long as Florida, and 100 miles (160 km) longer than Italy. Since much of it receives less than 10 in (254 mm) of rainfall a year, it is also technically a desert, although most of it is taken up by a rugged spine of mountains. The highest mountain rises to more than 10,000 ft (3,050 m). It is visible for 150 miles (242 km) and often snow-covered in the winter.

Because of its unusual gnarled-finger shape and the general absence of cloud cover, Baja California is one of the few places on earth that can nearly always be clearly identified from satellite pictures taken from 100 miles (160 km) above the earth. It also offers the most dramatic picture of movement along the San Andreas Fault, that great crack in the earth's crust which stretches almost the full length of California from the coast of Mexico. Twenty million years ago, the Baja peninsula was part of the mainland. It broke away sometime in the past, during a great earthquake. Like the rest of California, it has been steadily inching northward — it is now 250 miles (403 km) north of its original location.

The Baja peninsula is 800 miles (1,290 km) long and between 30 and 145 miles (48 and 234 km) wide. It is bounded on the east by the Sea of Cortez (now called the Gulf of California on most maps) and the Pacific Ocean on the west. The gulf once extended more than 200 miles (323 km) north of its present coastline, leading the first explorers to think they had found an island. The Spanish had been in Mexico for more than 200 years before they determined it was, in fact, a peninsula.

TIJUANA

In its early years, the Rancho Tia Juana beside the Rio Tia Juana was a sparsely populated spread not even worth a dot on the map. But when its northern boundary became the border between Mexico and the United States in 1848, it became more important. Still, only 200 people lived there at the turn of the century.

Nobody seems to know for sure when

a cooperative governor installed in Baja in the mid-1920's, American entrepreneurs moved in and built casinos in Tijuana and Ensenada. Below a picture of the old Agua Caliente Casino at the modern Tijuana Cultural Center is a brief explanation (misspellings and all). "Life in Tijuana changed in the twenties. The named "Dry Law" that restrained liquors sales in the United States, make that American citizen and tourists of all the world come to Tijuana to the casinos and the Hazard Games Horses, specially to the

Tia Juana became Tijuana. Some say the name derives not from the Spanish words for "Aunt Jane", but from a Spanish phonetic spelling of the Indian word *ticuan* or *tijuan,* which means "place by the water". Others say the American who built the gambling casino and racetrack at Agua Caliente misspelled it as Tijuana and the name stuck.

Whatever the origin of its name, modern-day Tijuana was shaped and defined by United States Prohibition, which lasted until 1933. "South of the Border" took on a whole new meaning; it was a place where people were free to drink and gamble and enjoy all the pleasures denied by law back home. With

"Agua Caliente Casino," the most important at the time and famous in all the world."

In 1925, the Tijuana Jai Alai Palace was built for playing and betting jai alai, a sport that originated several hundred years ago in the Basque region of Spain. Similar to racquetball or handball, the tiny hardball (*pelota*) is caught in a cusp-shaped cesta, or mitt, tied to the player's wrist and then hurled at the *fronton,* or front wall, at speeds of up to 182 mph (294 kph).

Mariachi bands roam the streets of Tijuana, two or three dollars for a song, the quickest and most enjoyable way of making money in this impoverished country.

South of the Border

The bullring offered an even more exotic sport outlawed in the United States. Famous bullfighters from Spain and Mexico came to Tijuana to mingle with glamorous movie stars, sports figures, and other high-rollers from the United States. Bullfights were presented from May through September. The older bullring, **El Toreo,** is on Agua Caliente Boulevard just east of Tijuana. A newer ring (claimed to be the largest in the world) is on the beach and is called the **Plaza Municipal.** The beach, or Playa de Tijuana, is separated from the tourist center of town by a steep range of mountains and has never been developed as a tourist facility center.

In 1935, Mexico's President Cardenas introduced sweeping reforms aimed at lifting his country out of the Depression. He nationalized the oil industry, seized foreign-owned lands, and prohibited gambling and betting in Baja. Although betting on horses, dogs, and jai alai was later restored, the ban on gambling has remained. Tijuana's gambling casinos thus became relics of the Roaring Twenties.

The Tijuana Chamber of Commerce claims that more than 24 million people visit the city every year, making it the "most visited city on earth". The "tourist" figures are doubtless correct if they include the multitudes who pour into Tijuana in the desperate hope of getting across the border to El Norte. Thousands are turned back every week but many hundreds risk imprisonment, even death, to reach the United States. Meanwhile, Tijuana's population has grown. It had 277,000 people in 1970; an estimated 1.7 million lived there in 1988.

Tijuana is a city of hope to the Mexicans. For tourists, some of the spirit from the casino days lives on, although the mood nowadays is decidedly younger and much closer to Fort Lauderdale than to Monte Carlo. Avenida Revolucion, the main street, seems like one long open-air discotheque. On weekends or holidays,

A sombrero salesman plies his trade on the Avenida de la Revolucion, in front of the fittingly Basque restaurant, Chiki Jai.

the music blares from every corner and the swinging crowds can be seen inching their way in and out of the discos. Adding spice — rather, salsa — to the American disco sound are the strolling mariachis. In the late afternoon, they gather at the Plaza de Santa Cecilia, a block-long walkway from the north end of Avenida Revolucion beside the old Hotel Nelson. The mariachis range from refined musicians in gold braid to street bums using their guitars to earn a few pennies for more

wine. The typical band includes trumpets, guitars, bass, accordion, and drums. The songs range from the familiar *Cielito Lindo* and *Malaguena* to the more obscure *corridos*, or folk stories, that endure from Mexico's many revolutions.

In Tijuana, you find an Americanized version of Mexican food. The base for most of it is the tortilla, a thin pancake-like bread made of cornmeal or flour. Folded in a pocket and deep-fried, it becomes a taco; soft and wrapped around meat or beans (or a mixture of the two) and guacamole (mashed avocados), it becomes a burrito. *Carne asada* is broiled beef and can be had in tacos, burritos, or

on a plate with beans, rice, and salad. *Carnitas* is boiled pork chopped and served the same way. A tortilla deep-fried flat becomes a tostada, spread with *seviche* (raw fish "cooked" in lime juice) or any of the other fillings. These are the basics, but in the restaurants and among street vendors, you'll find all kinds of creative refinements beyond the beans, chili, and tortillas. Around every meal, and available on every street corner, is a wide variety of luscious fruits that include mangoes on a stick and long slices of watermelon-sized papayas.

As for shopping, most of the souvenirs sold in Tijuana are mass-produced for the tourists. Among these are traditional woven blankets ($3 at most stands) and some very colorful pottery. For those with a discriminating eye, a much higher quality of arts and crafts can be found if you have the time to look for them.

At one end, Revolucion dead-ends into the road to Ensenada; at the other, it curves around and becomes the Boulevard Agua Caliente. Along this major thoroughfare out of town are the bullring, the golf course, the race track, and many major hotels and restaurants, the tallest of these being the twin green-glass towers of the 24-story Fiesta Americana Hotel.

Closer to the border and just off the main road from the United States, a new commercial and entertainment area is being developed along the wide, tree-lined boulevard called Paseo de los Heroes. The most striking are the buildings of the Tijuana Cultural Center, designed by the architect of the world-famous anthropological museum in Mexico City. Inside an enormous adobe-colored orb are huge exhibition spaces, a restaurant, and an "Omnimax Theater", a multimedia theater with a 180-degree screen. On permanent show here is the film *El Pueblo del Sol*, a dazzling tour of some of Mexico's most spectacular sights. Other films are also screened here. There are frequent performances of all kinds in the auditoriums of the adjacent building, including Mexico's famed Ballet Folklorico.

The most popular of Mexico's Catholic festivals is the feast of Our Lady of Guadalupe on December 12. It commemorates the Virgin Mary's apparition to a native Indian at Guadalupe.

HOTELS

At the old **Hotel Caesar** on Revolucion in the heart of downtown, the walls are covered with photographs and posters of famous bullfighters from an earlier time. The hotel was a meeting place for the city's most glamorous visitors and it was here that Caesar salad was first served. It's a bit seedy now, but the rooms are cheap ($26 for a single), by American standards, and clean. It is convenient to the jai alai games and the nightlife on Revolucion. Of course, the **Fiesta Americana** — two miles (three kilometers) east of town on Agua Caliente Boulevard — rises above all others (like a battleship in the desert). Locals brag that it is "just like yours in America". By that they also mean that here you pay American prices, three to four times the usual rates found elsewhere in Tijuana. The main restaurant is French. Just across the street, you'll find a delightful two-story alternative that charges one-third the rates of the Americana. This is the old **El Conquistador,** a sturdy old Spanish-style landmark, with balconies around an open palm-filled courtyard and a bar called El Quijote. The **Hotel La Lucerna** on the Paseo de los Heroes offers American-style luxury at a fraction of the cost of the Fiesta Americana.

Fiesta Americana, 4500 Caliente Boulevard, 430 rooms. Rates start at $70 a night per room per person. © 817000.

The following hotels offer more reasonable prices.

Caesar, corner of Fifth and Revolucion, 90 rooms, $26 single. © 880550.

El Conquistador, 700 Caliente Boulevard, 110 rooms, $37.50 single. © 817955.

Country Club, across from the Caliente Race Track, 90 rooms, $31 single. © 862301.

Lucerna, 10902 Paseo de los Heroes, 168 rooms, $37 single. © 840911.

Palacio Azteca, 213 Avenida 16 de Septiembre, 90 rooms, $40 single. © 865401. For reservations from the United States © (706) 686-5301.

Paraiso Radisson, No. 1 Agua Caliente Boulevard, 190 rooms, $39 single. © 817200.

Villa de Zaragoza, 1120 Madero Avenue, 42 rooms, $26 single. © 851832. For reservations from the United States, © (706) 685-1832.

RESTAURANTS

The best Mexican food in Tijuana can be found at opposite ends of Avenida Revolucion. Closer to the pedestrian crossing for the border is **Bol Corona**, one of Tijuana's oldest and most popular gathering places. The food is incredibly cheap and always good. Several blocks up Revolucion is **Tia Juana Tilly's**, the most

ABOVE: Ensenada offers a change of pace from Tijuana; the bars, such as the one opposite, are not raucous, and there is the nearby stretch of placid beachfront at Estero Beach.

famous spot in town for Americans. It has a large sidewalk cafe, an indoor dining room, and a huge bar area that is always busy with tourists. Tilly's adjoins the Jai Alai Palace. Those interested can place bets from their table, with the results of each game flashed on a screen in the bars and restaurant. Food to match the Basque sport of jai alai is offered by a tiny Basque restaurant called **Chiki Jai,** located just across the street from Tia Juana Tilly's, on the same side of Revolucion.

Across from the Jai Alai Palace is **Pedrin's,** another popular restaurant with Americans. It serves a rich array of Mexican seafood specialties, from *serviche* (raw fish marinated in lime juice) to the house favorite, the "Fountain of Youth" mixed platter.

The newer and better-quality restaurants are located along the Paseo de los Heroes. The **Alcazar del Rio** serves an international cuisine in an elegant Spanish setting. **Ochoa's** is a modern place, with live jazz and a menu of steaks and seafood. The **Guadalajara Grill** is second only to Tia Juana Tilly's for Americans visiting the bullring or racetrack, or for those coming south for an authentic Mexican feast.

Alcazar del Rio, 56-4 Paseo de los Heroes, one of Tijuana's most elegant restaurants; international cuisine. ℭ 842672. For reservations from the United States ℭ (706) 684-2672.

Bocaccio's, 2500 Agua Caliente Boulevard, Italian. ℭ 861845.

Bol Corona, 520 Revolucion. The best Mexican food at the cheapest prices in Tijuana, a popular meeting place for local business people. ℭ 857940.

Carnitas Uruapan, by general acclaim the best place in Tijuana for stewed pork fixed in a variety of ways.

Caesar's Palace, Fourth and Revolucion, above Le Drugstore, continental cuisine, hot Mexican buffet served daily for $6. ℭ 882794.

Chiki Jai, across the street from the Jai Alai Palace, at Seventh Street and Avenida Revolucion, Basque food. ℭ (706) 685-4955.

Las Espuelas, in the Plaza Rio shopping center, Mexican and continental cuisine. ℭ 840157.

Guadalajara Grill, Paseo de los Heroes at Diego Rivera Street. One of a popular Mexican chain of restaurants located throughout Mexico, in San Diego, and in Los Angeles. ℭ 802045.

La Lena, 4560 Agua Caliente Boulevard, American-style steakhouse near the golf course. ℭ 862920.

Ochoa's, 61 Paseo de los Heroes, elegant decor, seafood and steaks. ℭ 841857.

Pedrin's, 115 Revolucion, very popular seafood place for Americans attending jai alai games across the street. ℭ 854052.

Reno, 1937 Eighth Street, an elegant European-style restaurant in the heart of downtown Tijuana. ℭ 858775.

Tia Juana Tilly's, Seventh and Revolucion, adjoining the Jai Alai Palace, Mexican. ℭ (706) 685-6024.

SPORTS

GOLF: An 18-hole course is open to the public at the Tijuana Country Club (Club Campestre), on Agua Caliente Boulevard, three miles (five kilometers) east of downtown Tijuana.

JAI ALAI: The play begins at 8 pm in the Fronton Palace at Seventh and Revolucion every night except Thursday when the house is dark.

BULLFIGHTS: The most famous bullfighters in Mexico and Spain perform in Tijuana's two bullrings: El Toreo bullring, located on Agua Caliente Boulevard, and the Plaza Monumental, on the waterfront at the Playas de Tijuana. Fights are held on Sundays at 4 pm from May through September.

RACING: Some form of racing is held at the Agua Caliente Racetrack throughout the year. Thoroughbred horse races Saturdays and Sundays, with first post time at 12

OPPOSITE: In the markets of Tijuana, you'll find a colorful clutter of *pinatas* for sale.

noon. Greyhound races, 7:45 pm every day except Tuesday; afternoon greyhound races, 2:30 pm on Monday, Wednesday, and Friday.

SPORTSFISHING: **Gordo's**, 595 Calle Primera (First Street), the central building on the waterfront, also offers diving facilities. ✆ (706) 678-3515.

DIVING: **Aqua Mar,** San Marcos 788-7. ✆ (706) 676-0361; **El Yaqui**, Centro Commercial Valle Dorado – 3. ✆ (706) 676-6344.

ON THE ROAD FROM TIJUANA TO ENSENADA

On crossing the border, follow the signs to Ensenada 1-D (Direct) if you want to bypass Tijuana. From downtown Tijuana, go north on Avenida Revolucion and turn left at the dead-end. The first toll booths are just over the mountains west of Tijuana, overlooking the residential beach area and the huge new bullring built right on the oceanfront.

The toll amounts to $1.30 (65 cents at two stops) for the full route to Ensenada. The four-lane highway is in excellent con-

dition compared to other roads in downtown Tijuana or backcountry Mexico. It is also one of the most picturesque drives you'll find in this part of the country. To the east, the barren hills rise up to rugged peaks. Beyond them looms an enormous "Mesa Grande", the collapsed core of an ancient volcano that now forms a gigantic table-top mountain visible from the heart of United States California.

On the west, the toll road continues along the once wild and inaccessible coastline. Krutch could have predicted in his 1967 book about Baja that the roads would bring a dubious progress, with trailer parks and housing developments along the way. Still, since foreigners cannot own property here, this development has been very slow — there are still many long stretches of barren hillsides on one side and uninhabited cliffs and beaches on the other.

Directly offshore are the Coronados Islands (named after the four "crowned" royal martyrs, not the conquistador) which are now wildlife sanctuaries. Uninhabited except for a lighthouse keeper, they contain a few ramshackle ruins of the casinos that flourished there in the 1920's. You can see some wonderful photographs of these old casinos on the walls of **La Costa Restaurant,** a modern seafood place overlooking the islands. The specialty here is lobster. There are many cheaper places along the way, but La Costa is the best in terms of the view, the quality of service, and the fresh lobster and other seafood. Many old-timers would dispute this, however, saying that the **Baja Malibu Restaurant**, less than a mile (about one-and-a-half kilometers) south of La Costa, has more character and better lobster.

At Kilometer 30, you turn off to get to the **Rosarito Beach Hotel,** one of the grand old hotels in Baja. Surrounding the hotel is a dusty little town with very little to recommend it. The beaches here are black with silt. However, you can rent horses for $4 an hour anywhere along the beach and enjoy a ride along the shore.

The **Rosarito Beach Hotel** was an isolated getaway place for the glamorous international set in the days before jets. In the late 1950's, the hotel was closed for several years for trying to hold on to a part of that glamorous past, illegal gambling. Now, it is a somewhat faded old relic, but a charming one that is still very popular with Americans.

For many years, there was a Newport cigarette sign painted on a little beach cottage at Kilometer 44 on the toll road. To travelers in the know, that was no ordinary beachhouse, for there you could get the tastiest lobster in Baja for only $3. Word spread until less than 20 years later, you have hotels and motels and more than 25 lobster houses in the "lobster capital of the world". The new town is called Newport.

Just past Kilometer 53, you will find **Halfway House**, one of Baja's oldest and coziest restaurant-bars. Built in 1921, it looks like someone's old family beachhouse. The bar is famous for its margaritas; the widely imitated recipe is: $1\frac{1}{2}$ ounces tequila, $\frac{3}{4}$ ounce lime juice, $\frac{3}{4}$ ounce Cointreau, shaken with ice and strained.

At Kilometer 61, **Hotel La Fonda** is located atop a 100-ft (30-m) -high cliff with a full view of the ocean. Apart from the fantastic view, the food and service are also of top quality. Its hearty breakfasts make it a favorite first stop with many travelers. Lunch and dinners here feature not only the local lobster but quail as well.

At Kilometer 77, there is a modern residential community built around an 18-hole golf course that is open to the public.

Watch the signs for El Mirador because you will want to stop here for a truly breathtaking view. There are no guard rails of any kind and the viewing point drops (1,600 ft (488 m) straight down to the ocean, where the Bahia de Salsipuedes stretches south for 10 miles (16 km). On a small ledge about three-quarters of the way down, you can see tiny clusters of metal, the wreckage of cars driven off the steep cliff.

In January, **El Mirador** is one of the best places on the coast from which to watch the annual migration of the great

gray whales. Every year, the whales travel thousands of miles south to reach the isolated bays south of Ensenada, where they mate and give birth to their young.

About a mile (one-and-a-half kilometers) south of El Mirador, you can see the remnants of old olive orchards on both sides of the road. The dirt access road down to the beach at **Salsipuedes Bay** is very steep, and if it should rain, you'll be stuck until the road dries out. Salsipuedes means "Get out if you can".

HOTELS

Rosarito Beach Hotel, Kilometer 27.5 on the Tijuana to Ensenada toll road, 70 rooms, 80 suites. © (706) 612-11060.
Hotel Quinta Del Mar, 25500 Benito Juarez Boulevard, 143 rooms. © (706) 612-1145, (706) 612-1215.
Hotel Castel Le Club, within walking distance of the 25 lobster houses in Puerto Nuevo, has 150 rooms, 12 suites, 446 condominiums. © (706) 614-1345-48.
Plaza del Mar, Kilometer 51, 180 rooms and suites. © (706) 685-9152-58.

RESTAURANDS

Listed north to south, as you come to them on the Tijuana to Ensenada toll road:

At Hussong's Cantina OPPOSITE, the beer and cheer are both served in abundance and next door there's a busy boutique where you can buy souvenirs of the famous old bar. ABOVE: A lone horseback rider and sailboat share the open space at the Estero Beach Resort just south of Ensenada.

La Costa, at San Antonio, Kilometer 21.
Baja Malibu, Kilometer 23.
Halfway House, Kilometer 53.
La Fonda, Kilometer 61.

ENSENADA

The scenic drive down the coast is worth the trip in itself, but Ensenada is a lovely old seaport that offers a nice contrast to bustling Tijuana and a pleasant end to any journey. Like Tijuana, Ensenada's glory days were during Prohibition, when its lavish casino was a world-class attraction to the rich and famous. Unlike Tijuana, Ensenada reverted quickly to its small-town status when gambling was outlawed and the tourist trade dwindled. In recent years, Ensenada has become increasingly popular as a retirement center, especially for those who enjoy sports fishing.

It has remained a port of call for the major cruise ships from Los Angeles and San Diego to "the Mexican Riviera" further south, and there are daily visits by the *Ensenada Express* cruises from San Diego. But there is nothing here to compare with the fiesta atmosphere of Tijuana's Avenida Revolucion on weekends.

Like many spots in both Californias, Ensenada comes from a geographical term meaning "cove". One of the first Spanish explorers named the bay All Saints Bay, or Bahia de Todos Santos. But it was never more than a geographical point until the magnificent **Hotel de Playa** opened in 1930. The hotel's career was brief but dazzling. Its famous casino closed down five years after it opened and business faltered. Many international stars stayed here and American celebrities such as Charlie Chaplin, Al Capone, and Myrna Loy were married in the second-floor chapel. Gone are the elaborate interior decorations — inlaid marble from Italy, tapestries from France, and lamps from Morocco — but the old buildings and gardens, which now serve as a civic and convention center, retain a certain grandeur.

Ensenada's main industry is fishing. Colorful fishing boats line the waterfront which teems with people buying and selling the day's catch. There is a big open-air market for fresh fish. Alongside this are dozens of stalls where fish tacos and tostadas are sold with a mix of peppers, onions, and tomatoes. Reservations for sports fishing and diving can be made in the main building on the waterfront. There are several very good seafood cafes right off the docks. **Popeye's** may not offer the best in cuisine and decor, but it does have a full view of the bay.

In general, you will find the arts and crafts shops along the Avenida Lopez Mateos of a much higher quality (and price) than those sold in Tijuana. The government-owned Fonart store is located behind the old casino-hotel.

Seafood is the favored cuisine in nearly every restaurant in Ensenada. Even the American-style steakhouses also offer local lobster and abalone. At the top of everyone's list, however, is the French restaurant, **El Rey Sol,** which has offered the best in haute cuisine in Ensenada since 1947. The restaurant in the nearby **El Cid Hotel** is another elegant eating place. Perhaps the best mix of gourmet food and comfortable surroundings is found in the **Restaurant Del Mar**. It has a sunlit garden setting featuring the exhibits of Ensenada's finest arts and crafts store.

Of course, the most famous place in Ensenada is **Hussong's Cantina**, a popular drinking spot since 1892. The simple two-story clapboard building is a true relic of the old west; the front windows and inner walls are now covered with thousands of bumper stickers, slogans, and cards from all over the world. The tradition and the booze attract standing-room-only crowds throughout the year. You'll see Hussong's T-shirts, bumper stickers, and their own brand of beer all over California and other states. And there's a boutique full of Hussong souvenirs right next to the old bar. Diagonally across the street is **Papas and Beer,** which catches Hussong's overflow and has established a fairly raucous reputation of its own.

The **El Cid** is a grand old hotel in the dark paneled colonial style; at the end of Avenida Lopez Mateos is a Spanish mission-style hotel called the Mission Santa Ysabel. There are several American-style motels (a Travelodge and two Best Westerns), as well as a high-rise called the Villa Marina.

There are no beaches in Ensenada, but two miles (three kilometers) south off Highway 1 is the **Estero** (estuary) **Beach Resort**. The resort offers camping and hotel accommodation and has a patio restaurant with a full view of the wide beach and the estuary emptying into the ocean. Because of this confluence, swimming here can be hazardous. But the spot is very popular with the young crowd who find plenty to do in sunbathing, boating, and horse-riding on the beach. The Estero Beach Resort is also the end of the annual Newport to Ensenada Yacht Race.

From Estero Beach, you can see a high jut of land called Punta Banda. A drive of about 15 miles (24 km) will bring you to this point and a popular local attraction, **La Bufadora,** the blowhole caused when the tides hit the sheer cliffs and

shoot a spray of water 100 ft (30 m) into the air.

There are government checkpoints on the Trans-Baja road south of here and you will need papers to proceed.

HOTELS

El Cid Hotel, 1000 Lopez Mateos Avenue, 52 rooms. ✆ (706) 678-2401.

Estero Beach Hotel, 74 rooms. ✆ (706) 676-1001.

Hotel Mision de Santa Isabel, Avenida Lopez Mateos Castillo, 31 rooms (new addition to be completed in 1988). ✆ (706) 678-3616.

San Nicolas, Lopez Mateos Avenue at Guadalupe Avenue, 142 rooms. ✆ (706) 676-1901-04.

Villa Marina, high-rise American-style motel between Boulevard Costero and Lopez Mateos, downtown, 82 rooms. ✆ (706) 678-3321.

RESTAURANTS

Carlos 'n Charlies, 253 Boulevard Costero, local branch of the popular Guadalajara Grill chain. ✆ (706) 678-1554.

Carnitas Uruapan, on Calle Sanguines just south of town, same owners and menu as the popular Tijuana restaurant.

Casamar, 987 Lazaro Cardenas Boulevard, seafood a specialty, live jazz. ✆ (706) 674-0417.

Del Mar Restaurant, 821 Lopez Mateos Avenue, gourmet seafood. ✆ (706) 678-2195.

El Rey Sol, 1000 Avenida Lopez Mateos, an award-winning French restaurant, Ensenada's finest since 1947. ✆ (706) 678-1733.

El Toro, 999 Boulevard Costero, steakhouse. ✆ (706) 674-0694.

La Ermita, at Second and Balboa, lamb barbecue a specialty. ✆ (706) 676-3161.

A crusty old Mexican stands ready to sell a bunch of the bright-colored paper flowers you see throughout Tijuana.

Travelers' Tips

ARRIVING IN CALIFORNIA

Nearly all major domestic and international airlines have services to the huge airports in San Francisco and Los Angeles. Only in 1988 did the U.S. Customs service open facilities in San Diego to inaugurate a British Airways flight from London, which the city hoped would lead to a busier international schedule. Travelers to Los Angeles may find that one of the smaller domestic airports is more convenient, depending on their destination. Burbank Airport, for example, is more convenient to Burbank, Universal City, Studio City and other places in the San Fernando Valley; John Wayne/Orange County Airport is more convenient to Disneyland and points south of Los Angeles.

The Los Angeles International Airport ("L-A-X") the world's third busiest, is served by 67 different international and domestic airlines. The once difficult passage to and from the terminal was cleared up in a huge construction project completed in time for the 1984 Olympics in Los Angeles. Fitting for L.A., the new airport complex is wonderfully convenient to parking garages and car rental places.

San Francisco International Airport is only three places behind Los Angeles in the "world's busiest" rankings and visitors to the East Bay area — Oakland and Berkeley may find it more convenient to fly into Oakland International Airport. There are also several private charter companies located at the Oakland airport: Aero Services International, telephone: ✆ (415) 562-3210; Jetstream Aviation, ✆ (415) 638-7700; and Kaiserair, ✆ (415) 569- 9622.

MAJOR AIRLINES SERVING CALIFORNIA

The following is a list of the major airlines serving Los Angeles or San Francisco (or both) and their toll-free telephone numbers in San Francisco(SFO) and/or Los Angeles (LAX):

Aerolineas Argentinas, (LAX) ✆ (800) 333-0276.
Air America, (LAX) ✆ (800) 654-8880.
Air Canada, (SFO) (LAX) ✆ (800) 422-6232.
Air France, (SFO) (LAX) ✆ (800) 237-2747.
Air Jamaica, (LAX) ✆ (800) 523-5585.
Air New Zealand, (SFO) (LAX) ✆ (800) 262-1234.
Alaska Airlines, (SFO) (LAX) ✆ (800) 426-0333.
Alitalia, (SFO) (LAX) ✆ (800) 223-5730.
American Airlines, (SFO) (LAX) ✆ (800) 433-7300.
America West Airlines, (SFO) ✆ (800) 247-5692; (LAX) ✆ (800) 537-3273.
ANA, All Nippon Airways, (SFO) (LAX) ✆ (800) 235-9262.
Avianca, (SFO) (LAX) ✆ (800) 284-2622.
Braniff, (SFO) (LAX) ✆ (800) 272-6433 (BRA-NIFF).
British Airways, (SFO) (LAX) ✆ (800) 247-9297.
Canadian Airlines, (SFO) (LAX) ✆ (800) 426-7000.
China Airlines, (SFO)(LAX) ✆ (800) 227-5118.
CNAC (China National Airways Corporation) (SFO) ✆ (415) 392-2156.
Continental/Eastern Airlines, (SFO) ✆ (800) 258-1212; (LAX) ✆ (800) 322-8662.
Delta, (SFO) (LAX) ✆ (800) 221-1212.
Ecuatoriana, (LAX) ✆ (800) 328-2367.
El Al, (LAX) ✆ (800) 223-6700; or ✆ (800) 835-2848.
Finnair, (SFO) (LAX) ✆ (800) 223-5700.
Garuda , (SFO) (LAX) ✆ (800) 332-2223.
Iberia, (SFO) (LAX) ✆ (800) 772-4642.
Japan Airlines, (SFO) (LAX) ✆ (800) 525-3663.
KLM, (SFO) (LAX) ✆ (800) 777-5553.
Korean Airlines, (SFO) ✆ (415) 956-6373; (LAX) ✆ (800) 421-8200.
LACSA Airlines, The Airline of Costa Rica, (SFO) ✆ (415) 362-5995; (LAX) ✆ (800) 225-2272.
LAN, Chile Airlines, (SFO) (LAX) ✆ (800) 225-5526.
Lufthansa, (SFO) (LAX) ✆ (800) 645-3880.

Mexicana Airlines, (SFO) (LAX) © (800) 531-7921.

Northwest, (SFO) © (800) 225-2525 for domestic flights; or (SFO) © (800) 447-4747 for international; (LAX) © (800) 692-2345.

Pan American, (SFO) (LAX) © (800) 221-1111.

Piedmont Airlines, (SFO) (LAX) © (800) 251-5720.

Philippine Airlines, (SFO) © (415) 391-0470; (LAX) © (800) 227-6144.

Qantas, (SFO) ©) (415) 761-8000; (LAX) © (800) 227-4500.

Royal Jordanian Airlines, (SFO) © (415) 441-3500; (LAX) © (800) 223-0470.

Scandinavian Airlines System, (SFO) © (800) 221-2350; (LAX) ©) (213) 655-8600.

Singapore Airlines, (SFO) © (800) 742-3333; (LAX) ©) (213) 655-9270.

Southwest Airlines, (SFO) © (800) 531-5601; (LAX) © (800) 433-5368.

TACA International Airlines, (SFO) (LAX) © (800) 535-8780.

TWA, (SFO) © (415) 864-5731; (LAX) © (800) 221-2000.

United Airlines, (SFO) © (415) 397-2100; (LAX) © (415) 521-4041.

United Express (operated by WestAir), (SFO) © (800) 241-6522.

US Air, (SFO) (LAX) © (800) 428-4322.

TA French Airlines, (LAX) © (800) 423-7422.

Varig, (SFO) (LAX) © (800) 468-2744.

Yugoslav Airlines, (LAX) © (800) 752-6528.

CUSTOMS

Visitors to the United States should keep in mind that the country is involved in a massive drug war and literally thousands of law enforcement officers are stationed at the major points of entry with the single purpose of checking for illegal drugs. If you come into the States from one of the major drug producing countries — Mexico, Colombia, Thailand, Burma — you may be subjected to a thorough search

for no other reason than the passport stamps from those countries. If you are caught trying to bring in any kind of illegal drug, you will be dealt with severely.

Aside from the extraordinary security precautions regarding illegal drugs, the U.S. Customs are not that different from the major countries of Europe. With certain exemptions — the major ones are wearing apparel, jewelry, toilet articles, hunting and fishing equipment and any other personal effects — articles bought outside the United States are subject to a customs duty and internal revenue tax. Such articles, valued at more than $300 cannot be sold within three years unless a duty is paid to the District Director of Customs.

Non-Residents are also allowed to bring in a quantity of alcoholic beverages and tobacco without paying a duty on it. The U.S. Customs allows up to one liter of beer, wine or liquor to be brought in for personal use; anything over that will be taxed. U.S. Postal laws do not allow the shipping by mail of alcoholic beverages. As for tobacco, non-residents can bring in duty free up to 200 cigarettes (one carton), 50 cigars or 2 kg of smoking tobacco.

The laws regarding importation of motor vehicles are quite complex and you should consult with a United States Embassy or Consulate before attempting to bring in an automobile, airplane, motorcycle or any kind of vehicle even for personal use. In general, a vehicle may be imported for personal use up to one year. However, you must own the vehicle at the time and its arrival must coincide with your own; and all vehicles must meet United States air pollution, cost saving and safety standards. If you sell your vehicle within one year of your arrival, duty must be paid to the U.S. Customs.

Household effects and professional equipment are exempt for persons emigrating to the United States, but again, the rules here vary and are quite complicated. For example, theatrical scenery and wearing apparel are not considered professional equipment.

In addition to the exemptions already named, a gift exemption is allowed non-resident visitors to the United States. A gift valued up to $100 may be brought in duty free provided you plan to stay in the United States 72 hours and the article remains with you. An additional 100 cigars may be included under the gift exemptions, but no alcoholic beverages are allowed as gifts.

Non-Residents are allowed higher exemptions ($200 and 4 liters alcoholic beverages) if they are in transit through the United States and the articles will be going on to a place outside United States Customs jurisdiction.

Anything above the exemption rate up to $1,000 will have a flat duty rate of 10 percent charged, based on the article's retail value in the country of purchase. Articles purchased in "duty free" shops in foreign countries are also subject to customs duty in the United States.

Many fruits and vegetables, plants and seeds are prohibited from entering the United States. For more information on agricultural product, write to Quarantines, USDA-ATHIS-TTQ, Federal Building, Hyattsville, MD 20782, United States.

Firearms and ammunition may be brought in as sporting equipment, provided it is personal equipment that leaves with you when you leave the United States. For detailed information on firearms, write to the Bureau of Alcohol, Tobacco and Firearms, Department of the Treasury, Washington, D.C. 20226, U.S.A.

The United States prohibits the entry of any merchandise from the following countries: Cambodia (Khmer Republic), Cuba, Iran, Libya, Nicaragua, North Korea, Panama, South Africa, Vietnam.

The only restriction regarding money is that you must file a report (Customs form 4790) if you bring in or take out more than $10,000. Failure to file this report can result in civil and criminal penalties.

If you want to bring along a pet dog or cat from a rabies-free country, there are few restrictions. There are restrictions on other pets, however, and the traveler is advised to get the Customs' leaflet entitled, *Pets, Wildlife, U.S. Customs.*

The leaflet on pets and a general pamphlet called *United States Customs Hints, For Visitors (Non-Residents)* can be ordered from the Department of the Treasury U.S. Customs Service, Washington, D.C. 20229. The general information pamphlet is Publication No. 511.

CLIMATE AND CLOTHING

In San Francisco, they say, more than one clothier has made a fortune off of unwary first-time visitors who come unprepared for the city. They come expecting the dry warmth of southern California, only to find a damp fog setting in; they come expecting a laid-back casual place, when many restaurants require more formal dress.

In San Francisco, to be sure, you should come prepared, with rain gear, a coat and tie, or a fancy dress for evening wear. In the rest of California, the casual mode prevails and only the most exclusive places have any kind of dress code. Except in northern California you can forget about the rain gear. It's not true, as the song says, that "It Never Rains in Southern California;" but rain is so rare you don't really have to plan for it or worry about it spoiling your picnic.

One British actor said he had to leave Los Angeles because he "kept looking out the window, waiting for the rain that never come." What you should be prepared for, in the deserts in particular and southern California in general, is a sharp drop in the temperature when the sun goes down. It is a desert climate and the low humidity is, perhaps, its most attractive feature; but that means the thermometer will fall 30 or 40°F (0 to 5°C) and sometimes more at sundown. Likewise, when you travel from the low deserts to the higher mountains, you'll need a sweater or a jacket no matter how high the mid-day temperature rises.

As for the beaches, one nasty little secret about northern California is that the beaches are often fogged in; so often, in fact, many people in San Francisco prefer the inland "beaches" or banks along the Russian River where the sunshine is more predictable. In southern California you'll find people on the beaches no matter what the weather — in fact, the rougher the weather, the better it is for the truly dedicated surfers seeking the good waves bad weather brings. In general, the way to tell a tourist in southern California is somebody who goes in the water. The water is so cold most of the year, locals avoid it (in favor of volleyball, jogging or ogling) like the rare un-sunny day.

RAIL SERVICE

The poor or non-existent passenger rail service in California is a fitting memorial to the robber barons who made their fortunes off the American railroads. Never mind that the rails were laid on government property and that much of the construction was carried out through government subsidies, the private railroad owners by the 1950s realized that there was far more money to be made transporting freight than could ever be realized moving people, their original purpose. Amtrak, the government's own passenger service was established after the private rail companies either stopped passenger service altogether or made that service so poor and unpredictable nobody would ride the trains. The "Eastern corridor" between Washington and Boston was always profitable and service there never faltered. However in the American West, passenger train service all but disappeared for a time and even now the trains are few and far between.

The most successful route has become the line between Los Angeles and San Diego. It is a very picturesque route, right on the beach for several miles below San Clemente. There are also two of the country's grand old

train stations at either end. The one in downtown Los Angeles is located just below the historic Pueblo de Los Angeles district and is a wonderful art deco gem that has survived largely because of all the movies that have been filmed there. The old Santa Fe station in San Diego was built in time for the Panama Exposition there in 1915 and is a classic example of Spanish mission style.

There are nine trains daily between Los Angeles and San Diego; the fare is $23 one

way. Otherwise, best forget train travel in California. There is only one train daily between Los Angeles and San Francisco, leaving at 9:55 am and arriving at 9:05 pm. The fare is $70. There is only one train east from San Francisco and Los Angeles to Chicago, the fares for both routes are $192. The toll free number Amtrak is © (800) 872-7245.

Only San Diego and San Francisco have their own municipal rapid transit rail services. Decades late, the city of Los Angeles has finally begun construction of a subway

Casually dressed Californians watch a 4th July (Independance Day) parade in Sausalito, San Francisco.

system which will not be operable until the mid-1990s. In San Francisco, the subway system is called "BART", the Bay Area Rapid Transit, which runs across the city of San Francisco, under the bay to Oakland and on up the East Bay area. In addition to this streamlined system, the city also operates Caltrain, a commuter rail service for the southern part of the peninsula from San Francisco to San Jose.

In San Diego, you'll find a rail transit system at work that overnight became a southern counterpart of the cable cars in San Francisco. In establishing the San Diego Trolley, the city had two major advantages: there was existing track no longer used by the railroads already in place where the trolley should run; and not least of all, the bright red trolley cars go right to the border of Mexico, stopping at the U.S. Customs building at the Tijuana border. There were thus little construction cost involved and a ready market for tourists who wanted to see Mexico but didn't want to drive there. Tickets for the trolley line can be purchased at the stops; the fare for the full route is only $1.25.

CONSULATES

(SF) = San Francisco; (LA) = Los Angeles; (S) = Sacremento; (SD) = San Diego

Argentina, (SF) 870 Market Street, ✆ (415) 982-3050; (LA) 3550 Wilshire Boulevard, ✆ (213) 739-9977.
Australia, (SF) (415) 362-6160; (LA) 611 N. Larchmont Boulevard, ✆ (213) 469-430.
Austria, (SF) 950 Mason Street, ✆ (415) 397-7821.
Barbados, (SF) 712 Montgomery Street, ✆ (415) 421-8789; (LA) 3440 Wilshire Boulevard, ✆ (213) 380-2198.
Belgium, (SF) 170 Columbus Street, ✆ (415) 434-4400; (LA) 6100 Wilshire Boulevard, ✆ (213) 857-1244.
Bolivia, (SF) 870 Market Street, ✆ (415) 495-5173.

Brazil, (SF) 300 Montgomery Street, ✆ (415) 981-8170.
Cameroons, (SF) 147 Terra Vista Avenue, ✆ (415) 921-5372.
Canada, (SF) 50 Fremont Street, ✆ (415) 495-6021; (LA) 300 S. Grand Avenue, ✆ (213) 687-7432.
Chile, (SF) 870 Market Street, ✆ (415) 982-7662; (LA) 510 W. 6th Street, ✆ (213) 624-6357.
Colombia, (SF) 870 Market Street, ✆ (415) 362-0080; (LA) 3600 Wilshire Boulevard, ✆ (213) 382-1136.
Costa Rica, (SF) 870 Market Street, ✆ (415) 392-8488; (LA) 3540 Wilshire Boulevard, ✆ (213) 382-8080.
Denmark, (SF) 221 Main Street, 14th Floor, ✆ (415) 243-0705; (LA) 3440 Wilshire Boulevard, ✆ (213) 387-4277.
Dominican Republic, (SF) 870 Market Street, ✆ (415) 982-5144.
Ecuador, (SF) 870 Market Street, ✆ (415) 391-4148; (LA) 548 S. Spring Street, ✆ (213) 628-3014; (SD) 530 B Street, ✆ (619) 233-8640.
Egypt, (SF) 3001 Pacific Avenue, ✆ (415) 346-9700.
El Salvador, (SF) 870 Market Street, ✆ (415) 781-7924; (LA) 634 S. Spring Street, ✆ (213) 623-8823.
Finland, (SD) 530 Broadway, ✆ (619) 238-4433.
France, (SF) 540 Bush Street, ✆ (415) 397-4330; (LA) 9401 Wilshire Boulevard, ✆ (213) 272-2661; (S) 1831 Rockwood Drive, ✆ (916) 488-7659; (SD) 5440 Morehouse Drive, ✆ (619) 457-2338.
Germany, (SF) 1960 Jackson Street, ✆ (415) 775-1061; (LA) 6222 Wilshire Boulevard, ✆ (213) 930-2703.
Great Britain, (SF) 1 Sansome Street, ✆ (415) 981-3030; (LA) 3701 Wilshire Boulevard, ✆ (213) 385-7381.
Greece, (SF) 2441 Gough Street, ✆ (415) 775-2102.
Guatemala, (SF) 870 Market Street, ✆ (415) 781-0118; (LA) 548 S. Spring Street, ✆ (213) 489-1891.

Honduras, (SF) 870 Market Street, ℰ (415) 392-0076; (LA) 548 S. Spring Street, ℰ (213) 623-2301.

Iceland, (SF) 3150 20th Avenue, ℰ (415) 564-4007; (LA) 14755 Ventura Boulevard, Sherman Oaks, ℰ (213) 789-3308.

India, (SF) 540 Arguello Boulevard, ℰ (415) 668-0683.

Indonesia, (SF) 1111 Columbus Avenue, ℰ (415) 474-9571.

Ireland, (SF) 655 Montgomery Street, ℰ (415) 392-4214.

Israel, (SF) 220 Bush Street, ℰ (415) 398-8885; (LA) 6380 Wilshire Boulevard, ℰ (213) 651-5700.

Italy, (SF) 2590 Webster Street, ℰ (415 931-4924; (S) 5347 Folsom Boulevard, ℰ (916) 456-1950.

Japan, (SF) 50 Fremont Street, ℰ (415) 777-3533; (LA) 250 E. 1st Street, ℰ (213) 624-8305; (SD) Japan, Balboa Park, ℰ (619) 238-1177.

Jordan, (LA) 6033 W. Century Boulevard, ℰ (213) 216-4296.

Kenya, (LA) 9100 Wilshire Boulevard, ℰ (213) 274-6635.

Malaysia, (LA) 350 S. Figueroa Street, ℰ (213) 621-2991.

Malta, (LA) 5428 E. Beverly Boulevard, ℰ (213) 685-6365.

Korea, (LA) 5455 Wilshire Boulevard, ℰ (213) 931-1331.

Luxembourg, (SF) 1 Sansome Street, ℰ (415) 788-0816.

Mexico, (SF) 870 Market Street, ℰ (415) 392-5554; (LA) 125 Paseo de la Plaza, ℰ (213) 624-3261; (S) 1506 South Street, ℰ (916) 446-4696; (SD) 1333 Front Street, ℰ (619) 231-8414.

Netherlands, (SF) 601 California Street, ℰ (415) 981-6454.

New Zealand, (LA) 10960 Wilshire Boulevard, ℰ (213) 477-8241.

Norway, (SF) 2 Embarcadero Center, ℰ (415) 986-0766; (LA) 350 S. Figueroa Street, ℰ (213) 626-0338.

Pakistan, (SF) 211 Sutter Street, ℰ (415) 788-0677.

Panama, (SF) 870 Market Street, ℰ (415) 989-0934.

People's Republic Of China, (LA) 501 Shatto Place, ℰ (213) 380-2506.

Paraguay, (SF) 870 Market Street, ℰ (415) 982-9424.

Peru, (SF) 870 Market Street, ℰ (415) 362-5185; (LA) 6420 Wilshire Boulevard, ℰ (213) 651-0296.

Philippines, (SF) 447 Sutter Street, ℰ (415) 433-6666;(LA) 3460 Wilshire Boulevard, ℰ (213) 387-5321.

Portugal, (SF) 3298 Washington Street, ℰ (415) 346-3400.

Singapore, (LA) 350 S. Figueroa Street, ℰ (213) 617-7358.

South Africa, (LA) 50 N. La Cienega Boulevard, ℰ (213) 657-9200.

Soviet Union, (SF) 2790 Green Street, ℰ (415) 346-3400.

Spain, (SF) 2080 Jefferson Street, ℰ (415) 922-2995; (LA) 6300 Wilshire Boulevard, ℰ (213) 658-6050.

Sweden, (SF) 120 Montgomery Street, ℰ (415) 788-2631.

Switzerland, (SF) 235 Montgomery Street, ℰ (415) 788-2272; (LA) 3440 Wilshire Boulevard, ℰ (213) 388-4127.

Thailand, (LA) 801 N. La Brea Avenue, ℰ (213) 937-1894.

Turkey, (SF) 16 California Street, ℰ (415) 362-0912.

Venezuela, (SF) 870 Market Street, ℰ (415) 421-5172.

Yemen Arab Republic, (SF) 120 Montgomery Street, ℰ (415) 989-3636.

Yugoslavia, (SF) 1375 Sutter Street, ℰ (415) 776-4941.

NATIONAL PARKS IN CALIFORNIA

There are twenty wilderness, recreation and historic areas in California maintained as part of the U.S. National Park Service. Most of these are covered under individual headings. The Western Region headquarters for the park service is at 450 Golden Gate Avenue, Box 36063, San Francisco, CA 94102 and visitors can write to that address for more information on the parks in California. A camping guide to the National Parks is also available free of charge from the Superintendent of Documents, U.S. Government Printing Office, Washington, D.C. 20402. Another booklet on all facilities in all the parks can be obtained by writing to the Garner B. Hanson Conference of National Park Concessions, Mammoth Cave, Kentucky 42259. The following is a list of the National Parks in California and the addresses where information can be obtained about them:

Cabrillo National Monument, P.O. Box 6670, San Diego, CA 92106.
Channel Islands National Park, 1901 Spinnaker Drive, Ventura, CA 93001.
Death Valley National Monument, Death Valley, CA 92328.
Devils Postpile National Monument, c/o Sequoia and Kings Canyon National Parks, Three Rivers, CA 93271.
Eugene O'Neill National Historic Site, c/o John Muir National Historic Site, 4202 Alhambra Avenue, Martinez, CA 94553.
Fort Point National Historic Site, P.O. Box 29333, Presidio of San Francisco, CA 94129.
Golden Gate National Recreation Area, Fort Mason, Building 201, San Francisco, CA 9412.
John Muirr National Historic Site, 4202 Alhambra Avenue, Martinez, CA 94553.
Joshua Tree National Monument, 74485 National Monument Drive, Twentynine Palms, CA 92277.
Kings Canyon National Park, Three Rivers, CA 93271.
Lassen Volcanic National Park, Mineral, CA 96063.
Lava Beds National Monument, P.O. Box 867, Tulelake, CA 96134.
Muir Woods National Monument, Mill Valley, CA 94941.
Pinnacles National Monument, Paicines, CA 95043.
Point Reyes National Seashore, Point Reyes, CA 94956.
Redwood National Park, 1111 Second Street, Crescent City, CA 95531.

Santa Monica Mountains National Recreation Area, 22900 Ventura Boulevard, Suite 140, Woodland Hills, CA 91364.
Sequoia National Park, Three Rivers, CA 93271.
Whiskeytown-Shasta-Trinity National Recreation Area, P.O. Box 188, Whiskeytown, CA 96095.
Yosemite National Park, P.O. Box 577, Yosemite National Park, CA 95389.

EARTHQUAKES

Don't be misled by all the jokes. Earthquakes are a very serious matter in California. There's not much you can do about the initial jolt, but you can take cover before the aftershocks hit. Most people are killed by falling plaster or beams, so get under a table, a doorway, or anything that offers protection. Keep a flashlight with good batteries on hand at all times, have a supply of bottled water and canned food, and know where to shut off the gaslines. Advisories are broadcast every day on California radio and television stations by the state Earthquake Preparedness Commission.

SWIMMING

Visitors are advised to be cautious about swimming at any of the California beaches. As picturesque as they may seem from a distance, the waters can be rough and the undertows in many places are very dangerous. Don't swim if there are no lifeguards around. Don't be fooled by the ease with which the young surfers handle the rough waters; these people are expert swimmers who know what they are dealing with.

FREEWAYS

For many years, the freeways in Los Angeles seemed decades ahead of their time. They were a quick and efficient way of getting from one part of the sprawling city to another. But those days are long gone.

The freeways are now desperately inadequate to handle the millions of cars that use them. In general, avoid the freeways during rush-hours – between 7 and 9 am, and 4 and 6 pm. A small amount of planning can save you from getting caught in one of those massive traffic jams that can leave you sitting still for up to an hour.

HOTELS, RESTAURANTS, AND SPORTS

CALIFORNIA IN GENERAL

Hotels and motels of America's major chains are found in California. While many of these, such as Hilton and Sheraton, started out as luxurious facilities in the major cities, they are now quite ordinary. Only Hyatt has managed to maintain a consistently high standard of luxury in its hotels – except for the original Hyatt at the Los Angeles airport, which is no better than the average Holiday Inn. Ask plenty of questions before making reservations using the following toll free (800) numbers. Find out the exact location of the hotel, its distance from the places you want to see, and the facilities it has to offer.

Best Western: ✆ 1-(800) 528-1234
Hilton: ✆ 1-(800) 445-8667
Holiday Inn: ✆ 1-(800) 465-4329
Howard Johnson: ✆ 1-(800) 654-2000
Hyatt: ✆ 1-(800) 228-9000
Marriott: ✆ 1-(800) 228-9290
Ramada Inn: ✆ 1-(800) 272-6232
Sheraton: ✆ 1-(800) 325-3535

Inexpensice Hotels and Motels
Budget: ✆ 1-(800) 824-5317
Comfort Inns: ✆ 1-(800) 228-5150
Motel 6: the cheapest of all has no toll free number; the central reservation number for California is ✆ 1-(505) 891-6161.
Quality Inns: ✆ 1-(800) 228-5151
Super 8: ✆ 1-(800) 843-1991
Travelodge: ✆ 1-(800) 255-3050

CURRENCY EXCHANGE

While most of California's cities are major international tourist stops, you won't find services such as currency exchanges as common here as in the major world capitals. It is best either to come with traveler's checks or to exchange your money at the air terminal or border crossing. Once

inside the state, there are only a small number of exchange offices in the major cities. The Bank of America offers exchange services in its major downtown offices and most branches, however no other local bank will exchange currency. Deak International also has exchange offices in downtown San Francisco and San Diego; however, there is a service change and notes are general higher than they would be in the air terminal or border crossing exchange places.

ABOVE: The Los Angeles Freeway system is not quite so complex as it might appear in this picture of the major interchanges; however, it is still best to avoid the freeways during morning and late afternoon rush hours.

CAR RENTAL

Car rental offices are located convenient to the baggage check out or customs offices in all major airports in the State. However, most travelers will want to make reservations for a car rental at the same time reservations are made for air travel; this is the only way to insure that the particular car you want to rent will be ready and waiting when you arrive. Travelers to sunny southern California may want to take advantage of the convertible cars that can be rented from Budget rental cars.

The services offered by rental car agencies throughout California vary from place to place, even within the same agency. If you plan on traveling into Mexico, check with the agency first. Some do not allow their cars to travel into Mexico; others will provide the Mexican insurance necessary for such travel.

The following is a list of the toll free numbers of the major agencies found in every part of the state. If you're looking for budget prices, the best deals can usually be made through the small local agencies. For long-term leases, the best bets are the major auto dealers such as Ford or Chevrolet.

Alamo: ✆ 1-(800) 327-9633
Avis: ✆ 1-(800) 331-1212
Budget: ✆ 1-(800) 527-0700
Courtesy (formerly Ajax): ✆ 1-(800) 824-3232
Dollar: ✆ 1-(800) 421-6878
Hertz: ✆ 1-(800) 654-3131
National: ✆ 1-(800) 328-4567
Sears: ✆ 1-(800) 527-0770

TRAVELER'S AID SOCIETY

The International Traveler's Aid Society has offices in the major California cities. A private organization funded by its members, Traveler's Aid is set up to offer emergency relief or practical advice to travelers in trouble or in need.

In San Francisco, the telephone number for Traveler's Aid is ✆ (415) 781-6738; in Oakland, the number is ✆ (415) 444-6834; in Los Angeles, the Traveler's Aid number is ✆ (213) 625-2501; in San Diego, the number is ✆ (619) 232-7991.

In Los Angeles, the Los Angeles County Medical Association operates a physician referral service from 9 am to 4:45 pm Monday to Friday. Visitors should keep in mind that the United States and South Africa are the only countries that do not have any kind of health insurance. If you are injured in an accident, there are emergency rooms in the county hospitals that are required to treat you; however, no hospital will admit a patient without proof of insurance or some other proof of your ability to pay for treatment.

In Los Angeles, the 24 hour Traveler's Aid Hotline is ✆ (213) 686-0950.

In San Francisco, there are several clinics that offer outpatient services: Access Health Care, at 1604 Union Street at Franklin, ✆ (415) 775-7766 and at 26 California Street at Drumm, ✆ (415) 397-2881; The Medical Center at the University of California, San Francisco, is at 500 Parnassus at Third Avenue, ✆ (415) 476-1000; San Francisco General Hospital is at 1001 Potrero Avenue, telephone: ✆ (415) 821-8200 or dial 911 for 24-hour emergency service.

MEXICO

There are virtually no restrictions on visitors to the border areas. No papers of any kind are required for visits up to 72 hours to the border towns, including Ensenada.

VISAS

Tourist cards are required for any visit 30 miles (50 km) beyond the borders, excluding Ensenada which is 65 miles (105 km) south. Cards are good for 30 days and can be extended up to 180 days. They can be obtained from travel agents, airlines, or Mexican consulates. Tourists of all ages are required to carry these cards at all times. In addition, minors under 18 years of age must have notarized letters from both parents; those traveling with only one parent must carry a letter from the absent parent. These restrictions are aimed at discouraging teenagers who flock to the border towns to avoid the drinking laws in the United States.

The Mexican Consulate in San Diego is located at 1333 Front Street, Suite 200, San Diego, CA 92101. ✆ (619) 231-8414.

TOURIST INFORMATION

The best source of specific information on Baja is the Tijuana/Baja Convention and Tourism Bureau at 7860 Mission Center Court, San Diego, CA 92108, ✆ (619) 299-8518, or toll free in California, ✆ (800) 522-1516. This office provides information for conventions or individual tourists, makes hotel reservations, and arranges car insurance.

The most common complaint of visitors to Mexico is "Montezuma's Revenge", a severe form of diarrhea caused by the body's adjustment to a different set of bacteria. Since all hotels provide guests with bottled water to drink, there must be a basis in fact. Again, common sense is the best guide here: be careful where and what you eat, and drink only bottled water.

CURRENCY

The currency of Mexico is the peso. The rate of exchange alters daily owing to rampant inflation in the economy. In 1975, the exchange was 12.50 pesos to the dollar; in 1988, it was 2,300 pesos to the dollar and rising. However, in the border areas described here, you will find a fair exchange in most shops, restaurants, and hotels – and there is really no need to change money since dollars are accepted everywhere.

RETURNING TO CALIFORNIA

If it seemed easy going south of the border, be prepared for all manner of inconveniences coming back into the United States. The law enforcement bureaucracy you encountered in Mexico is nothing compared to the thousands of local, state, and federal officials assigned to the United States side of the border. This crossing is not only the busiest border crossing in the world, but also a major artery for illegal drugs entering the United States.

If you appear the least bit suspicious in dress or behavior, it is likely that you will be waved over to the "secondary" area where a more detailed questioning and thorough search of your vehicle will take place. In general, United States citizens with nothing to declare at customs are waved on through. However, foreign travelers who have stamps from any of the major drug-producing countries may find themselves routinely subjected to searches.

A number of pocket guides about U.S. Customs can be obtained either from the local customs office or by writing a postcard to the U.S. Customs Service, P.O. Box 7407, Washington, D.C. 20044.

United States citizens may bring back up to $400 worth of goods purchased in a foreign country if they are for personal use. This can include 100 cigars, 200 cigarettes, and a liter of wine, beer, or liquor. Remember to keep all receipts as U.S. Customs may ask for proof of purchase. A duty of 10 percent is levied on all purchases over $400 up to $1,600.

The main border crossing at Tijuana has become so congested that you often have to wait two to three hours to get back into the United States. To relieve this situation, a new crossing has been opened at Otay Mesa, northeast of the city. To reach the new crossing, follow signs to the "Aeropuerto", go past the airport toward Mexicali, and then follow signs (left or north) that say "Garita de Otay".

Both border crossings are best avoided at morning and evening rush-hours. The worst time of all is Sunday afternoon and early Sunday evening. The best times are after 10 pm and before 7 am.

The borders at Tecate and Mexicali are closed at night and open only from 7 am to 10 pm.

Severe restrictions are imposed on agricultural products coming from Mexico. Violations could result in long delays at the border, or fines. In general, anything that can carry plant pests or animal diseases is prohibited. A special permit is required to bring in any kind of seeds or plants. Banned items also include raw or cooked pork, eggs, and live birds. There is, however, a long list of permitted items, including most nuts, bananas, blackberries, cactus fruits, dates, dewberries, grapes, lychees, melons, papayas, pineapples, strawberries, avocados, and nearly all vegetables except potatoes and okra.

CAR RENTAL SOUTH OF THE BORDER

In general, United States rental cars cannot be taken into Mexico. However, two agencies in San Diego, **Southwest** and **Dollar Rental Cars,** provide Mexican insurance and their cars can be taken across the border.

Motorists are advised not to drive at night. Except for the Tijuana–Ensenada toll road, the roads in Baja are narrow and there are very long stretches between service stations.

DRIVING AND AUTO-INSURANCE

The most important warnings about travel in Mexico relate to automobiles. United States or any other foreign insurance is not valid in Mexico. Moreover, an automobile accident is considered a felony and everyone involved will be detained until financial responsibility is determined. You will either have to pay cash on the spot or provide proof of Mexican insurance. Mexican insurance can be obtained, for a modest fee of $6, from travel agencies or offices located under huge billboards on the United States side of the border. The largest and most convenient of these is called **Instant Mexico Auto Insurance Services.** There is a drive-in window and all that you need to do is prove that you own the vehicle. You can also obtain hunting and fishing licenses here. The agency publishes a very good road guide to Baja California. And if you want to learn Spanish as you ride along, you can buy cassette tapes with lessons here. For travel on the mainland of Mexico, all cars are required to have permits, but these, too, can be obtained easily.

BUS SERVICES FROM SAN DIEGO

Greyhound provides a bus service from the San Diego terminal at 120 W. Broadway to Tijuana's North Terminal on Avenida Madero. Buses leave every hour, from 5:15 am to 11:30 pm; fares are $4 one way and $8 round-trip.

One of the most popular rides to the border is on the **Tijuana Trolley**. The trolley goes from the Santa Fe Railway terminal downtown to the border, with frequent stops through downtown and south to the border. The fare is $1.25 for the full route; trains run every 15 minutes.

Gray Line Tours offers a three-day excursion into Baja, from San Diego to San Felipe to Tijuana. It also has shopping tours to Tijuana three times a day. Gray Line Sightseeing Tours is located at 1678 Kettner Boulevard in San Diego. ℂ (619) 231-9922.

Quick Reference A–Z Guide
to Places and Topics of Interest with Listed Accommodation, Restaurants and Useful Telephone Numbers